INFORMATION
AND
RECORDS MANAGEMENT

INFORMATION AND RECORDS MANAGEMENT

A DECISION-MAKER'S GUIDE TO SYSTEMS PLANNING AND IMPLEMENTATION

Milburn D. Smith III

Q

QUORUM BOOKS

NEW YORK
WESTPORT, CONNECTICUT
LONDON

Library of Congress Cataloging-in-Publication Data

Smith, Milburn D.
  Information and records management.

  Includes index.
  1. Records—Management.   2. Information resources
management.   I. Title.
HF5736.S58   1986   651.5   86–638
ISBN 0–89930–111–8 (lib. bdg. : alk. paper)

Library of Congress Catalog Card Number: 86–638
ISBN: 0–89930–111–8

First published in 1986 by Quorum Books

Greenwood Press, Inc.
88 Post Road West, Westport, Connecticut 06881

Printed in the United States of America

The paper used in this book complies with the
Permanent Paper Standard issued by the National
Information Standards Organization (Z39.48–1984).

10 9 8 7 6 5 4 3 2 1

Copyright Acknowledgment

Exhibits are reprinted courtesy of The Omni Group, Ltd.

Contents

Exhibits

PART 1

RECORDS MANAGEMENT AND INFORMATION PROCESSING: THE IMPACT OF INFORMATION-PROCESSING TECHNOLOGIES

1

The Traditional Role of Records Management

1.1 RECORDS ARE ASSETS

In the fall of 1985, Hurricane Gloria swept north along the eastern seaboard and, after crossing over Long Island, made landfall near the Connecticut–Rhode Island border. A senior executive in a major corporation who had just moved his company's headquarters from New York City to Connecticut found his new location without electricity for four days after the weather cleared. Since his staff was denied access to documents and records, his entire operation was paralyzed. He wondered what would have happened if the hurricane's center had struck closer to his headquarters. Besides the threat to life, without all those files, letters, memos, and documents, his organization might have suffered a fatal blow.

In the winter and spring of 1985, the IRS was beginning to use a new computer system to handle the returns of 1984. Not far into the filing period, it became evident that the transition was not going to proceed as smoothly as had been planned. In fact, data were lost when some returns were disposed of before they had been fully transcribed. Vital records had been jeopardized.

These two examples provide very brief illustrations of the need for, and the power of, records. Records contain the information that is the lifeblood of any organization, without which it could not function. Records management, therefore, is a vital task for all companies or organizations.

This book is intended to serve as a guide for those involved in records management and who are confronted with the technological advances taking place today. We believe that with preparation, knowledge, and experience, the problems facing those involved today in records management can be successfully solved. The goal of this book is to provide a wide range of information on matters that affect records management, so that more-informed and better decisions can be made.

1.2 WHAT IS A RECORD?

From the time symbols were first preserved on the walls of caves, records have allowed man to function in a variety of endeavors. Progress up until the most recent 50 or 60 years in records technology was slow, but we are now witnessing technological innovation at an exponentially accelerating rate.

For the purposes of this book, we can generally state that records are kept to document the spectrum of business activities. A record is any form of recorded information. The medium itself may be paper, film, microfilm, magnetic media, or optical disks.

The various records media fall into several broad categories. Electronic media include magnetic disks, diskettes, magnetic tapes, and optical disks. Electronic media are used for large-volume or production-type records, or for records with widespread use (such as general ledger, historical account data, or statistics).

Microphotographic media include microfilm or fiche and computer-output microforms and are used for information that requires the multiple generation of records, quick access, or storage over longer time frames (such as employee benefits profiles, stock certificates, and customer account records).

Paper-based records are maintained in a hard-copy form such as memos, letters, contracts, and project files. The main benefit of this medium is to provide short-term reference and to maintain vital records with important information, such as legal documents.

Voice and video media are used for the storage of voice documents and full-motion video. Voice and video records come in a variety of formats including audio minicassettes, audio cassettes, $1/2$-inch, $3/4$-inch, 1-inch, and 2-inch videotape. In the future, the industry will be moving to digital media such as laser-readable disks for the storage of both audio and video data.

Whatever the medium, records have a four-phase life cycle based on their relative business value over time: first, the period in which records are created; second, a period of active and frequent use; third, a phase of semi-active or archival use, when they are stored mostly for reference purposes; and finally, a period when they become obsolete and should be destroyed.

At each of these stages in the record's life cycle, some form of control, dictated by appropriate policy, is necessary. Without this, the system will fast become ineffective.

When dealing with computers, the term "record" is used in yet another, specialized manner. A computer record is a set of related data pertaining to a particular individual, transaction, or item of information. A computer record in an employee file would consist of various fields such as the employee's name, age, date of employment, salary level, benefits package, health plan options, and so on. While we will refer to computer records at various points in this book, we shall use the term "record" in its broader meaning.

1.3 THE CHANGING ENVIRONMENT

For several decades, the United States has been shifting from a predominantly manufacturing-based to a service-based economy. For the first time in our nation's history, a majority of the labor force—53 percent—are "information workers," that is, white-collar professional and clerical employees. Clearly, today is an information age—a fact by now so widely touted that few would dispute it.

With all the technology and human resources dedicated to pursuing and communicating information, one would think that the field of records management should have entered its golden age. Never before has the need for records tracking, processing, storage, and retrieval been so great. And never before has technology been so capable of meeting this need.

Nevertheless, the records manager of the 1980s does not have an easy task, as the information age poses considerable challenges as well as opportunities. For instance, while computers have become increasingly powerful, affordable, and usable, they are primarily designed for the handling of electronic information, or soft data. Unfortunately, the records manager has to cope with a variety of formats: not only the magnetic tape used by most computer systems, but also film, audio and videotape, and, of course, paper.

Computers are not only changing how records are stored and retrieved, they have also generated more records to control. Today there are more than 18 million clerical workers tracking America's daily output of 370 million pages of new business document originals, 1.9 million pages of computer output, and 1.9 billion copies. A majority of the Fortune 1000 companies have experienced a measurable increase in paper output since 1983. The American Paper Institute forecasts an escalation in the use of bond and writing paper, as well as business forms, through the year 2000.

The paper glut may come as a surprise to many, since computer advertisers have been promoting a vision of the paperless office of the future for several years. It is certainly no surprise, however, to professionals in today's businesses, especially those who are involved in establishing records-management programs for their departments, divisions, and companies. Computers don't provide automatic solutions, and we are still a long way from replacing paper with a single integrated electronic system (see Exhibits 1.1 and 1.2).

Although it is ironic that office machines seem to have contributed to the paper glut instead of solving it, there are explanations for the present state of affairs. For one thing, copiers and printers can produce documents faster and cheaper than ever. For another, automation has increased the complexity and variety of available information. But a more fundamental problem has been in establishing compatibility and conformity across computer systems.

In the area of personal computers, for example, IBM's PC has emerged as a de facto standard, spurring the sales of "IBM compatibles." Nevertheless, most large companies today have computers from a variety of vendors which are incapable of communicating effectively with each other. Where communication is available, in many cases it occurs only at the most rudimentary level, where the exchange is less valuable. Since paper is the common denominator among these various systems, it remains the universal medium.

1.4 A BRIEF HISTORY OF RECORDS-MANAGEMENT DEPARTMENTS

A good illustration of the importance of records management is provided by the federal government. At the National Archives in Washington, D.C., the Declaration of Independence is preserved and displayed in a unique storage facility. The document is held at ground level for public viewing in a gas-pressurized, double-walled glass case. The inner case is designed so that it would descend through a shaft to a vault deep in the underlying bedrock in the event of a physical disaster. Here, it is hoped, the document would be able to survive. The records of the founding fathers would be available for later generations.

Such an arrangement is notably unique and reflects the significance attached to the document. While very few records managers will have to face such a preservation need, the illustration does point out the value attached to records management and control services.

Historically, the federal government has been a pioneer in the area of records management. In the private sector, records management is gen-

Exhibit 1.1
Impact of Office Automation on Paper Explosion

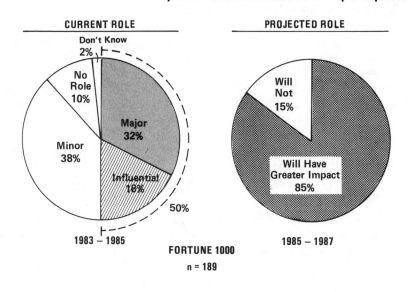

CURRENT ROLE

PROJECTED ROLE

Don't Know
2%

No
Role
10%

Major
32%

Minor
38%

Influential
18%

50%

Will
Not
15%

Will Have
Greater Impact
85%

1983 – 1985

1985 – 1987

FORTUNE 1000
n = 189

Exhibit 1.2
Directions in Paper Consumption, 1983–1987

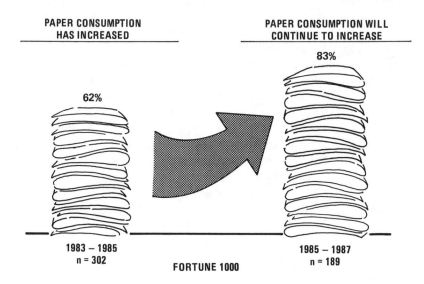

PAPER CONSUMPTION
HAS INCREASED

PAPER CONSUMPTION WILL
CONTINUE TO INCREASE

83%

62%

1983 – 1985
n = 302

FORTUNE 1000

1985 – 1987
n = 189

erally considered to have emerged as a business function in the early 1950s. Earlier, no dedicated business group or department was responsible for records management.

1.4.1 The Federal Government's Action

At the end of World War II, President Harry S. Truman recognized the need for an orderly program of records management and records disposition. Although originally designed to handle the massive amounts of records generated by the war, these programs affected all the branches of government and, later, the private sector. In 1947 President Truman signed the Lodge-Brown Act, establishing the Commission on Organization of the Executive Branch of the Government. The commission, chaired by former President Hoover, came up with a number of recommendations and conclusions:

- Write into law a Federal Records Act to provide for the more effective creation, management, preservation, and disposition of U.S. government records.
- Create a Records Management Bureau in the Office of General Services which would include the National Archives.
- Establish a records-management program in each department and agency of the federal government.

From these recommendations two laws were written and passed. In 1949 the Federal Property and Administrative Services Act came into being, which gave the administrator of the General Services Administration (GSA) the authority to survey government records and promote improved practices and controls. It also placed the National Archives under the auspices of the GSA. In 1950, the Federal Records Act was passed. This legislation gave the administrator of the GSA broad powers over all federal records and made records disposal programs mandatory for all federal agencies.

In 1953, President Eisenhower convened a second Commission on Organization of the Executive Branch of government, once again headed by former President Hoover. This commission found that current legislation required a great deal of useless paperwork to be filed by companies and that in a great number of cases there were overlaps, redundancies, and misfiles. The commission came up with two major recommendations. The first consisted of three proposals:

1. that the President shall establish a federal government records-management program;
2. that the GSA be given supervisory responsibility for all paperwork management programs throughout the executive branch; and
3. that the Records Service and the National Archives be consolidated under the GSA.

The second recommendation was that a single official in each agency be charged with the responsibility for a reduction of paperwork in that agency. A further result was that the GSA established records-management guidelines and, in 1955, published its *Guide to Records Retention Requirements*. This volume continues to be updated annually and may be obtained from any Government Printing Office outlet.

Government regulations continue to have a profound effect on private companies and their records management. The Privacy Act of 1974, the Paperwork Reduction Act of 1980, and the recently amended Freedom of Information Act are but three examples. In many organizations, particularly those which are under a high degree of government regulation, such as the pharmaceuticals industry, the legal aspects of records management and records retention requirements are a special skill.

1.5 DEFINING RECORDS MANAGEMENT

While the federal response to a growing records-management problem was being formulated and carried out, corporate America developed specific departments or divisions of general administrative services to manage its own records needs.

The records-management function, it should be clearly established from the start, is involved in each phase of the records life cycle: generation, active use, inactive use, and disposal. A common misconception is that the records manager is involved only in the last two areas—that is, the semi-active and destruction phases.

A comprehensive records-management program concerns itself with the control of records from their creation through the active and inactive stages to their disposition. When properly executed, such an approach should aid in the control of the unnecessary proliferation of copies and make the retrieval and utilization of records more efficient.

With overhead costs such as personnel and rent comprising between 80 and 90 percent of overall records maintenance costs, the control of these increasingly expensive resources is a prime concern of the records manager. The records manager's objective is therefore twofold: to efficiently generate, retrieve, and use all necessary records efficiently, and to minimize associated costs.

Given this objective, how does records management differ from information management? To return to our earlier definition, records contain data. Records are therefore the substance, or the building blocks, of information. Information, however, is contextual. Put in another way, one cannot have information without data, but one can have data without information.

A record must be viewed within the context of an organization to be meaningful and have value. In isolation, a record of a specific transaction, discussion, or agreement is often meaningless. Because records are form or medium oriented, whereas information is contextual, blurring the distinction between the two can create problems. While records are static and finite, information is changing and ongoing.

1.6 SCOPE OF A RECORDS-MANAGEMENT PROGRAM

Because of the wide-ranging scope of records management and its impact on the entire company, records management has been receiving increased attention in recent years. Additionally, its importance has increased because of external factors such as the expanding scope of federal and state requirements for records retention and the increasingly litigious environment of American society.

What specific responsibilities comprise records management? Since records management should address all phases of the record's life cycle, it should encompass the following responsibilities:

• Records generation and control (including forms analysis and reports analysis)

• Processing records

• Records storage and retrieval

• Records conversion (for example, from paper to microfiche)

• Records retention and elimination

• Vital records protection

• Records delivery

• Analysis of cost

Clearly, there is a great deal of overlap in these areas. Improvements made in one area, therefore, will have varying degrees of impact on the other areas. Looking at these functional areas in terms of the records life cycle, it becomes clear that certain actions are emphasized during each stage. Exhibit 1.3 is a reiteration of the functional areas of records management, with each area corresponding to the applicable phase of the life cycle.

Exhibit 1.3
The Relevance of Records Management to Different Phases in the
Records Life Cycle

Phases in the Life Cycle:

1 - Generation

2 - Active

3 - Inactive

4 - Destruction

Functional Areas and Life Cycle Correspondence:

Records generation and control	1
Processing records	2
Records storage and retrieval	2
Records conversion	1,2
Records retention and elimination	2,3,4
Vital records protection	3
Records delivery	2
Analysis of records cost	1,2,3,4

1.7 TRADITIONAL ISSUES IN RECORDS MANAGEMENT

For a records-management program to be successful, a number of issues must be addressed in the early stages of the program. These issues are often divided into three areas: organizational issues, financial issues, and operational issues.

1.7.1 Organizational Issues

The first organizational issue that should be addressed is the range or scope of the records-management program. In smaller and many medium-sized companies this may not be an issue, as a companywide effort would be the only one contemplated. In larger organizations, however, a departmental or functional area for implementing records management may be proposed.

The operating level to which the records-management group reports is an issue of fundamental importance. Obviously, the higher the level in the organization, the more likely is it that records management will be seen as a strategic, rather than simply an operational, function. The evidence suggests that companies are taking records management more seriously today, just as information management has emerged in the last few years as an area of strategic importance.

Records-management programs which are organized on a company-wide basis have some inherent advantages. A companywide program may eliminate potential problems, such as cross-departmental "culture" or "translation" gaps. Furthermore, a piecemeal program does not take advantage of economies of scale and efficiencies of standardization which uniform programs offer.

On the other hand, organizing records management on a departmental basis can preserve the integrity of the function and ensure that the records program remains responsive to users on the local level. The advantages and disadvantages of centralized and local records-management planning offer no clearly prescribed solution. Different firms have chosen different solutions.

In the Fortune 1000 companies today, records management most often reports to administrative service and MIS (management information systems) departments. But in some companies, records management reports to the legal or accounting departments. (This issue will be explored in greater detail in Chapter 3.)

1.7.2 Financial Issues

The allocation of costs and benefits in any records-management program is a difficult task. Costs are often spread throughout a number of operational areas. Similarly, benefits from effective records management can be felt throughout the organization. The goal of a comprehensive records-management program is to allow the organization to meet its objectives more effectively and competitively.

While the benefits of effective records management are hard to track, a records manager will have to provide a concrete statement of costs and benefits in order to sell any records program to top management. As a first step in any cost-benefit analysis, a thorough audit of the company's current records-management system should be carried out. Alternative systems and equipment packages will have to be examined in terms of hard savings potential. Once the selection and implementation of records equipment has been carried out, cost tracking must be continued for an ongoing evaluation of the program. Part 3 of this book examines this process in detail.

1.7.3 Operational Issues

Operationally, records management must serve the business needs of its users within the firm as a whole and in each specific department in particular. At times, the firm's global needs and the department's local needs come into conflict. For instance, it may be decided that by organizing a centralized records-management system, the firm can drastically reduce costs in both equipment and labor to the firm as a whole. On the departmental level, however, the customary way of doing things may be so disrupted by the change that a records retrieval task that used to take only a minute now takes half an hour.

In implementing a records-management system, managers must be aware of the unofficial or "invisible" network within which information is stored and through which it is shared. Such a network is invisible in the sense that it is not explained in any manual of standard operating procedures. In fact, only the participants in such a network know anything about it. For example, suppose within a particular department five individuals are responsible for customer complaints. Because no one else in the firm is charged with this responsibility, they have evolved their own custom-made data base. But, if the firm wants to organize a global customer account data base that incorporates all the information relating to each customer, this data base will necessarily appropriate all of the data on customer complaints. The five individuals will have to learn an entirely new system. The system will probably be located at some remote, less convenient spot. And the net effect on the customer complaint group will be disruptive. The intention of the new centralized system may have been to reduce costs and improve efficiency, but because of the invisible network, the new system accomplished neither. This example serves merely as an illustration of the issues involved. These problems also will be taken up later in a more systematic fashion.

QUESTIONS AND ANSWERS

Q. What is a record?

A. A record is the physical representation of information in one of a variety of forms or formats available. The medium itself may be paper, film, microfilm, magnetic media, or optical disk.

Q. What is the volume of paper records in U.S. business?

A. The proliferation of paper records is accelerating and shows no sign of slowdown. Eighteen billion clerical workers currently track America's daily output of 370 million pages of new business document originals, 1.9 million pages of computer output, and 1.9 billion copies.

Q. What are the stages in a record's life cycle?

A. Records have a four-phase life cycle. Initially, there is the period in which records are created; second, a period of active and frequent use; third, a phase of semi-active or archival use, and finally a period when the records become obsolete and should be destroyed.

Q. What are the origins of records management?

A. Records themselves have existed since the earliest days of our history. Various forms of records management have also been in effect for a very long time. Modern records management, however, had its beginnings in the actions taken by the federal government after World War II to deal with its growing records-management problem.

Q. What is the goal of records management?

A. The goal of records management is to coordinate the financial, human, and equipment resources required to meet an organization's storage and retrieval needs.

Q. What are the principal records costs?

A. While the accurate determination of all costs in a records-management program is a difficult task, personnel and rent comprise between 80 and 90 percent of overall maintenance costs.

Q. What is the relation of records to information?

A. Records contain data which are the substance or building blocks of information. While data can exist in isolation, information is only meaningful in reference to a particular question or task.

Q. What is the scope of records management?

A. Records management includes responsibilities in the following areas:

- Records generation and control (including forms analysis and reports analysis)
- Processing records
- Records storage and retrieval
- Records conversion (for example, from paper to microfiche)
- Records retention and elimination
- Vital records protection
- Records delivery
- Analysis of cost

Challenges for Records Managers in the Information Age

2.1 NEW TECHNOLOGIES CHANGE THE FACE OF RECORDS MANAGEMENT

Today we live in a world marked by the most sophisticated information-processing tools man has ever known. Where information was once limited by our own memories or by the dimensions of a file cabinet, the computer revolution has changed the nature of the game entirely. The development of the tiny computer chip has given users in business, government, science, and education a remarkable range of affordable and portable processing devices. This potential power has been made more accessible with new and powerful software programs. Now everyone from students to chief executives can use computers to gather, store, sift, and analyze information.

American business has been at the forefront of the computer revolution. This invasion of computer technology and office automation has had a strong impact on traditional records-management techniques and practices. In fact, office automation has been one of the contributing factors to an increased demand for records management and records control.

2.1.1 Micrographics

Microfilm media have been available for over 30 years, primarily as a method for archival storage. Businesses began using microforms to store inactive documents in a miniature, cost-effective format. Additionally, microforms offered greater longevity than paper or other media for archival storage.

Today, new technological developments are revolutionizing micrographics use. Computer output microfilm (COM) allows digitally encoded documents to be written directly on fiche cards or filmstrips. COM allows microfilm storage directly onto the microfilm without an intermediate hard copy. Letters, memos, and reports which have been typed on a word processor or PC can thus be saved on microfilm and then filed or reproduced for distribution. Similarly, computer system outputs, which previously consumed reams of printout paper, can be transposed to film directly and stored. COM technology is spurring increased micrographics use and changing the way records managers carry out their duties.

2.1.2 Storage and Retrieval Systems

New hybrid storage and retrieval systems which wed computer technology with advanced storage techniques are rapidly changing the records-management world. These systems offer extremely large storage capacity and automatic high-speed image retrieval. The components of these new systems include on-line computer data bases for indexing, multifunction workstations, COM for records storage, robotic technology for storing and archiving microfilmed records, optical character readers for hard-copy input, and optical disk data storage. These new systems can be tied into a local area network (LAN), thereby allowing remote access and widespread document distribution.

2.1.3 Optical Disks

Optical disk (OD) technology has been in the wings of the office automation revolution for a number of years. Most records managers have already heard reports of the impact optical disks will have in revolutionizing the storage, access, and manipulation of document images. From a purely technical perspective, the capability of optical disks to compact and quickly access data is impressive. The major factors which have prevented their widespread use to date are the lack of a practical erasable technology, relatively high equipment costs, lack of industry-wide standards, and a not-yet-established legal standing for their use as evidence. Technological advances are, however, beginning to overcome many of these drawbacks.

The OD systems now available perform admirably under the current conditions of user demand and user access. Further, many recently released COM and CAR (computer-assisted retrieval) systems are designed for the future addition of OD storage and library modules. The unique strengths of OD storage will be used to supplement the existing media which managers are already familiar with.

2.1.4 Artificial Intelligence

Another area of advancing technology that records managers should be aware of is artificial intelligence. Artificial intelligence is a branch of computer science which attempts to imitate or simulate human cognitive behavior. Such actions would include reasoning, problem solving, learning, game playing, and natural speech recognition. In the last decade or two, computer scientists working on artificial intelligence have emphasized game playing, machine vision (for robotics), knowledge-based or "expert systems," voice recognition, and natural language capability.

These last three areas—expert systems, voice recognition, and natural language systems—will have the greatest impact in the modern office. Although practical applications of these developments are five to ten years away, some benefits of the research are currently being seen in related areas such as system integration and new applications software.

Voice recognition will have a major impact on document generation and word processing. It is already being used, albeit in a limited fashion, to initiate computer commands in several commercially available packages. In the future, voice recognition will be used for document input and could conceivably replace or augment the traditional keyboard.

2.2 OFFICE AUTOMATION—MOVING INFORMATION TECHNOLOGY INTO THE FRONT OFFICE

Technology is not only affecting the tools of records management but shaping records-management practices. In fact, records management is being redefined by the entry of computers and computer processing into the front office. Of course, computers have been a vital tool for most businesses for several decades. But it is only in the last decade that computer use has become widespread among not only data-processing specialists, but a much broader community of end users, including managers, professionals, clericals, secretaries, and other support staff—in short, the full range of office workers.

2.2.1 Back-Office Processing

In the early days of computer use, data processing was a highly specialized activity. Many companies began to create departments of data processing (DP) or management information services (MIS) beginning in the 1960s. The idea was that a dedicated computer department could handle all of the computing needs of the organization. Further, data-processing professionals required systems programming and analysis expertise to run the computers. Not only did end users lack these skills, but they also felt there was no reason for them to gain computer expertise.

The relationship between the data-processing and end user departments was developed in this early period of corporate computer use. Systems analysts from the data-processing department would confer with end users to determine their computing requirements for applications such as sales orders, billing and receipts, payables, and inventory accounting. The systems analyst would submit his or her systems design to a programmer in the DP department, who would then write the actual program.

The processing at this time was done in batch mode. In other words, the tasks were queued in the computer and run sequentially. Upon completion of these tasks, the computer would then produce a queue of output reports.

Computerization offered companies several benefits in terms of increased speed and accuracy of data handling. Computers were used for applications at a clerical level, supporting or displacing clerical personnel. However, there were several problems with data processing which soon became apparent to data-processing professionals and the business executives they serviced.

The first problem had to do with the nature of the data-processing department's interface with end users. Systems analysts, while well versed in data processing, often lacked the business expertise to translate users' needs into effective systems. End users, on the other hand, often miscommunicated their needs to data-processing specialists or needed to introduce new kinds of information into inflexible systems.

Another problem had to do with the technology itself. Batch processing did not allow users (technically proficient or otherwise) to query their computer systems interactively. In order to get any information out of the computer, a report had to be designed, fed into the computer, and queued behind any other outstanding jobs. Data-processing backlogs became inevitable, and data-processing departments had to impose schedules on end users, who quickly became impatient for the information they needed.

2.2.2 Front-Office Processing

The next stage in the history of corporate computing occurred with the development of powerful minicomputers. Based on new developments in integrated circuitry, the minicomputers were able to handle vast amounts of data at fast processing speeds. The new machines were smaller than the previous generation of computers, and less expensive. A host of new suppliers became serious players in the computer industry based on their minicomputer products.

Along with increasing miniaturization, newer generations of computers were able to handle interactive, as opposed to batch, processing. This meant that users could literally interact with a computer in "real time," rather than wait for a special report to be written and run.

It was not until the advent of the microcomputer, however, that computers began to appear in the front office. Smaller than a minicomputer, the microcomputer was small enough to sit on a user's desktop, like a "dumb" terminal. Unlike a dumb terminal, however, which has no intelligence (processing capability), microcomputers could be used to write and run independent programs without the assistance of a larger device.

The first front-office function to be automated was secretarial, through the development of the dedicated word processor. While a word processor can simply be a program which runs on a computer for creating, editing, and printing text, a dedicated word processor is a microcomputer that is designed primarily for word processing. Dedicated word processors quickly became popular in companies with a requirement for a high volume of typing, particularly repetitive typing such as form letters and mass mailings. While some companies placed their word processors in an automated typing pool, or word-processing center, these machines were soon seen appearing on secretarial desktops.

Microcomputers quickly moved from the secretarial to the professional's desktop with the advent of the electronic spreadsheet. VisiCalc was the first of a multitude of such spreadsheet packages to become popular and quickly spurred the sales of Apple, IBM, and other microcomputers. Today there are literally hundreds of applications software packages available for microcomputers. The most popular applications continue to be word processing, spreadsheets, and database management packages, in addition to business graphics, calendaring and scheduling, and electronic mail.

For the records manager, the implications of front-office processing are enormous. More and more users are creating, handling, storing, and retrieving documents electronically. The microcomputer is becoming not only a tool for a user's individual needs (hence the name "personal computer"), but a window on a company's electronic data base. In addition to the benefits offered by front-office processing in terms of increased record integrity, speed of processing, and quicker and more efficient communications, however, there are dangers. These dangers include possible user resentment of the new tools, misuse, and a lack of security from electronic tampering.

2.3 USING INFORMATION COMPETITIVELY

A few years ago, most corporate executives knew little about computers and office automation. For the most part those who had in-house information-processing systems were unaware of the potential of these machines and what they might provide for their companies.

Today, corporate awareness not only of computers but of information management has changed radically. Business executives are now far more concerned than in the past with what their information systems are providing—and not providing. Management is increasingly aware that in today's business environment, information management is not just an aid to better bookkeeping, but also a key competitive weapon.

Some of the ways in which businesses are using information technology to increase their competitiveness include automated product development, better financial management, and computer-assisted customer service. In the area of marketing, information technology is being used in improved market intelligence, sales, and telemarketing. The technologies are making new businesses possible. Some companies are even selling extra processing power to provide new services for their clients.

In this way information processing is altering the very nature of business from the ground up. The ability to collect, manage, and enhance information is having a profound effect on a broad range of industries.

2.4 THE BENEFITS OF AUTOMATED RECORDS MANAGEMENT

The primary benefit of integrative office automation (OA) is that the records manager today can have a degree of total information flow control never before possible. OA has affected each stage of the record life cycle and, like it or not, the office of yesterday is gone forever. The advent of cheaper, more powerful, and easier-to-use systems is partly responsible. Just as important is the fact that organizations are only now beginning to actually realize and enjoy the benefits of information technology and office automation which had been heralded for so long.

Fortunately for records managers, the automation of information management provides the tools as well as the need for controlling this enormous potential. For example, the union of database management software with computer output microfilm or optical disks allows for systems with performance features never before possible. Not only can very large image or document bases be reduced and stored on highly efficient media, but advanced cataloging and indexing methods can be utilized. This allows users to access records in a variety of novel ways and also allows records managers to update and maintain the currency of the classification system much more quickly and thoroughly.

Some of the other principal benefits of records-management automation follow.

2.4.1 Reduction of Human Intervention

Automated records-management systems eliminate much of the physical paper handling associated with the active and inactive phases of the records life cycle in more traditional systems. When documents are no longer stored on paper in hundreds of thousands of file cabinets, clerks need no longer be sent to physically retrieve them. Instead, the user sits at a video screen linked to an integrated CAR system and conducts a document search utilizing a procedure customized for that type of industry or even particular company.

Having identified the document and its identification number by means of a key word, invoice number, or chronological index, the user then calls up an image of the document on the screen and reviews it for the desired information. If necessary, a hard copy can be produced on a laser or other type of printer. Different systems allow for various levels of access activity, and these should be matched to the user's need level.

2.4.2 Increased Access Speed and Accuracy

Access time in automated storage and retrieval systems varies depending on the level of sophistication and the components used in a particular system. Because these systems store an accurate image of the original document, all of the information contained therein is available. This includes nontextual data such as drawings, graphs, and charts as well as signatures.

2.4.3 Reduced Space Requirements

The earliest users of microfilmed records wanted to take advantage of the medium's information compaction ability. Space savings in automated systems remains a principal benefit. With rents steadily increasing, freeing up storage space is a prime factor for advanced records-management systems.

Automated systems also save space through the elimination or reduction of multiple copies of documents required for use by different departments or individuals, often at different locations. Eliminating these multiple copies with an on-line central storage and retrieval facility can increase space savings by more than a factor or two or three. Total companywide savings can therefore be greater than at first anticipated.

2.5 CHANGING USER DEMANDS

We have already seen that records-management technology has undergone a great amount of change over the last five to ten years. There is no evidence that this process of technological evolution is coming to an end. In fact, the evidence suggests that the rate of technological change is accelerating. Today, for example, inexpensive microcomputers have the same amount of memory and processing speed as much larger minicomputers of ten years ago.

Adjustments must be made not only for new equipment, but also for the changing demands of those who make use of the tools in carrying out their daily responsibilities. In 1983 most records managers and information specialists in large companies saw a greater demand for document management in their companies compared with the previous two-year period (see Exhibit 2.1). In fact, 94 percent of those who saw a change said there was a "greater" or "much greater demand" for document management than in the recent past.

According to these professionals, increased user demand is being driven by a variety of factors. Foremost among these are security concerns. Users are demanding that greater restrictions be placed on sensitive information to prevent unauthorized disclosures, misinformation, and outright piracy. Additionally, the need for better decision-making is making itself felt from users who expect better service and more timely information from modern, computerized systems. Other factors driving user demands are space constraints, regulatory requirements, and greater competitiveness.

As a means of illustrating these changing needs, let's follow the creation of a business proposal through the processes, tools, and data sources used to come up with a finished product. Initially, the individual who is charged with such a task would first create the proposal outline. The author would then in all likelihood need to consult several sources of information. These could range from internally generated market data, financial projections, and customer correspondence to external sources such as financial reports and business periodicals.

Today, the author could very likely find that these diverse sources are all stored on different media. He or she may have to assemble a mix of paper-based, microfilm based, and on-line database information. Once the information has been assembled, the proposal generator would then most likely want to manipulate the data for a number of scenarios. The next step may be to depict these results in graphs or other visual forms and then to incorporate these into a document. The writer would then circulate the proposed document among his or her colleagues for comments, integrate these changes, prepare a final document, and finally present it for action.

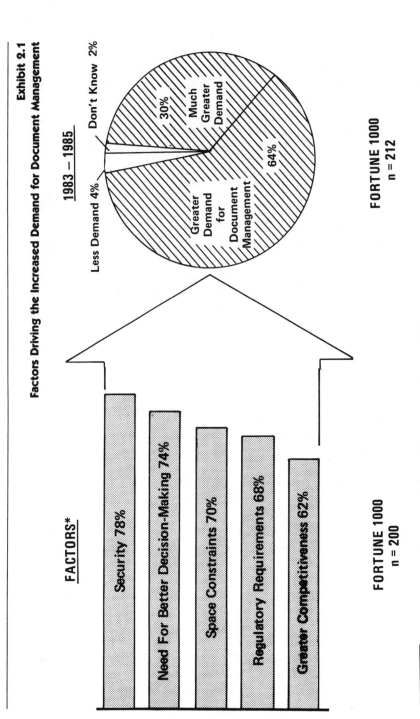

Exhibit 2.1

Factors Driving the Increased Demand for Document Management

1983 – 1985

Don't Know 2%

Less Demand 4%

30%
Much Greater Demand

64%

Greater Demand for Document Management

FORTUNE 1000
n = 212

FACTORS*

Security 78%

Need For Better Decision-Making 74%

Space Constraints 70%

Regulatory Requirements 68%

Greater Competitiveness 62%

FORTUNE 1000
n = 200

*Rated as "extremely important" in increased demand for document management

From this illustration we can see that the research effort and the various steps in producing and distributing the document place novel demands on the company's records system. The various tools and resources of data processing, word processing, and other departments must be combined into a unified whole.

The demand for integrated records management comes from a number of areas within a company. This includes sales, product development, marketing, finance, and accounting. Records managers must ensure that users' needs are met in the most timely and cost-effective manner available.

The pressures put on records managers is illustrated by how they rate their companies' records handling systems in terms of retrieval time, file integrity, and security. Exhibit 2.2 shows the percentage of records managers and MIS professionals who are not very satisfied with their systems performance for the three major types of documents: corporate or vital documents, active documents, and personal documents. A substantial number of these professionals see room for improvement in all three areas, particularly file integrity. Further, a greater percentage of MIS professionals are dissatisfied than records managers, illustrating the potential for conflict between these groups as their areas of responsibility overlap. We shall explore the relationship between records management and MIS in greater detail in Chapter 3.

2.6 RECORDS MANAGERS AND CHANGE

The role of the records manager is currently undergoing fundamental changes. This chapter has already discussed many aspects of this change, including new technologies, the changing role of information in the business world, and new user demands. In response to this altered environment, records managers must recognize their new role and begin to adapt to it. These new roles are giving records managers a new level of responsibility. As information becomes more and more important, both as a tool of the company to carry out its mission and as a potential revenue-generating commodity, the stewardship of that information carries added importance.

In looking at new opportunities for records managers, one should keep in mind that changes in the environment have created a need for a different breed of managers. They must exhibit a greater degree of flexibility and adjustability than their counterparts of ten years ago. The modern records manager must be technically versed. The array of equipment, systems, and technologies can be confusing unless the records manager has a framework for evaluating competing systems.

To date, records managers as a group remain largely unaware of some of the latest technological developments affecting their field. For ex-

Exhibit 2.2
Dissatisfaction Index: Document Handling

TYPE OF DOCUMENT	PARAMETER			RESPONDENT GROUP
	RETRIEVAL TIME	FILE INTEGRITY	SECURITY	
Corporate/Vital	16%	32%	15%	Records Managers
	34%	33%	21%	MIS/DP
Active	22%	36%	23%	Records Managers
	35%	41%	36%	MIS/DP
Personal	24%	35%	22%	Records Managers
	36%	37%	40%	MIS/DP

FORTUNE 1000
n = 302

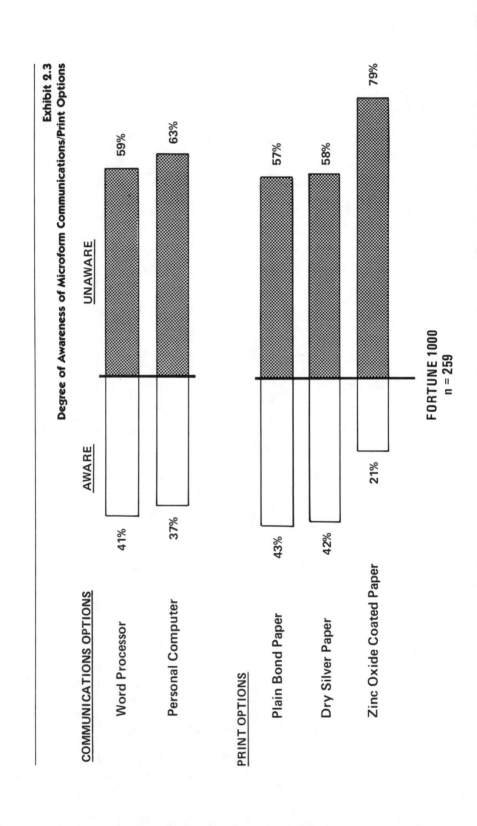

Exhibit 2.3

Degree of Awareness of Microform Communications/Print Options

COMMUNICATIONS OPTIONS

AWARE | UNAWARE

Word Processor — 41% / 59%

Personal Computer — 37% / 63%

PRINT OPTIONS

Plain Bond Paper — 43% / 57%

Dry Silver Paper — 42% / 58%

Zinc Oxide Coated Paper — 21% / 79%

FORTUNE 1000
n = 259

ample, in the Fortune 1000 companies, a majority of records and MIS professionals were unaware that microforms can be interfaced to desktop devices such as a word processor or personal computer (see Exhibit 2.3). Further, a majority of these professionals were unaware of the various print options on the latest generation of microform printers. Records managers have had to begin to address their need for ongoing training in new technologies in order to make informed decisions about new systems for their companies.

This chapter has, in a sense, posed the challenge for the future: to master new technologies, meet user requirements, and exercise records-management control in such a way that it can be most effective. While the new tools are powerful, the automation of information processing has created a greater range of records to be managed. Although automation can be a double-edged sword, it cannot be ignored any longer. The only viable option is to control its enormous potential. Fortunately for records managers, the task is not impossible, but it will require training and re-education.

Clearly, records managers need to examine the framework for decision-making at their own firm. If records managers are to be responsible for the performance of document and information management systems, then they must be given a strong voice in determining what systems will be implemented.

QUESTIONS AND ANSWERS

Q. What is the current state of records management?

A. Computer technology and the spread of office automation are having a strong effect on traditional records-management techniques and practices. New tools and systems are changing how records are handled and used.

Q. What are the principal new technologies?

A. The new technologies include microcomputers and applications software, advanced micrographics systems, automated storage and retrieval systems, optical disk, and artificial intelligence.

Q. What is to be gained from information technologies?

A. Information technologies can help the members of the organization achieve business goals in a more efficient and effective manner. More specifically, costs and time can be saved, and a greater range of functions can be at the disposal of personnel.

Q. What is the new role of information?

A. Information is increasingly being seen as a product of a company's operations and as a potentially valuable commodity or resource that can generate income. Information and the new technologies are affecting product development, financial management, customer service, marketing, and sales operations.

Q. What are the principal benefits of records-management automation?

A. The principal benefits include: a reduction of human intervention, increased speed and accuracy, and reduced space requirements.

Q. How does one describe the "new" records manager?

A. New managers will be more flexible and more technically versed than their predecessors. Additionally, they must be capable of examining, evaluating, and selecting companywide information management systems.

3

The New Role of the Records Manager

3.1 PLACEMENT OF THE RECORDS-MANAGEMENT FUNCTION

Given the pressures on records managers, both in terms of increasing user demands and the need to master new technologies, where does the records manager fit into the corporate hierarchy? As discussed in the last chapter, records management is only one of several corporate functions dealing with the management of information. Thus, the records manager will coexist with specialists in personal computing, telecommunications, office automation, and data processing.

In the past, records management was considered an administrative science and, as such, under the authority of the administrative or administrative services department in most large companies. However, in the last few years there has been a growing movement toward placing records management under the aegis of the data-processing or MIS department. The argument for integrating records management and MIS is twofold. First, records management is increasingly concerned with storing and retrieving information from computerized systems. Since the MIS department is the source of expertise on computers, decisions about computerized systems should be made in concert with MIS.

The second part of the argument for integrating records management with MIS is that MIS is not only the source of computer expertise but, more broadly, the custodian of information handling throughout the company. According to this argument, records management is a specialized MIS function that makes decisions about the physical records through which information is stored and retrieved.

One of the assumptions underlying this argument is that there should be a centralized authority responsible for information handling in the company. Historically, this has been the MIS department. In the last chapter we saw how office automation has pushed information technologies, such as word processors, personal computers, and intelligent terminals, down to the end user. Along with the tools has come the responsibility for managing information. In the future, advances in information technology and the spread of computer expertise may dictate a fundamental change in the role of the MIS department. Indeed, the evidence suggests that this shift has already begun to occur.

3.2 OFFICE AUTOMATION POLICYMAKING

The new end-user technologies are reshaping the role of the records manager, since records managers must concern themselves with the ways in which records are stored and accessed. While in the past this has meant paper-based systems, today the records manager must oversee a variety of automated and semi-automated systems, incorporating a variety of media.

If we lump these end-user technologies under the umbrella "office automation," then we must ask who is responsible for office automation in this broader sense in corporate America today.

Exhibit 3.1 displays the profile of OA policymakers in the Fortune 500 industrials and service companies, medium-sized companies (the next tier below the Fortune 1000), and small companies (defined as having from 10 to 100 employees). In the large firms, OA policy is most often set by an interdepartmental committee, next most often by a single department with responsibility for office automation. In striking contrast to the large firms, the medium-sized and small firms typically assign OA decision-making to the company president or an interdepartmental committee, rarely to a dedicated department. Noticeably, across all companies, regardless of size, user departments rarely set their own office automation policies.

Who sits on the interdepartmental committee? Exhibit 3.2 shows the distribution of the policymaking committee in the Fortune 500 industrial companies. MIS or data processing is the department which most often sits on these committees, along with administration, finance or strategic planning, end users, and telecommunications. MIS is typically the most influential member of the committee.

When OA policy is set by a single department, that department is MIS in 71 percent of the industrial 500 firms (see Exhibit 3.2). The num-

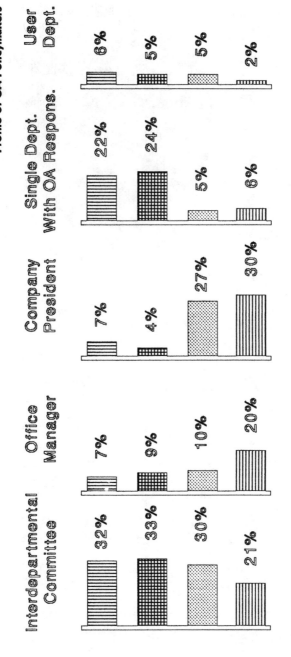

Exhibit 3.1
Profile of OA Policymakers

Interdepartmental Committee

- 32%
- 33%
- 30%
- 21%

Office Manager

- 7%
- 9%
- 10%
- 20%

Company President

- 7%
- 4%
- 27%
- 30%

Single Dept. With OA Respons.

- 22%
- 24%
- 5%
- 6%

User Dept.

- 6%
- 5%
- 5%
- 2%

FORTUNE 500 INDUSTRIALS FORTUNE 500 SERVICE

MEDIUM-SIZED COMPANIES SMALL COMPANIES

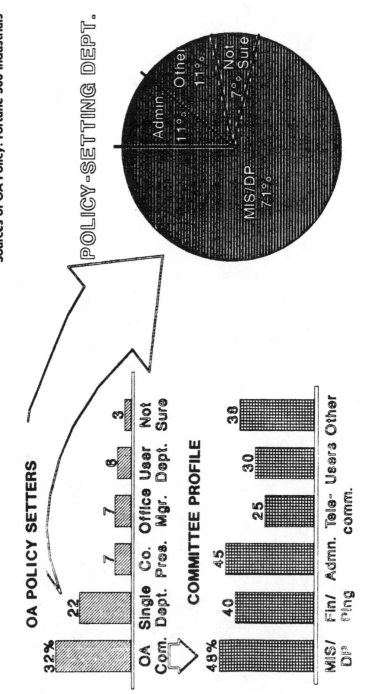

Exhibit 3.2
Sources of OA Policy: Fortune 500 Industrials

OA POLICY SETTERS

32%	
22	
7	7	6	3

OA Com. | Single Dept. | Co. Pres. | Office Mgr. | User Dept. | Not Sure

POLICY-SETTING DEPT.

Admn. 11% | Other 11% | Not Sure 7%

MIS/DP 71%

COMMITTEE PROFILE

4.8%	
40	45	25	30	38

MIS/ DP | Fin/ Plng | Admn. | Tele-comm. | Users | Other

bers are strikingly similar in the service 500 companies. The conclusion is clearly that MIS is the single most important group in setting OA policy in the largest companies, either as the centralized decision-making department or as the most influential voice on an interdepartmental committee.

3.3 STRATEGIC ISSUES IN OFFICE AUTOMATION POLICYMAKING

Whereas MIS was solely concerned with large-scale data processing in the past, today it has expanded its role to include the myriad components of office automation. This has meant a shift in focus and responsibility of the MIS department. Exhibit 3.3 shows the new strategic issues confronting MIS in the area of office automation.

Rather than developing and maintaining systems, as it has done in data processing, MIS is playing the role of standard-bearer and gatekeeper. The rush by end users in the last few years to purchase affordable microcomputers is a perfect example of the movement of technology decision-making, on a personal or even departmental scale, toward the end user. To meet this challenge to its autonomy, MIS is

- establishing standards and protocols,
- setting methods for evaluating equipment,
- establishing vendor of choice lists for office technologies,
- developing needs assessment methodologies,
- choosing office technologies and services which can be acquired, and
- establishing corporatewide OA objectives.

The implications for the records manager is that he or she will have to make decisions in light of MIS objectives. Further, when purchasing particular components of automated records systems, the records manager will have to adhere to MIS policies, guidelines, and architectures.

The evolution of the MIS department is also instructive for the records manager of the 1980s and beyond. Just as MIS is playing the role of standard-bearer as end users gain increasing control of office technologies, so too must the records manager set policies, standards, and guidelines on records use and communicate these to end users. Today, the records manager cannot realistically expect to maintain physical control over all of the company's records. In the case of computerized files, anyone with access to a terminal (given company-specific restrictions) can get at the files. However, the records manager can take steps to ensure that corporate records activities adhere to uniform guidelines set by the records department.

Exhibit 3.3

Strategic Issues in Office Automation: The Fortune Companies

PERCENT OF COMPANIES WHOSE OA POLICIES COVER THIS ISSUE:

Issue	Fortune 500 Industrials	Fortune 500 Service
Method of Evaluating Equipment	78%	80%
OA Objectives	91%	89%
Needs Assessment	90%	94%
Standards and Protocols	87%	90%
Vendor of Choice	89%	85%
Technologies That Can Be Acquired	80%	84%
Services That Can Be Acquired	79%	86%

FORTUNE 500 INDUSTRIALS   FORTUNE 500 SERVICE

3.4 DECISION-MAKING FOR DOCUMENT STORAGE AND RETRIEVAL SYSTEMS

The records-management function is being reshaped by the introduction of automated document storage and retrieval systems into American business. Who is making the decisions about these systems today? Are they being selected by a centralized records-management department? Are they left up to end users? Or have these systems been selected and purchased by the MIS department?

The decision-making process for these systems is a good illustration of the state of records management today and the challenges facing records managers. Exhibit 3.4 illustrates that in the Fortune 1000 companies, these decisions are made by a centralized group in only 32 percent of firms. In most firms (46 percent), the decision-making is "controlled decentralized"; in other words, the decisions are left up to individual departments or divisions within the company but monitored and influenced by a centralized authority, such as records management or MIS.

Who is the authority when these decisions are made by a central body? As illustrated in Exhibit 3.4, there are a variety of players involved. While records management is most often the decision-maker, other groups include MIS, OA committees, administrative services, records committees, and purchasing. In a quarter of the cases, the centralized body is a collection of groups acting in concert (such as records management and MIS).

The diversity of voices involved in selecting document storage and retrieval systems indicates that records management today is in a state of flux. While the records manager is often called upon to select these systems, in many companies he or she has no choice but to work around systems which have been chosen by other departments without his or her advice.

One of the reasons that the records-management department has not yet emerged as the dominant voice in the selection of storage and retrieval systems is the lack of computer expertise in records management. As records managers become increasingly proficient in computer systems, however, one would anticipate that they will play a greater role in the selection and purchase of storage and retrieval systems. Without the records manager's input, there is an obvious danger that such systems may be inappropriate from the viewpoint of the company's records requirements.

3.5 RELATIONSHIP BETWEEN MIS AND RECORDS MANAGEMENT

Earlier in this chapter, we discussed the argument for integrating the records-management and MIS departments. Exhibit 3.5 shows the status

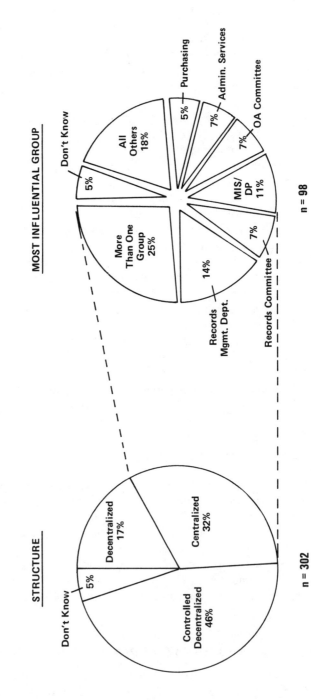

Exhibit 3.4
Decision-Making in the Fortune 1000: Document Storage and Retrieval Systems

STRUCTURE

Don't Know
5%

Decentralized
17%

Centralized
32%

Controlled
Decentralized
46%

n = 302

MOST INFLUENTIAL GROUP

Don't Know
5%

All
Others
18%

Purchasing
5%

Admin. Services
7%

OA Committee
7%

MIS/
DP
11%

More
Than One
Group
25%

7%

Records
Mgmt. Dept.
14%

Records Committee

n = 98

Exhibit 3.5
Relationship between MIS and Document Management

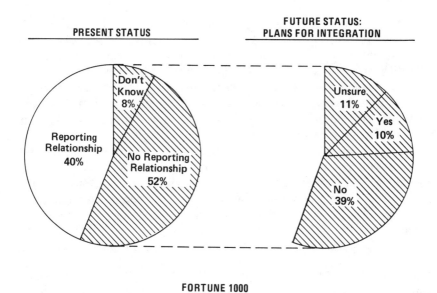

PRESENT STATUS

FUTURE STATUS:
PLANS FOR INTEGRATION

Reporting Relationship 40%

Don't Know 8%

No Reporting Relationship 52%

Unsure 11%

Yes 10%

No 39%

FORTUNE 1000
n = 302

of that integration in the Fortune 1000 today. In 52 percent of Fortune 1000 companies there is no reporting relationship between the departments, compared to 40 percent where such a relationship exists. Further, among companies where there is no reporting relationship today, only a minority plan to effect that integration in the near future. Roughly two-thirds of these companies plan to keep the two areas separate for at least the next two years.

There are several advantages to integrating records management with MIS. Foremost among these is that each area has unique expertise to share with the other. In companies where no such relationship exists, records managers will have to take steps to ensure that lines of communication remain open between the two departments so that decisions which affect both areas can be made jointly.

3.6 INFORMATION RESOURCE MANAGEMENT

We have seen that the corporate milieu in which the records manager operates is rapidly evolving as MIS and records-management professionals are called upon to master new technologies and meet new responsibilities. In Chapter 1 we outlined the traditional functions of the records manager. While the goals of the records manager today remain essentially the same, the steps taken to meet these goals are changing as information systems throughout a corporation are implemented and modified.

"Information resource management" is a label for a new approach to managing the corporate information infrastructure. While information management relates to the words and data generated by computerized or semi-automated systems, information resource management is dedicated to establishing controls over the staff, equipment, and services that generate that information. This includes the traditional records-management responsibility for the creation, processing, retrieving, storing, and use of information.

Many companies today are moving toward information resource management as a solution to their need for integrated information systems development, maintenance, and use. This shift in management philosophy offers several benefits compared with the compartmentalization of computing, business services, records management, and office automation which still remain in many companies today. Information resource management is particularly well suited to the technological developments that are bridging previously diverse disciplines such as data processing, telecommunications, and office automation. These technological advances will be discussed in detail in Part 2 of this book.

3.7 SELLING RECORDS MANAGEMENT TO TOP MANAGEMENT

All the benefits of information resource management will remain only goals unless implemented. Once a course of action is decided upon or arrived at by consensus, the support of at least two groups must be obtained. The first is the support of upper management. This is followed by support from end users.

The records manager will have to take different approaches to gaining the approval of these two groups. This is because the needs and concerns of each group are distinct. Success depends on early identification of these distinct needs and the development of a strategy to address them.

One of the first steps to be taken is to determine organizational readiness. Concerning top management, a number of issues can result in reluctance or resistance. One of the most obvious obstacles to top management support can be unawareness of a problem or need. "What's wrong with the way things are now?" is often a first reaction. This may be because the symptoms of a poor records or information management system are not evident. Delays in solving customer problems or inquiries, for example, are often blamed on poor coordination of departments or many other extraneous factors.

An additional area of concern or objection by top management to a new records-management system is the issue of increased costs. While a substantial initial capital outlay may be required, this is an area where it is difficult to quantify the benefits of success. Part of this concern is becoming alleviated as upper managers realize the new role of information and the importance it can have on bottom-line results and increased competitive advantage. For example, new automated information systems can greatly alter the way financial data and resources are handled. Much better and more timely cash and financial management can be exercised, resulting in the reduction of uncertainty and a reduced float. Even direct links to a company's bank are possible with today's electronic networks, eliminating delay in transaction times and confirmations.

The second group which must be addressed by the records manager is the end users. Active involvement in systems study and design helps to alleviate the resentments caused by implementing new tools and procedures. Besides system selection, an effective implementation plan must be formulated. Successful plans anticipate difficulties and establish clearly defined mileposts and objectives.

3.8 NEW RESPONSIBILITIES FOR RECORDS MANAGERS

The task facing records managers is neither simple nor easy to accomplish. But it is not impossible. "New" records managers must possess the skills that will allow them to carry out the expanded responsibilities. Specifically these new responsibilities would include the following:

Technology planning. The availability of new and more powerful tools means that new ways of designing systems must be developed. Senior management is looking to the records and information specialist to provide leadership in making the transition to new technologies. Today, the focus is changing from standalone to multifunction and multi-user systems. Driven by high demand and the growing realization that information is a strategic tool, the new technologies result in systems which are much more complex and which need to be designed with future developments in mind.

Information-systems strategic planning. This area is a high-level activity which links information and records management to the strategic plan of the corporation. It dictates the way in which such systems support corporate goals and strategy. In instances which are becoming more and more frequent, advanced information systems are actually influencing the strategy of the firm itself by increasing productivity or profitability or by allowing for the development of new products and services.

Human resource management, including computer literacy or education programs. Computer-based technology requires new skills and abilities of those interacting with the systems. A large majority of American companies provide computer skills training. Understandably, the larger companies provide a higher level of in-house training compared with smaller companies. While in-house training may often be used for existing employees, companies are increasingly requiring computer skills of job applicants. Records managers are being called upon to provide skills development not only for their own staff, but for a broad base of end users.

Support and consultation. This area should show steady growth in demand over time. Records managers will be required to communicate the potential of new and developing information resource management systems. They will also be called upon to modify or update these systems as user requirements change. In some companies, the records manager may become part of an internal consulting team, retained on an as-needed basis.

QUESTIONS AND ANSWERS

Q. Where do records-management departments report in most businesses today?

A. Traditionally, records management has reported to the administrative or administrative services department. In about 40 percent of the Fortune 1000 companies, records management reports to the MIS department.

Q. What is the argument for integrating records management and MIS?

A. The argument for integrating records management and MIS is that the MIS department is the source of computer expertise at a time when records are increasingly being handled electronically. Further, MIS is generally the corporate custodian of information handling and the body responsible for setting information objectives and policies.

Q. Who is in charge of office automation policymaking in most businesses?

A. In the Fortune 1000, office automation policymaking is usually the responsibility of a dedicated department (typically MIS) or an interdepartmental committee. In smaller firms, OA policies are set by an interdepartmental committee or the company president.

Q. What is meant by the term "information resource management"?

A. Information resource management is an approach to centralized control of a company's staff, equipment, and services dedicated to information generation. This would include the creation, processing, storing, retrieving, and use of information.

Q. What skills should records managers possess to meet these new responsibilities?

A. Records managers are being called upon to provide technology planning and evaluation, end-user education, and end-user support and consultation. Meeting these needs will require expertise in computer and related technologies, analytical skills, and oral and written communication skills.

PART 2

THE TOOLS OF RECORDS MANAGEMENT

4

Manual Filing Systems

Despite the potential inherent in automated records management to revolutionize filing, automated systems have not yet created the paperless office. Most records systems still consist of a mixture of computer retention and manual filing. Documents such as vital company records must be kept in hard copy for legal and administrative purposes. Manual filing systems, then, have not become obsolete. Furthermore, it would be impossible to effectively automate a company's record program if its manual system were not up-to-date and well organized. Simply having a good manual filing system is a prerequisite to undergoing any sort of records-management overhaul. This chapter will lay out the basic principles of classification and the tools of storage. The rest of this section will explain the tools of automated management.

4.1 TYPES OF FILES

File classification has several different aspects. First, there must be a method for finding particular documents. Document identification, whether numerically or alphabetically, and document location are thus crucial components of any classification scheme. Second, individual documents have to be sorted into different categories, each of which becomes a file or a file series. File series can consist of anything from correspondence to invoice notices to pension records. Obviously, classification schemes for each group of records will vary depending on the content and type of file. Even more generally, file series are categorized according to how they are used by the company, whether for legal or financial reasons or only for conducting normal day-to-day business. Again, these factors are important in determining where files should be kept and how they are organized.

For example, records such as charters, deeds, and contracts are known as archival or inactive vital records. Specifically, vital records are those that a company would need to start its business from scratch if everything else were destroyed. Other documents in this category would be tax and pension records, patents, property leases, and accounts receivable documents. These records normally comprise less than 2 percent of a firm's document inventory and are almost never consulted during daily operations.

Other inactive files must be kept to meet legal and administrative requirements, but they do not demand special security measures. These records range from historical correspondence and internal memos to general business records and reports. Most of them were frequently used at one point but have entered a different stage in the records life cycle. In their inactive phase, they may be used for occasional reference but need not be readily accessible. Finally, every company has sets of active files—employees actually use them every day. Active series are usually recently generated documents like letters and memos, or consistently used information like payroll files or accounts payable.

Obviously, each of these file categories demands different treatment. Vital records require a high level of security, with limited need for accessibility. Inactive records need to be located where people can get at them if necessary and without taking up valuable space. Active records require means for speedy and convenient retrieval by particular employees.

4.2 CLASSIFICATION SCHEMES

Once documents are grouped according to content and use, each file series must be given an internal organization. No one filing system can accommodate all types of series, so it is best to have a grasp of all the available methods.

The simplest form of organizing a group of documents is alphabetically by name. It is a well-known method which doesn't have to be taught to new staff members and doesn't require a special index. Alphabetizing by name works best with personnel and customer files or with special adaptations like geographical place names. Even such a simple system has its drawbacks, however. Large series are often hampered by misspelled or misfiled names. Some alphabetizing rules, such as those governing acronyms like IBM or WNYC or the infamous Mac's and Mc's, are unclear or generally unknown. If a company has many such special cases, it could develop its own rule book, but more likely a guide like *Rules for Alphabetical Filing* (prepared by the Association of Records Managers and Administrators) will suffice.

Another way to avoid alphabetical confusion is to adopt a phonetic indexing of names. In certain instances, considerable amounts of time are wasted searching for uncertain spellings. Systems like Soundex operate by assigning a combination of letters and numbers based on consonant sounds. Obviously the trouble it takes to learn such a scheme is only worthwhile for very large filing enterprises such as state criminal records.

With a standard alphabetical format, documents can be filed by subjects or key words as well as by names. Obviously these classification schemes require more thought, as designating subject headings with cross-references is not always a clear-cut task. Key word indexing involves pulling out significant words in the title or text which identify the document's content. If you take this type of referencing one step further, an entire document can be condensed into a one-sentence or one-paragraph abstract. Abstracts can be retrieved through the use of a subject or key word index. The advantage of all these content-oriented filing systems is that they provide more visible information about a file than a mere name or number could offer. However, subject categories must be standardized in order to avoid confusion. To this end, records management should create detailed functional headings and subheadings which can accommodate most of the firm's records.

Some documents, like purchase orders, invoices, or checks, are most easily accessed by number. Numeric filing schemes assign a sequential number to each document. The simplest type of numeric file is chronological, but obviously a date gives the least amount of information about the documents the file contains. A more complex number system would take the date as well as the document type into its code. Although numerical files require a reference index in order to find a document, they have the advantage of being easily cross-referenced and less unwieldy than word title files. When document numbers do get unwieldy, say over five digits, documents can simply be filed according to the last two digits. Otherwise, for smaller files, consecutive filing should be adequate.

To make any of the schemes mentioned above more accessible, color coding can be a useful highlighting tool. In a numbering system, each digit from zero to nine can be assigned a different color. Likewise, letters of the alphabet, calendar years, or departments can be similarly coded. Instituting such a filing support device is relatively simple, as color codes can be purchased ready-made. Training to use color coding is also fairly basic, as long as the colors are distinctive and the code is easy to remember.

4.3 FILING EQUIPMENT

Efficient storage is the cornerstone of an economical and accessible records program. Because of the unique demands of each office, in terms of available space, quantity of documents, and type of use, choosing and arranging file equipment will be one of the records-management team's primary responsibilities. Ideal records storage requires durable equipment designed for specific uses. It must provide the greatest amount of filing capacity per square foot without sacrificing convenience and accessibility. Other criteria include security requirements and fire protection, the need for expansion and mobility, the size of the documents, and the speed with which they must be retrieved.

4.3.1 Vertical Filing

The most traditional storage container is the vertical filing cabinet with either four or five drawers. It is most convenient for departmental storage of limited document series. With more than several cabinets stacked together, vertical filing becomes an inefficient use of space, but for individual offices with one or two primary users, it can still be the best option. Although retrieval is not instantaneous, documents can be removed without sifting through or removing entire files. Physical access to the files, which can be problematic for multiple users, is adequate for a one-secretary office. Also, limited security is fairly easy to achieve, by simply putting locks on confidential drawers. However, for highly confidential or vital records, these metal cabinets provide inadequate protection. Locks can be picked or otherwise violated, and metal is extremely vulnerable to heat.

4.3.2 Lateral Filing

For small offices or personal files, lateral filing is another familiar cabinet option. Lateral files are wider and narrower than vertical ones, so that documents are filed from left to right as opposed to front to back. As such, the cabinets need about 25 percent less aisle space for maneuvering drawers. And, because of their narrow width, they are useful as room dividers in open landscape office environments. In reference to other filing criteria, lateral cabinets have similar advantages and disadvantages to vertical ones, although vertical cabinets are considerably cheaper. They provide limited security, convenient but slow retrieval, and are fairly easy to move. In addition, laterally filed documents are slightly less susceptible to fire, but specially insulated files must be purchased to provide real protection.

4.3.3 Open-Shelf Filing

Another option for the small to medium-sized office or department is open-shelf filing. Documents are stacked from left to right, as in lateral cabinets, but there are no drawers or doors to pull out or open. Open shelving can be ideal for file series which are frequently used by several people at once. It is also an extremely efficient space user, because no aisles are needed for moving drawers. An additional plus is the ease of reaching top shelves and viewing their contents, which speeds up retrieval time. And finally open shelving provides the cheapest per square foot filing option available.

There are drawbacks, however, which dictate when these units can be appropriately used. Exposed files may be unappealing or unsuitable for client reception areas. Open shelves can also collect dust and dirt, so that good air-conditioning or ventilating equipment is a must. A more serious problem is the complete lack of security and fire protection which the exposed units afford. As an added inconvenience, all the contents must be removed and the shelves disassembled in order to relocate files.

4.3.4 Compactible Filing

Where space is more of a premium than speed or multiple access, compactible files are an option to consider. More complicated to install and more costly than any of the equipment described so far, compactible files consist of a series of open-shelf units which slide along tracks. These units can be packed together without the normal aisle allowance between each row. Aisles are created as necessary by pushing apart the appropriate unit, either manually or automatically. Obviously, only one set of shelves can be accessed at any time, so that speed and visibility are considerably reduced. Predictably, such a system is also fairly costly to purchase and requires some technical expertise to install and to move. But all these drawbacks may be compensated for if expanded storage capacity makes the difference between moving to a new office space and staying put. Space considerations are likely to be especially crucial in high-rent urban areas.

4.3.5 Automated Files

Automated files are the ultimate in paper storage systems. As such, they are the most costly both to install and to maintain. The motorized unit is shaped like a huge metal box, and files are stored in shelves inside the enclosed box. To retrieve any file, an operator simply pushes a button, and the appropriate shelf is moved directly in front of him or her. The advantage of automated files is the speed with which documents can be effortlessly retrieved from such a high-density unit. But, like compactible files, they are difficult to move. Furthermore, if they break down, you may be left without any access at all. A good maintenance contract with the vendor can alleviate some repair nightmares, but if the vendor's maintenance center is not located nearby, delays can occur. Some files are equipped with manual cranks, but these are so inconvenient to use that it may not even be worthwhile to operate them. The decision to purchase automated files should thus be carefully considered.

Although they represent the state of the art in hard-copy filing, the investment in automated storage systems might be more profitably directed toward computerizing the records (methods are fully described in the following chapter of this book).

4.4 LOCATION OF FILES

When situating your firm's active and inactive files, several factors need to be taken into account. Convenience, available floor space, security, lighting and ventilation, and room for expansion are some of the most important considerations. In addition, any firm's location strategy will depend on the type of business it does and on its management style.

The first decision to be made is whether the company's records will be centralized or decentralized—that is, whether they will be collected in one area or located in each department. If the system is completely decentralized, each department would make its own records decisions. Or, as a compromise, a central managing department can set standards and procedures for files located in the departments.

A central file room would operate like a library, with borrowing regulations and close supervision. This centralized arrangement has the advantage of saving space and equipment as well as the need for multiple copies of documents. In addition, files would always be processed by the same filing staff, thus reducing the chance of mistakes or miscalculations. Departmental users will not react favorably, however, to inconveniently located central filing rooms. In large or spread-out office spaces, such a system might not even be feasible. In this case, an ideal compromise might be a distributed decentralized system where the records management staff works to establish consistent procedures throughout the company. Another alternative would be to build a mixed system by centrally locating only those file series commonly used by several departments.

4.4.1 Records Storage

Whether or not the firm's active files are scattered throughout the departments or located in an active records center, inactive records should be stored together, if at all possible. Creating a storage area not only reduces the costs of duplication and inefficient space utilization, but also standardizes control of the company's memory bank. A well-organized records center reflects and influences the relative efficiency of the entire business. It must balance the demands of inexpensive long-term storage with adequate retrieval speed.

When choosing a location for the records center, on-site options are preferable for convenience. A center within the building also minimizes the cost of transferring records from active to inactive status and of retrieving records for reference. The balancing factor in these cost considerations is, of course, floor space. On-site records centers are normally located in basements to reduce the stress of so much weight, but renting or acquiring such an area may be prohibitively expensive in urban centers. This option is most attractive for small to medium-sized firms with unused space.

Companies with more extensive records may want to pursue one of several off-site options. If the firm has the available land, it could build an adjacent center to house its records. If not, renting warehouse space is probably the cheapest off-site alternative. However, its attractiveness is limited by the difficulty in retrieving. Thus, with a separate records building, the firm can staff it with records-management personnel and good phone service to facilitate requests for information. A warehouse, on the other hand, provides no such services. Getting at any document involves notifying the warehouse company and sending someone from the company down to dig out the record.

A more costly alternative to the leasing of warehouse space is the use of a commercial records center. For the extra money your firm receives a variety of services, from document search to destruction. The level of services does vary, so it's best to check carefully into the schedule of charges and services provided. For instance, some centers will only retrieve entire boxes of records, while others will search for specific documents. Again, some will deliver requests, while others require that you pick them up. In addition to services, the facilities should be fully evaluated, as some have better fire protection or climate control for records preservation.

Wherever you decide to store your firm's records, and whatever classification schemes you employ, it is important that these decisions are seriously weighed. Although manual filing may seem routine and commonplace in this age of electronic storage, it is far from obsolete. Before any firm can even consider the automated storage tools discussed in the next chapters, it must gain control of its manual systems.

QUESTIONS AND ANSWERS

Q. What role in the age of office automation does a manual filing system play in the modern office?

A. Advances in computer-based technology and automated information management systems have still not created the paperless office. Paper remains the primary medium for information sharing and for personal work. The majority of records systems operating now consist of a mix of computer retention and manual paper-based systems. Up-to-date, well-organized systems are also the basis for an automated program. They must therefore be examined and understood before moving ahead.

Q. What are typical methods of classification in a manual system?

A. Documents are first grouped in file series according to their content and use. Then, for internal organization, each series is further classified. Common methods include alphabetizing and numerical ranking which includes chronological indexing.

Q. What are the major types of equipment used in manual filing?

A. Vertical files, lateral files, and open files are the most common and widespread types of hardware. Additionally, more specialized types of files include compactible files and automated files for paper.

5

Imaging Systems

5.1 MICROFILM: A TOOL FOR RECORDS MANAGEMENT

Paperless information storage has been commonplace in many businesses since the 1920s. Micrographics, or the art of recording documents on microfilm, opened the paperless era. Today it is still an essential component of most corporate records-management programs. In fact, although some experts predicted that microfilm would be made obsolete by developments in office automation, the opposite has occurred. State-of-the-art image management systems now seek to integrate micrographic and computer capabilities to create even more effective document storage and retrieval programs. Meanwhile, new storage media like optical disks have been developed to complement micrographics in the record-management systems of the future.

The microfilm industry continues to grow steadily and evenly, supported by a product that produces predictable benefits. A recent study conducted by the Association for Information and Image Management (AIIM) showed that acceptance of microforms by people working in records management is on the rise (see Exhibit 5.1). This chapter will review the various alternatives in document imaging, from the most familiar technologies to the most advanced.

Exhibit 5.1

Attitudes Toward Image Technologies

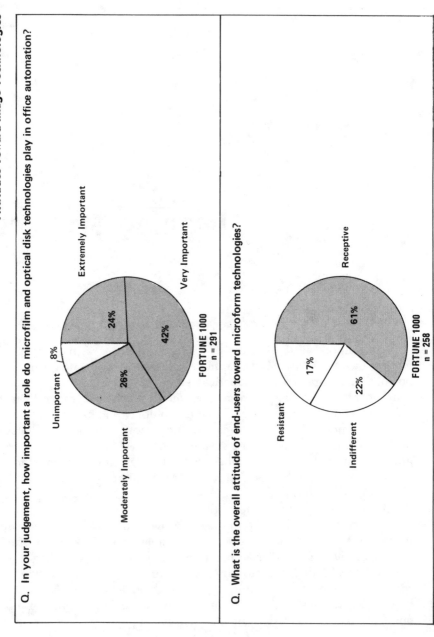

Q. In your judgement, how important a role do microfilm and optical disk technologies play in office automation?

Extremely Important

Very Important

Unimportant 8%

24%

42%

26%

Moderately Important

FORTUNE 1000
n = 291

Q. What is the overall attitude of end-users toward microform technologies?

Receptive

Resistant 17%

61%

22%

Indifferent

FORTUNE 1000
n = 258

There are good reasons for microfilm's staying power. When micro-filming was first introduced over 60 years ago, its primary function was to conserve space. As the cost of office space and the production of documents continued to climb at a rapid rate, the demand for space-saving devices intensified. Microfilm's potential in this regard is obvious. For example, the contents of a four-drawer vertical filing cabinet, such as those discussed in the last chapter, can be included on five or six rolls of 16mm microfilm. Rather than filling 14 cubic feet of storage space, the film occupies no more than 6 percent of a cubic foot. The original file cabinet could hold approximately 1,000 rolls of film, or the equivalent of nearly 250 such cabinets full of paper documents. Depending on the type of document and filing equipment, space reduction can be as high as 98 percent.

Besides saving space, storing documents on microfilm can provide better protection than paper filing. First, microforms can be more easily shielded against unauthorized access. It is more difficult to tamper with microfilmed records than with hard-copy originals. By filming a series, both content and sequence can be fixed. In addition, microforms are often used as back-up copies for important documents. Because they require such limited space, the same document can be kept in different locations for maximum security. For example, if a fire or other natural disaster should destroy an on-site records center, an off-site microform center would be invaluable in helping a firm rebuild its business.

Although microform storage offers space and security advantages for vital and inactive records, micrographic developments since the 1950s have made it profitable to microfilm active records for several applications. A 1985 AIIM study pointed out that there are as many companies using microfilm in their active records programs as in inactive storage. Active files frequently need to be referenced frequently and updated. Originally micrographics were most useful for long-term storage, since it is difficult to call up a single document from a roll of film or a cartridge or add to a series once it has been photographed. In active records applications, records control and retrieval has become the primary focus. Searching for documents in file drawers and desks has always been time-consuming, while microform retrieval systems can access individual images within seconds.

Besides its ability to save space and speed in document access, microfilm offers other benefits (see Exhibit 5.2). In selecting storage media, its physical stability is a crucial factor. Certain types of microfilm, like silver gelatin, are capable of meeting specified archival standards. For most documents without archival requirements, microforms offer more consistent durability than does paper. The longevity of paper documents depends on the quality of paper used, but common business paper has a high acidic content. Sulphite paper is cheaper than that with a higher

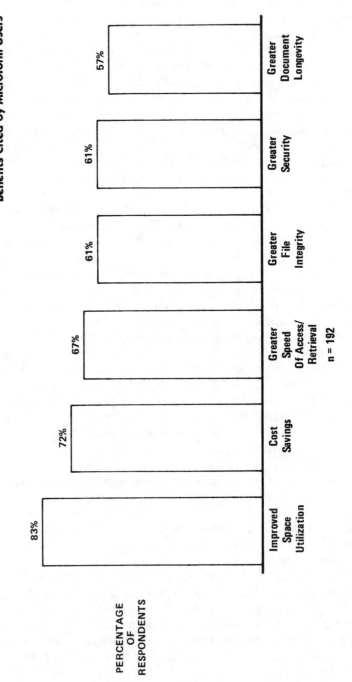

Exhibit 5.2

Benefits Cited by Microform Users

rag content, and thus more widely used, but it is also more vulnerable to physical decay.

If microfilm is to be used to store important documents, records managers must consider the legality of microfilm for the application. Because many federal and state regulatory agencies require that documents be kept for a specified period of time, it is crucial to find out if a microfilm version of a record meets the legal standards. For most applications, organizations can satisfy retention schedules and legal requirements with photographic records, including microfilm. Microfilm, of course, has the advantage of representing the entire original document, from scribbles in the margin to signatures. Because of this, businesses are usually free to destroy paper documents in the course of the routine process of records control and to substitute microfilm for them.

There are, however, some limitations on the legality of microfilm documents. Usually it must be demonstrated that paper which has been replaced by film has been destroyed according to a regular and well-defined schedule which accords with normal business practices. In addition, certain documents must be kept in their paper form. In some closely regulated industries, like pharmaceuticals or insurance, regulatory agencies usually enumerate the types of records to which this restriction would apply. If microfilming is permitted, there may be other standards, such as archival standards, which must be met. Finally, states have varying rules on the admissibility of microfilm as evidence in a court of law. Some states simply require paper enlargements of the image; others may insist on using the paper original if it is available. To be secure, the legal guidelines governing microfilm retention should be researched.

If microfilm's potential for records storage is to be fully evaluated, cost comparisons must of course be made. Cost factors will be different in each situation, so justification must be figured on a case-by-case basis. For example, the primary savings which a records manager would expect from microfilming inactive records would be in storage and equipment costs. In setting up an active records program, however, improvements in labor productivity would probably weigh more heavily in the cost evaluation. Whatever the specific microfilm application, it is liable to represent a substantial capital investment. Many businesses have invested large sums in micrographics equipment. An average figure cited by firms is over $30,000, with the largest portion of the investment devoted to integrated systems technology. Standalone computer systems for microfilm storage and retrieval run anywhere from $10,000 to several hundred thousand dollars, depending on their sophistication. Once a system is set up, however, cost savings in document storage accrue fairly rapidly.

Of course, records managers must be aware of user response to micrographic equipment. As is the case in implementing any new technology, office systems are only as productive as the people who use them. Workers may prefer familiar pieces of paper to computer screens just as secretaries may prefer using traditional typewriters over computer keyboards and terminals. But resistance to change can be overcome with adequate training and education.

It is also important to emphasize that up to now no significant decline in work efficiency or alertness as a result of prolonged use of display terminals has been found. According to certain quantifiable factors, such as reading rate, visibility, and comprehension, performance remains unaffected. Some new users do experience fatigue, but this discomfort seems to pass with continued use of the microfilm reader. The upshot of all these advantages is that micrographics is a flexible field with applications in a wide variety of departments and industries. But before exploring the ways in which micrographics can contribute to records-management programs, it is helpful to take a look at the records storage alternatives.

5.2 OPTICAL DISKS

Micrographics remains a healthy industry partly because of the embryonic state of competitive technology. Optical disks are recent innovations whose cost is still prohibitive except for the highest volume jobs. Optical disks make use of video recording technology and are about the size and shape of a record album. As video tools, they were originally designed for recording pictorial images and used in training and home entertainment applications.

Recently, however, disks have been developed that can read text, making the potential for paper storage reduction phenomenal. They can store up to 20,000 pages of printed information in digital form. The disks record data by the use of a laser scanner which burns holes onto the surface of the disk. The most effective way to use optical disks for records management is in conjunction with computer retrieval systems. Thus, the disk could store vast amounts of digital information while the computer was programmed to keep track of it.

Despite the disk's tremendous potential, its present uses are limited by the steep costs of laser technology per unit of stored material. Only qualified technicians with sophisticated equipment can put data on the disks; whereas micrographic media can be created by an organization with its own resources. In addition, once a disk has been made, there is as yet no economical way to update it. Its only practical use thus far has been in storing very large, non-expandable data bases like encyclopedias. Nevertheless, research is continuing, and it is most likely that the integrated records-management system of the next decade will consist of some combination of microforms, optical disks, and computer-assisted retrieval. At this point, however, traditional microforms provide the best records-management tools for most businesses. For this reason, the remainder of the chapter will be spent on the mechanics of micrographics.

5.3 MICROFILM TYPES

The most common microfilm on the market today is called silver halide or silver film. It is made by applying a silver halide emulsion to a polyester, acetate, or triacetate base. When light passes through the film, the part of the film emulsion that was hit by light solidifies. The image of the document is preserved in the areas not struck by light, much as a cutout silhouette portrait uses the contrast of black and white to outline the subject. Silver film is normally used for photographing original paper documents.

Vesicular film was recently developed for the purpose of duplicating microfilm. In most cases, it is made from a polyester base and coated with a layer of light-sensitive material. Vesicular film comes in all the standard film sizes and is capable of copying all other original rolls of film.

Diazo microfilm is used for contact printing and is generally employed for continuous-tone copy, engineering drawings, and some computer output microfilm (COM) processes. Again, it consists of a polyester or acetate base which is covered with a layer of diazonium salt, dye couplers, and a stabilizing agent. Also, dry silver microfilm has been developed for use in COM cameras that employ an electron or laser-beam recording method.

5.4 MICROFILM FORMATS

Microfilm is the word used to describe the various forms in which microfilm can be found. The original roll microfilm still exists, but it now shares the field with such nonserial forms as aperture cards, microfilm chips and jackets, microfiche, ultrafiche, and ultrastrip. All the forms have their particular advantages and disadvantages, and most firms use several different media in an effort to best utilize available space and to meet the access needs of various users. Despite the diversity, the respondents favored microfiche by an overwhelming majority, with 16mm film running a distant second, and 16mm cartridges holding third place. Although roll film is still the most widely used, the preference for microfiche demonstrates how completely micrographics has been incorporated into all areas of records management. This film medium is mainly used in active records retrieval systems while roll film is reserved for inactive storage.

5.4.1 Serialized Microforms

As their name indicates, serialized microforms store images sequentially on a continuous roll. Roll microfilm is the most economical and most common method of storing low-access documents. The three types of serial forms are open reel, cartridge, and cassette film. Inexpensive production is often the primary consideration in filming large quantities of infrequently used records, and a single 100-foot roll can hold more than 2,000 documents. In these cases, the inconvenience of accessing a single image is somewhat compensated for by the speed with which serialized documents such as books, newspapers, reports, and computer listings can be reduced for cheap storage. Because a roll of film records a fixed sequence of images, it is also difficult to update, although reels can be spliced in order to add information.

Roll films come in different widths, thicknesses, and lengths. The most common width is 16mm film, which is capable of photographing all documents smaller than legal-size forms. 35mm and 105mm are also widely used for larger records such as maps, engineering drawings, newspapers, and large books. Most 105mm, however, is normally cut into microfiche, but details on this medium will be provided later in the chapter.

Microfilm thickness can vary from a minimum of 2.5 mil to 7 mil. The key variable in choosing film thickness is space, as the thinnest available film could fit twice as much footage on a reel as the thickest. On the other hand, thin film is less durable and thus less attractive for frequently accessed documents.

Open reel is obviously the cheapest and oldest form, consisting simply of a length of microfilm, usually 16mm or 35mm wide, wrapped around a spool. Cartridges and cassettes are improved versions of the serialized open reels. They are simply plastic containers that are designed to hold and protect the roll of film, and their purpose is to speed the handling and loading process. Both are easy to work with and can be loaded automatically on an appropriate reader for convenient viewing. The major difference between them is that cartridges contain only one reel, while cassettes hold two fixed reels. Thus, cassettes do not need to be either threaded or rewound when they are removed from the reader. However, the existence of two reels makes the cassettes bulkier to store and more expensive to purchase.

There are several ways of identifying and retrieving specific images off cartridges and cassettes, making them more versatile than open reels. One approach is to develop targets to separate document groups. Odometer indexing, on the other hand, can be used to measure the distance from the documents or document groups to the beginning of the film. Frames can also be numbered according to a sequential manual index. In more complex electronic retrieval schemes, this numbering system can be translated into machine-readable blips or image count marks. An appropriate reader could thus automatically count frames and advance to the desired image.

Because of the innovations in retrieval techniques, cartridges and cassettes play important roles in the computer-assisted retrieval systems discussed later in the chapter. But this convenience comes at a price, as both the forms themselves and the readers which give users rapid access are considerably more expensive than open reel equipment.

5.4.2 Unitized Microforms

Unitized microforms differ from serial forms by allowing direct access to any record unit without having to advance a roll of film to the appropriate location. That is, they set up a one-to-one correspondence between the microform—whether an aperture card, a jacket, or microfiche—and an individual record. In roll film, on the other hand, the reel probably contains many unrelated records on it. Therefore, serialized microforms are easier and cheaper to film while unitized microforms are simpler and more inexpensive to reference. Unitized forms are thus well suited to handling the frequent retrieval of individual documents.

One of the oldest forms of unitized microfilm is the aperture card. It was developed in the 1950s for dealing with engineering drawings which were difficult to store and retrieve because of their unwieldy size and format. Its basic form is that of a computer keypunch card, usually 3 inches by 7 inches, which can hold keypunched text and data. It also, however, contains a slot or aperture where a single frame of 35mm film can be affixed.

This combination of media makes the aperture card very flexible and easy to retrieve. The keypunch portion of the card provides columns of information which can be used to sort and recall the drawing recorded on the film. And, as opposed to full-size drawings, the cards can be conveniently stored in normal filing cabinets or fed into any one of a number of automated retrieval units.

Microfilm jackets are another early development in the field of unitized microforms. They were designed to meet the need for updatable files, capable of accepting new information. The microfilm jacket consists of two plastic sheets with columns into which strips of 16mm or 35mm film can be inserted. Although jackets come in a variety of sizes, the most commonly used format is 4 inches by 6 inches, with four channels holding 12 frames each. The updating procedure is simple. Whenever frames become obsolete, they are removed; when new information must be added, it is inserted into empty slots until the card is full.

A variation on this form is the card jacket, which is a paper index card fitted with transparent plastic sleeves for the microfilm. The advantage of the card jacket is that it can record written information for easy reference and indexing. Microfilm jackets, on the other hand, usually use color coding or notching for retrieving batches or groups of jackets. Notching can either be top cut for manual recognition or bottom cut for automated retrieval.

Jackets are especially useful because they allow roll film to be transferred to a unitized form. Since many businesses recorded documents on reels before any other forms were invented, conversion to jackets is a feasible way to make these documents part of an active records program. Producing jackets is a multifaceted process. The roll film must first be exposed and processed, then cut into strips and inserted in the plastic containers. Much of it, however, can be accomplished by various automated and semi-automated devices. Cameras exist which both process and cut film, and insertion can be done automatically by a tool called a jacket loader. Jackets are distinguished from apertures in their capacity to hold a series of related records in discrete units. This format allows each element of the file to be simultaneously available. Thus, it is a particularly useful medium for keeping complex files like personnel or insurance case files. For example, a card jacket could display the frequently accessed employee information, like social security number, name, and address, in eye-readable form, while more detailed records like appraisals or recommendations could be stored on the strips of film.

Similar in design and format to the microfilm jacket is microfiche—currently the most popular form of microfilm in business use. Like the jacket, the fiche is a series of images stored in a grid pattern on a 4-inch by 6-inch card. The number of images on each sheet of microfiche is determined by the reduction ratio, which is normally 24 for paper documents and 42 to 48 for computer output microfiche. However, there does exist a special form of fiche, appropriately named ultrafiche, which can reduce documents up to 400 times their original size.

Since the 1970s and the invention of updatable microfiche, this microform now offers a one-step updating process to replace the multistep task of adding information to jackets. Because of nonsilver photographic media, which can be reused without losing sensitivity, a master fiche can be put back into a camera. New images can be inserted into any unused space on the exposed film. In some cases, the film is completely erasable, so that obsolete documents can be conveniently destroyed. The effect is to turn a sheet of microfiche into the miniature equivalent of an expandable paper file.

Microfiche can be created in several different ways. The fastest way to produce fiche is with a computer output microfilm device (COM), which generates fiche from computer data. For source document production, paper can be photographed with a step-and-repeat camera or copied from any other film media.

Although microfiche has many advantages as a storage media, it makes the most sense when applied to high volume files like large reports, catalogues, directories, and manuals. Because of the ease with which it can be duplicated, it is especially valuable for those multipage documents which need to be frequently updated and widely distributed. For lower volume tasks involving paper records, the investment in equipment cost and time is probably not worth it. In these cases, jackets are often adequate and more cost-effective.

Two other types of unitized microfilm are the microchip and the ultrastrip, but both are usually custom designed and thus too expensive to be commonly employed. Ultrastrip consists of a piece of microfilm with a very high reducing ratio and requires a clean-room environment to produce. It is made by copying another piece of microfilm with less reduction capabilities. The chip is a tiny piece of cut film which also contains highly reduced images and is stored in an electronic retrieval device. Both chips and strips are often components of high-speed electronic retrieval systems and, as such, contribute to the advancing integration of micrographics and data processing.

5.5 MICROFILM CAMERAS

The current versatility of microforms would be unthinkable without the several decades of innovations in microfilm camera equipment. Special cameras record full-size images onto miniature forms like microfilm, for example. However, no one camera can yet produce all the available microforms, so it is necessary to spend some time matching microform needs with camera equipment. For a more detailed description of microfilm cameras than the one that follows, your best reference is the Association for Information and Image Management (AIIM) consumer handbook called *All About Microfilm Cameras*.

5.5.1 Rotary Cameras

Microfilm cameras are grouped into planetary and rotary types. Rotary cameras are built for high-speed production of legal size or smaller, single-sheet documents. Using a technique that allows both document and film to move simultaneously while filming is taking place, these cameras can be fed up to 1,000 pages per hour manually and more with machine feeding. Some cameras can even film two-sided documents, but most are limited to recording one side at a time. Documents are fed in, filmed as they move past the shutter, and pushed out to the retrieving tray. Most of these cameras use 16mm film, which can be stored in open reels, cassettes, or cartridges, or cut into aperture cards or jackets. Some important features to consider when choosing a rotary camera are automatic exposure control and indexing capabilities. Manual lighting control requires that an operator decide how much exposure is needed for a group of documents, but an automatic device allows more precise reading of light requirements and thus more even exposure. Cameras which record indexing codes or blips on each frame of film are extremely useful. When coded film is combined with a microfilm reader capable of sorting through the index, the retrieval process is speeded up considerably.

Despite the benefits of speed and reduced labor costs, rotary cameras do have their limitations. Documents that are to be filmed must be in good condition to be moved across the rotating belts. Also, not all types of paper will stack neatly in the out tray, so a stacker may need to be purchased for controlling flyaway papers. In addition, most rotary cameras will only take documents up to 14-inches and sometimes 18-inches wide. Length, however, is not a problem, and some cameras can even be fitted with a device that allows continuous feeding of unbursted computer printouts. Regardless of their size, documents must be cleared of all paper clips, staples, or other foreign materials before they are ready for processing.

5.5.2 Planetary Cameras

Planetary cameras are so called because both the film and the document remain stationary during the photographing process. For this reason, the quality of the image produced is much greater than that of the rotary camera. The document to be filmed is placed on a flat surface, the copyboard, which holds it in place. The camera is mounted above the board, either at a fixed or variable height. Lighting is externally monitored. Other features have varying levels of sophistication. For example, copyboards can be obtained which are electrostatically charged to keep documents stationary. Cameras with movable filming units can be adjusted to various reduction ratios. Exposure time can be set by photoelectric cells which measure the documents' reflected light. And planetary cameras can be fixed with an automatic feed device which speeds up the loading process.

Planetary cameras are most useful for photographing documents in bound volumes or of larger dimensions. They are also gentle enough to accept brittle or fragile sheets of paper. The cameras come in a variety of sizes, and the larger models can handle documents up to 45-inches wide on 35mm or even 105mm film. These large machines are often used to reduce engineering drawings to frames which fit on aperture cards. A more complex camera, called the processor planetary, can film, process, and mount the 35mm image on a card in one step.

The most obvious drawback of the planetary camera is the slowness of the production process. Models with automatic feed are an exception. In addition, the larger cameras are considerably more expensive than standard rotary cameras. Unless the camera will be consistently used for photographing delicate archival material or large drawings, it might be wise to have such documents processed by an outside microfilming service.

A variation of the planetary camera is the step-and-repeat camera. This model is designed specifically for the creation of 105mm microfiche. The film can be cut into fiche-sized sheets either before or after it goes through the camera. The camera's special feature is that it can position images according to a microfiche grid and automatically create a microfiche format. An assembly device inside the camera moves the film after each photograph and positions it for the next exposure. The cost of step-and-repeat cameras, however, has inhibited their use in the creation of microfiche from paper documents.

5.6 MICROFILM READERS AND READER-PRINTERS

Microfilm readers are probably the most important equipment purchase associated with microfilm use. Buying cameras can be avoided by hiring a film service or by renting for a one-time conversion effort. Readers, on the other hand, make microfilm accessible to the users. Without appropriate readers, the microfilm is virtually useless except as archival material. There are several types and sizes of readers, all of which are appropriate for different locations and uses. The two basic forms of microfilm readers are front and rear projection. In one case, the viewing screen is located in the rear, while in the other, it is positioned in front. Choosing this feature depends on office lighting and user preference, but the most common projection format is rear. In terms of size, there are four general designs: portable units, desktop models, lap readers, and larger freestanding models. Lap readers and portable models can fit into briefcases or desk drawers and are meant for individual use. Some can even run using batteries. Obviously, desk and freestanding readers are larger and are designed for regular and permanent office use.

Apart from its general physical characteristics, a reader must be chosen for the microforms that it is capable of displaying. Serialized readers usually provide the least versatility, while some microfiche readers have interchangeable lenses for aperture cards and jackets as well. Roll film readers consist of two spindles operated by either a hand or machine crank. To view cassette or cartridge roll film, special readers which can accept the particular type of plastic case or brand of film are necessary. This fact should be kept in mind when microfilm is being created, as incompatible brands could lead to the purchase of unnecessary, costly machines.

Microfiche readers are cheaper and more flexible than the cartridge and cassette readers, since many brands on the market today can display all unitized microforms. The reader is constructed of two glass plates between which the sheet of fiche is inserted. Identifying images on a sheet is accomplished with the help of a pointer and a built-in grid pad which matches the grid pattern on the microfiche itself. In order to accept documents with different reduction ratios, a fiche reader can either be equipped with removable lenses or with a single zoom lens that can be adjusted accordingly.

Readers should also be scrutinized for user comfort. If users spend long hours in front of the screen, the reader should have a sharp, uniform, easily focused image. Screen finish can be either dull to help reduce eyestrain or shiny to sharpen the picture. Illumination levels and print type vary, and users are bound to react positively to different models. Finally, screen angles should take account of the size of the user; some models even provide adjustable screens. The bottom line for evaluating all these factors is comfort or user friendliness. To help make choices in these areas, the user's expressed needs should be taken into account. Many vendors will even allow a firm to use a model for a trial period before final purchase is made.

Microfilm reader-printers improve on simple readers by being able to convert the microfilm back to a paper document. They are equipped with a paper supply, a device for getting the hard copy to the user, and, most important, one of several methods of transferring the screen image to a sheet of paper. The precise copying process depends on the model, and there are several options you should be aware of. Print quality varies, as does print size and cost per print. Some printers produce 8-and-a-half-inch by 11-inch copies while some create sheets up to 30 inches long.

While reader-printers can be convenient, there are some pitfalls in owning one. First, they cost more than readers. And second, it is easy to neutralize the benefits of microfilm use and storage by creating needless paper copies which then get filed or thrown away. It is best, therefore, to limit the number of printers and to keep production under strict control.

5.7 COMPUTER OUTPUT MICROFORM (COM)

Allusions have been made throughout the chapter to the interface between computer technology and micrographics. In fact, the survival power of micrographics has been increased by its integration with advanced forms of electronic storage and retrieval systems. The linking of data processing and micrographics technologies has opened new doors for the management of active records.

Computer output microform (COM) is produced directly from a computer, without a paper document ever being created. In other words, the COM recorder replaces the printer on a computer terminal. Thus, the recorder can take machine-readable data from the computer and translate it directly into human-readable data in a micro format, either 16mm, 35mm, or 105mm microfiche.

The most obvious advantage of COM is the reduction of paper output and the consequent savings in storage space. In addition, it is much cheaper to create a few frames of film than the sheafs of paper which are necessary to replace them. Finally, a COM recorder can create film at a much higher speed than a printer puts out paper, especially if you include the time it takes to collate, staple, and burst.

However economical a COM recorder is to operate, its initial setup costs are high, starting at around $100,000. Therefore, it may not make sense to purchase a recorder unless predicted volume will outweigh the cost of having an outside service perform the task. In addition, COM is not appropriate for all production needs, especially not for data bases that need to be frequently updated. The creation and management of data bases, however, goes beyond the scope of micrographics technology. In the next chapter we will explore the computer implications of integrated systems.

5.8 COMPUTER-ASSISTED RETRIEVAL (CAR)

CAR systems are another facet of the marriage of computers and micrographics. In fact, they were able to combine the best of both worlds— to take the sorting and classifying power of a computer and mix it with the inexpensive storage capacity of microfilm. CAR is thus able to benefit records management by handling some of the chronic problems of manual filing and retrieving systems—that is, to help reduce error and to save time searching for files and setting up complex classification schemes. A CAR system is able to call up randomly filed microform images according to a computer-generated and -maintained index. Indexes can be established by software programs, or retrieval parameters can be typed in manually.

QUESTIONS AND ANSWERS

Q. Why use microfilm?

A. Sixty years ago when microfilm was first introduced, its primary benefit was space conservation. Today this is still a reason for its widespread use, and advanced storage and retrieval systems take advantage of this. Microfilm can also provide greater longevity and security than paper. All these add up to reduced cost.

Q. Is all microfilm the same?

A. No, various types of film have features suitable for different applications. These film types include silver halide, vesicular, diazo, and dry silver.

Q. What about microfilm formats?

A. There are numerous microfilm formats available to users; in fact, the term microform was coined to include all these. The most popular formats are fiche, 16mm and 35mm roll film, and 16mm cartridges.

Q. What are serialized microforms?

A. Serialized microforms store images sequentially on a continuous roll. These include reels, cartridges, and cassettes. They differ from unitized microforms, which allow the user to directly access any image without having to advance a roll of film. These include aperture cards, microfilm jackets, and fiche. One type makes it easier and simpler to film, the other easier and simpler to access.

Q. How are documents filmed?

A. Filming can be handled in-house or done by an outside jobber or service. There are two main types of microfilm cameras—planetary and rotary. In planetary cameras, both the film and document are stationary during the exposure period. These are usually manual systems and feature high quality and versatility. In rotary cameras, both document and film move simultaneously during exposure, allowing for much higher automatic volume production.

Q. What is available in readers and printers?

A. A wide array of equipment is available. This is probably the most important equipment purchase associated with microfilm use. User needs should be carefully assessed, and a trial period is often a good idea.

6

Computer Literacy and Office Automation for Records Managers

6.1 RECENT DEVELOPMENTS

Recent developments in the field of records management (RM) have gone hand in hand with the availability of new technologies. If a records-management system lacks the flexibility to incorporate new technology, it will become obsolete not long after it is installed. This is especially crucial as the technological revolution accelerates.

The office automation (OA) revolution and the underlying fundamental shift of the American economy toward service industries has dramatically affected the magnitude of the task facing records managers. As the work force becomes more service oriented, management of information becomes a more important and all-encompassing task. Information is the primary product of the office and the main ingredient to the decision-making process.

As a by-product of this information flow, U.S. businesses generate an estimated 600 million pages of printed computer output, 250 million photocopies, and 80 million letters every working day. To this daily production is added the 400 billion documents that are now stored in 38 million four-drawer file cabinets. With the number of new documents growing at approximately 20 percent per year, the total amount of information stored doubles every four years. To date, the automation process has intensified the flow of paper creating a veritable deluge.

Corporate expenditures on OA equipment show rapid growth. By the year 1990 business purchases of office equipment will hit the $6 billion mark—three times the current sales figure for office equipment.

If OA technology generates so many paper records, will the computer-aided OA revolution help those responsible for managing the flow of information? The answer is a guarded "yes." Although improvements in records control have been slow to date, they are gathering momentum. New technologies for handling information have changed the way in which documents are communicated. We are witnessing the appearance of computerized workstations and data communication networks, with capabilities for word processing, electronic mail, facsimile transmission, and business graphics. These facilities are fast replacing traditional typewriters and filing cabinets and changing irrevocably the way business is transacted.

6.1.1 Information Digitization

Integrated circuit technology has enabled digital storage and transmission of information. Computers process and store information electronically as digital pulses. Everything is coded in such a way that it can be represented by a series of on-off electrical states. Data communication switches are digitally controlled. Digital techniques have transformed the traditional means of storing, retrieving, and transmitting data records.

Rendering information in digital format offers distinct advantages over traditional forms of information storage, communication, and manipulation. Digital techniques increase the speed of data communications, reduce paper and paper-handling costs, and reduce the long-term overall labor costs. Integrating online data access and records management allows instant document retrieval. Applying customized computing power to various forms of data enhances the speed with which data is processed and enables the two-way flow of information.

6.2 HUMAN-READABLE OR MACHINE-READABLE DATA

Data can be recorded onto a storage medium in either human-readable (HR) or machine-readable (MR) form. HR forms include writing, printing, and other visual displays from cave paintings to graphs, while MR forms include both the older analog and the new digital forms of electronic data storage and transfer. Naturally, MR data are not directly accessible to the human eye; they require some sort of intermediary machine to interpret for human use.

In the new world of MR data, machines store and process the data.

The human user sees only the final product in HR form. Machines can communicate directly with one another, not only within an office (intra-office) but also from one office to another (inter-office).

Electronic mail systems (EMS) and central database management systems (DBMS) allow companies to bypass traditional paper-based mail, to gain speedier service, and, in the case of more advanced systems, to file transmitted records automatically. Video displays (sometimes termed soft copy) provide the interface between MR data and HR data. Video displays translate the digital, machine-to-machine data stream into an HR format so that the data may be studied or changed. Until a final hard copy is desired, video displays provide electronic handling of digital documents, instant data correction, and records-management automation.

6.3 COMPUTERPHILIA AND COMPUTERPHOBIA

Computers have been known to bring out extremes in people. At one end are those who embrace the technology and become experts practically overnight. At the other end of the spectrum are potential users who feel threatened by the computers. The members of this latter group are often older workers in middle or upper management, and therefore they can exert an influence out of proportion to their numbers. Given these two countervailing attitudes toward computers, how does the records manager strike the proper balance?

Computerphilia, or the love of computers, can result in extreme actions which do not usually have the desired outcome. The department or section head who after some experience with computers goes out and purchases a PC for every desk is one example of such an extreme response. Computers do not offer overnight packaged solutions to business problems. Mass applications of computer power do not result in increased performance or better bottom-line results through some magical transformation.

Like everything else, computers have their limitations. For instance, a computer will not solve a problem that is poorly defined. Computers work only when they are used to accomplish a specific, well-defined task. Computers are highly efficient at sorting through and collating large amounts of data. Unless it is well organized, more information is not necessarily better. Computers do not instantly improve bottom-line results. While computers can create impressive cost savings in many areas of business, such savings are not a quid pro quo of computer use. In fact, as has been mentioned repeatedly, the computer revolution has brought about a paper explosion and has broadened the records-management function. The "paperless" office dream of 10 or 15 years ago is just that—still a dream.

The computer will not reduce personnel needs overnight. Computers should not be seen as substitutes for people. Rather they should be seen as tools which can be used to enhance the efficiency and productivity of workers. As the sole means of records management, paper has severe limitations imposed by the high cost of copying, the high cost of space, the cost of labor-intensive document handling, and the physical limits of speedy and accurate filing and retrieval.

Computers and electronic technologies permit much speedier and more accurate handling of documents. Paper is no longer necessary to many applications. But, when computers are used instead, all data have to be digitally encoded, including past records. Computer systems are complex and expensive and often require organizational change. While some tasks may be eliminated, computerization should allow you to get more out of each dollar spent, and not necessarily reduce the total dollar outlay.

Computers solve problems that call for subjectivity. This should be obvious, but many business tasks blur the subjective-objective distinction. Computers make great support tools—their use in financial and business planning attests to this—but a final decision requires qualitative as well as quantitative input.

Computers will not replace paper completely in the near future. Although in years down the road a significant reduction in paper use, especially for records, may be expected, information must still be put into HR form. While screens are useful, a need for hard copy will also persist.

Finally, computers are not always right. The concept of infallibility, although much less prominent than in the early years of the computer revolution, may still affect beginning users of computers. For years computer users and programmers have used the acronym GIGO—garbage in, garbage out. It still holds true today. Computers are unforgiving with small errors. Because they function at such a high speed, they compound small errors very quickly into major ones. While the machines normally operate flawlessly, one cannot become complacent and stop checking up on them.

Computerphobia, or the exaggerated fear of computers, on the other hand, is not a sensible attitude either. Computers are tools with special requirements and capabilities. The producers of new generations of software are increasingly aware of objections made by first-time users with little or no computer knowledge and experience. User friendliness is more than just a marketing slogan and has been incorporated into all the major successful canned software programs. A program must be user friendly if it is to gain wide acceptance in today's market.

Avoiding change has never been a viable solution for dealing with change. Just as you would expect your doctor to keep up with developments in the medical world, so does the business environment expect its practitioners to keep current. Today's hardware and software also make this a realistic possibility for the modern professional. Computer-phobia can be overcome through exposure and knowledge.

6.4 WORD PROCESSORS AND COMPUTERS

First-generation word processors began the shift in business comput-ing from the back to the front office. The addition of computing power to office terminals expanded their use in the office exponentially. They are used not only to enter and review data, but also to establish an end user connection to mainframes and an interoffice communication net-work. The evolution of a link between microcomputers and large systems has allowed the development of integrated information-processing sys-tems. The integrated systems affect all stages of records management.

Multifunction microcomputers are designed to do more than simple word processing and text editing. They can store large amounts of in-formation, access mainframe data bases, communicate with one another, and become the links in a computer-based messaging system (CBMS) which can be used for internal as well as external electronic mail.

Microcomputers are able to perform these tasks because they incor-porate data communication facilities. Information from the microcom-puter is transferred through a modem, which translates the digital pulses to analog current, like that carried over the telephone line. Electrical signals can travel over a communication channel to any destination: a central storage unit, a mainframe data base, word processors, or other types of peripheral equipment such as printers, phototypesetters, or the new digital compatible photocopiers. Communicating terminals allow the user to draw information directly from a number of sources during the preparation of a report. When they are used to create a document which is to be reviewed at a distant point, two important benefits are realized. An original document may be created quickly and stored cheaply on a magnetic disk, for instance. Once stored on the system, it may be transmitted with the push of a button. Any further changes to be made on the document can be done at any location on the network without the need for retyping the entire document. Instant soft-copy displays replace paper hard-copy, which has to be physically shuttled back and forth between contributing parties.

Two-way communications raise the microcomputer to a new level of functionality. Access to data stored at local or central facilities is possible, and all without the use of file clerks or other human intermediaries. In an online menu-directed system, outside data or information is called up sequentially during original document preparation and transferred directly to the new document without being rekeyed. Time is saved and errors are reduced. Efficiency is thereby improved.

Another important feature of smart word-processor integration in an automated office is that records management can also be automated. Two-way communication between workstations and a central or local storage facility automatically provides a record trail and classification of stored data which is available for future reference. All internally generated documents can be stored and made accessible or purged over time without the separate filing and records-management steps needed for hard-copy systems. All the traditional records-management functional areas of creation, storage-retrieval, processing, replication, distribution, archiving, and destruction may be handled with computers. Computers and enhanced communication abilities allow for greater integration, and with this process comes greater productivity through the elimination of duplication of effort in copying, rekeying, and rehandling of information.

As information managers and professionals look at their equipment needs and purchasing policies, a distinction between PCs (microcomputers) and word processors is usual. Issues such as the main function of the position—text processing or data processing—are examined. If it is word processing, standalone word processors can provide simple and efficient service. PCs can also perform with excellence all the needed word-processing tasks. In other words, the line which has been distinguishing the two is fast fading. PCs and word processors can no longer be viewed in isolation. Combining the two allows for truly integrated information processing and management.

6.5 OPTICAL DISKS

Optical disks (OD) are a technological breakthrough that would extend the memory capacity of computers still further. They have been on the periphery of day-to-day usage for many years. Records managers have heard it before: Optical disk technology is going to revolutionize the information storage industry. Finally, the time for optical disks has come. Commercial products and systems have hit the marketplace, and a number of end users are experimenting with the new systems.

Optical disk technology, as a means of compact and highly accessible data storage, offers many advantages over microfilm and magnetic storage media. The remaining disadvantages should be overcome in the near future, thereby increasing the acceptance and use of optical disks. New technological developments require a considerable period of quiet activity before reaching a critical mass and bursting forth upon the scene. The more familiar a records manager is with the basics of OD technology in the early stages of its emergence, the easier it will be to evaluate and keep abreast of improvements as they occur.

6.5.1 The Future of Optical Disk Technology

Optical disk technology should soon overcome a number of limitations that have prevented its widespread use to date. At this time, the optical disk (OD) is a permanent medium to which information may be written only once. There is not yet a universally accepted, industrywide standard system. The cost of producing OD is still high because the volume of sales has not yet reached the point where costs will fall rapidly. Finally, optical disks are not yet accepted as a storage medium for legal evidence. These technological and early constraints should fall in the next few years, and it is widely recognized that the full capabilities of an OD system clearly outweigh its limitations. Extremely dense data compaction abilities (up to 60 times those of magnetic storage), high-speed random-accessibility, and the portability of memory disks are the key advantages of optical disks. With so many high-tech manufacturers concentrating on different aspects of OD technology including erasability, developments should be forthcoming.

Currently, records managers should examine their present system, pay special attention to micrographics usage, and attempt to formulate systems in which OD technology can slowly be phased in as an enhancement. Current storage methods need not be displaced by OD technology. Rather, OD can be used as an adjunct facility and applied where its special strengths can be best utilized. Integration of disk technology into a company's information network should increase the power and capacity of the total information system.

6.6 OTHER SYSTEMS

The automation of office work has affected many different areas of the modern business organization. Records managers, who need to be conversant with computers and computer technology as it impacts the creation, processing, maintenance, and disposition of business records, find themselves confronted by a variety of electronic media and an array of electronic devices. This section will list and briefly highlight some of the more common systems that a manager is likely to encounter. A more in-depth treatment of all of these areas would require another volume in and of itself. Therefore, those interested in a specific medium should consult more specialized information sources.

6.6.1 Local Area Networks

A local area network is a communications system that interconnects two or more communicating devices and is limited in geographic scope, usually under 50 miles. It further provides a structured medium which allows many types of equipment and applications to be linked, including data processing, word processing, video, voice, and electronic mail. Its power lies in its ability to coordinate all the operations within an organization. A local area network allows every device on the network the potential to communicate with every other device. For the information resource manager, a LAN can ensure that all a company's activities are based on the same central data and information base. For a data-processing manager, a LAN can centralize control of an organization's newly distributed computing system and ensure device compatibility. Or it could act as a tool for creating and enforcing a uniform filing system for all of a firm's records.

As envisioned, a LAN can serve as the central trunk for the orderly growth of communicating and computing functions within a company. Although it can allow a firm to make great strides in resource sharing and functional integration, compatibility problems, physical installation, and choices of speed, protocols, and flexibility have prevented LANs from becoming firmly established. Without widely accepted standards and procedures, more time will be needed for LAN-based systems to become commonplace for information management. For now however, the LAN is a powerful tool for integrating various computer-based and automated functions.

6.6.2 Teleconferencing

Teleconferencing permits two or more groups of people in different locations to communicate using modern telecommunications facilities. As an alternative to face-to-face meetings, it can save considerable travel time and costs. The term teleconferencing is not a precise one and spans a range of systems and communication levels. A teleconference may simply involve voice transmission or may include video transmission as well.

In its most basic form, a teleconference can be set up with a conference call. Because such a meeting requires no special equipment and utilizes common carrier lines, it has the lowest cost. At the opposite end, the most expensive and sophisticated system is the full-motion, two-way video conference. In such a meeting the participants both see and hear each other, and because this requires such a large amount of transmission capacity, it is much more expensive. The growing transmission capacity of satellites and the emergence of fiber optic cable with high-speed data transmission capacity should soon reduce these costs. Teleconferencing will then become a more widespread and accepted communications tool.

6.6.3 Voice Store-and-Forward Systems

Traditional telephone communication requires a simultaneous two-way conversation between parties. Empirical studies show that two-thirds to three-quarters of all business phone calls are not completed on the first attempt resulting in the activity euphemistically labelled "telephone tag."

Voice store-and-forward (VSF) systems are meant to overcome this shortcoming. It allows a caller to leave a recorded voice message directed at a particular person. In this respect it resembles a conversational telephone answering machine. However, the technology of these systems can do much more than answering machines. VSF systems act as true voice processors. Utilizing computers, they digitize voice messages and store them on magnetic disks until called for. Unlike the telephone answering machine, these systems act as a central voice message exchange providing a service to tens, hundreds, or thousands of users. The VSF records a caller's message and directs it to an electronic mailbox which can be for an individual, several individuals, or even a department, under the control of the caller.

The message recipient is provided in turn with a sequential series of accurate messages which he or she can review, save, erase, or forward to others. Substantial cost savings are achieved with such systems, as both executives and secretarial time devoted to telephone messages, both received and originated, is sharply reduced. The same applies for paper messages, and where calls are directed to more than one party, hard-copy memos can also be reduced.

6.6.4 Videotex

Another method of conveying information which bypasses the paper medium is videotex. Videotex is a two-way computer-based communication system which is designed for the display and retrieval of information. The system is composed of three essential components: a communications network, a host computer, and an end-user access station or terminal. This terminal can consist of a number of types of equipment ranging from a dedicated CRT and keyboard, to a modem-equipped personal computer, to a TV set coupled with a pushbutton telephone in some public access systems.

In utilizing a videotex service, the user views a simple and straightforward index and is provided with clear instructions on how to proceed. No special knowledge or training is required, so the information data base can be accessed by a wide variety of end users. Outside of the United States, for example in Europe and Canada, public government-sponsored videotex services are a rapidly expanding industry.

Overall, videotex can be divided into three general classifications. First, public database services such as those mentioned in Europe and Canada offer to a wide subscriber base information retrieval in such areas as at-home shopping, public and cultural affairs notices, public library information, and banking.

Second, limited user-group services are available to specialized users of commercial and proprietary information. Fees are usually charged on a pay-as-used basis, and examples of this type of service are specialized news services, stock market information services, or data bases for the legal or medical professions.

The third and final level of videotex service is the in-house or private system. These are often based on a mainframe or distributed processing network and handle specialized information needs and user services. Examples could be in-house systems used by banks to handle customer accounts and systems used by universities for student registration.

6.6.5 Facsimile (FAX)

Facsimile units are so named because the output copy is a replica or facsimile of the original document. Facsimile units electronically encode the data from an original document, letter, photograph, chart, or technical drawing and transmit it over telephone lines to a location where the document is reconstituted. It is a form of instant communication which circumvents the slow delivery and increasing cost of conventional mail service. Furthermore, FAX transmits pictorial documents as well as text. In fact, most of the recent advances in FAX technology originated in Japan, where complex written language incorporating Chinese characters created a strong need to transmit graphic data.

FAX use is spreading rapidly. New installations exceeded 80,000 units in 1984, bringing the total to nearly half a million. The International Telephone and Telegraph Consultative Committee (CCITT) of the United Nations divides FAX into four types or levels of service. Group 1 equipment transmits an 8-and-a-half-inch by 11-inch page by analog signal in six minutes over a telephone line. Group 2 digitizes the signal and reduces send time to three minutes. Group 3 machines further reduce transmit time to 15 to 30 seconds per page and double the horizontal and vertical resolution. This class can also incorporate features such as document storage, auto-dialing, priority listing, and the like. The final level, Group 4 equipment, reduces redundant information in the document before it is transmitted and usually utilizes more advanced telephone networks or systems.

With improved laser printers that boast quality far above the thermal printers now widely used, and the increased demand for "instant" communications, FAX use should grow steadily. Further integration of these units into total information systems will provide a further impetus.

6.6.6 Electronic Mail (E-Mail)

Electronic mail describes a wide variety of different technologies used to electronically transmit textual and graphic data. This transmission can take place within a company on its own local area network (LAN) or externally on public carriers or on a number of specialized services. It differs from FAX service in that hard copy at each end is not a prerequisite, and in practice it more likely replaces the telephone as a means of communicating messages. CRT display terminals are the ideal and most common means of message creation and receipt. The real value of E-Mail is that it allows users to control their own time. Messages are written once and forwarded, and the receivers can accept and respond to the messages at their own convenience. Telephone tag, ritual telephone talk, and constant interruptions are avoided.

Because E-Mail utilization requires a communications network to be in place, they are nearly always added on, or are adjuncts to, existing PC or smart word-processing networks. For companies with several remote locations, a public E-Mail service may be a viable and cost-effective option.

6.6.7 Graphics

Computer graphics have become commonplace as the cost for the necessary hardware and software has fallen. Advances in printing technology have special impact on the spread of graphics use. New laser printers can perform a variety of tasks with a quality level unheard of only a few years ago. Computer-generated graphics offer a special ability to combine text and data. Text and graphics may be incorporated in a single document and, in a single creative process, carried out on one multifunctional workstation. For records managers, the increasing use of graphics affects directly the selection of storage media. High-density storage media such as optical disks and micrographics are particularly suitable for graphic data.

6.6.8 Laser Printers

Laser printers use a directed, amplified light beam to form character images. These images are then transferred to paper by a reprographic method which uses an electrically charged plate surface and an adhering toner. Laser printers are therefore inherently faster than impact printers.

Most laser printers have a unique advantage in that they can reproduce in two formats. In their portrait mode, they approximate typeset printing. In their landscape mode, they can be used to produce graphics and forms. For the records manager this latter ability can be especially useful. It can move both forms design and forms production in-house.

Recently, low-cost laser printers have been introduced, and quality levels and capabilities of the higher-end machines have been enhanced. These developments should increase the potential applications of laser printers to include the printing of technical service manuals, educational and training materials, customer proposals and quotations, and financial reports. Because they operate with mechanisms that are simpler than impact printers, their price-performance ratios are approaching that of the traditional printers. Laser printers will become more widely used as their operating characteristics improve and their price decreases.

6.6.9 Computer-Aided Design and Manufacturing

Computer-aided design and computer-aided manufacturing (often jointly referred to as CAD/CAM) can be an important source of records in firms which are design or engineering oriented, or which are involved in manufacturing. As the terminology itself implies, CAD and CAM are closely related computer-based activities which have a wide range of application in many industries. Many of the advances in office automation are permitted by the use of CAD/CAM in the design, prototype, and manufacturing stages of advanced solid-state electronics. CAD/CAM is also widely used in such industries as aerospace, automotive, consumer appliances, architecture, and civil engineering.

Because CAD/CAM systems rely on computers and digital technology to manipulate large quantities of data, these systems often draw on a diversity of tools, ranging from mainframes to minicomputers to advanced line plotters. Records and information resource managers should be familiar with the basics of such systems if they are used by their organization or company. The increasing use of robotics and other forms of automation on manufacturing lines is expected to increase the use of CAD/CAM throughout the remainder of this century.

6.7 COMPUTER LITERACY AND TRAINING

For an employer there are a number of types of training that can be used to construct a user training program. Pre-employment training, induction or employee orientation training, vendor training, specialist training, and on-the-job training are all applicable methods.

In an office that uses computers, some level of formal training must be institutionalized. The sophistication of the equipment and the increasingly complex functions that can be performed require skilled personnel. Productivity gains can only be realized if hardware and software capabilities are maximized by their human operators.

The reader should by now be thoroughly convinced of the expanding role of computers in the modern office. More and more office workers therefore must be computer literate. With computer skills required for employees at all levels, many companies are noting shortages in personnel who have the requisite computer skills.

To compound the difficulty of the hiring process, the structure of the labor market has changed dramatically over the last few years. More than half of American women are now working, most of them in white-collar jobs. But expanded managerial options mean that skilled support staff are harder to find. These facts point to the importance of training within a company's overall strategy.

Any training program will have plenty of obstacles to overcome. Convincing nonusers that computers will enhance and simplify their jobs is not always an easy task. Managers in particular continue to express fears and doubts about the usefulness of computers to their jobs. Most seem to be confused by computer command structures and baffled by software programs. Negative attitudes toward computer use also focus on work quality considerations, such as boredom, loss of creativity, and lack of human interaction.

On the other side of the coin, however, most managers seem to feel that learning is worth the effort—that the time saved using a computer will outweigh the time spent mastering it. Generally, computer users express more enthusiasm about the benefits of automation than do nonusers. One clue to be derived from this information is that the more exposure people have to computers, the more favorable their outlook toward them becomes.

6.7.1 Creating Training Programs

Training objectives have both general and specific facets to them. For this reason, it is usually advisable to break employees into distinct training groups. While it may be a general goal to achieve companywide computer literacy and records-management ability, professionals need to use different software applications than do secretaries or clerical workers. To this end, a training program should cover four distinct sets of activities or goals. First, it should take advantage of such an overhaul to offer remedial training in those traditional office skills which are still useful. Second, it should take care to reinforce existing office procedures and to educate workers about newly created ones. Third, it should deal with more abstract notions of business and departmental goals and game plans. Finally, training must address the new technology, with both general computer education and specific operating instructions.

6.7.2 Office Skills

Other than possessing the basic skills addressed above, clerical workers need to be proficient in coordinating all sorts of office-related activities. As secretaries take on more delegated professional tasks and as individual workstations become more self-sufficient, it is crucial to decentralize such paraprofessional skills as time management and prioritization and planning techniques. As with the basic tasks, none of these more sophisticated skills is new to the business world or unfamiliar to any good personnel department. Indeed, part of the training challenge is to get employees to apply the old skills to novel applications. For example, procedures regulating document production and retention will be adapted to serve a company's distributed or centralized processing system. Likewise, some office tasks will have disappeared completely, others will take less time, and still others will be newly created.

6.7.3 Corporate Computer Literacy Program (CCL)

Training individuals in specific skills is, in a sense, a prerequisite to establishing a successful computer literacy program. Such a program should represent the culmination of the office automation process and the integration of all its human and technological components. As such, it involves much more than training on specific machines. Simply, CCL would seek to instruct workers at all levels and in all fields of information resource management on how the automated office affects both their own positions and the objectives of the company as a whole.

The modern records manager has a vital role to play in this companywide transformation. All levels of personnel, from top management to temporary or part-time staff, need to interact with a company's record system to control and influence information flow. Therefore, because computers are increasingly used in records management or corporate information resource management, a computer literacy effort must include segments on document and image control. Although advanced systems have astounding capacity and capabilities, as we shall see in the next chapter, the power of machines can only be unlocked with human skill.

QUESTIONS AND ANSWERS

Q. What major development continues to influence computer usage, office automation, and records management?

A. The digitization of increasing amounts of information, records, and communications has transformed the office. Information may be processed, communicated, and stored at a lower cost, with greater efficiency, and on a more timely basis.

Q. How has the role for the back office or DP department changed?

A. Advances in microcomputer technology which took place in the 1970s have allowed inroads to be made on the DP department's control of business computing. The true developments with the greatest impact were the proliferation of more powerful and cheaper PCs and the development of smart word processors with computer and database access capabilities. Such equipment expands the role of the front office and dilutes the relative monopoly of the back office over data manipulation and information systems management.

Q. How can the spread of computerphilia and computerphobia, which sometimes results from the increased use of computers, be handled?

A. Computers must be seen as tools. Extreme reactions for or against computers do not make sense and can be dangerous. Education and planned introduction are the best methods for dealing with or avoiding either extreme response.

Q. What can microcomputers do in the modern office?

A. Stated briefly, the addition of computing power to office terminals has expanded their role exponentially. They provide a means of entering and reviewing data or information (such as reports and letters), and they have established communications links between office machines and individuals both within and outside the office. Important for the records manager, they can automate virtually every records-management task.

Q. Is computer training and literacy necessary?

A. With the expanding role of computers in the modern office, the need for new computer-related skills is strong and growing. To meet this requirement, some level of formal training must be institutionalized so that the full benefits of the new equipment can be realized.

7

Automated Storage and Retrieval Systems

7.1 INTEGRATING COMPUTERS AND MICROGRAPHICS

Microfilm is an information storage medium with which records managers have long been familiar. Although used primarily for archival storage, the use of microfilm has spread widely over the last 20 years because of the explosion in the use of paper engendered by the emergence of computer technology in the office. Recent technological developments provide ways to link electronic data storage and manipulation with micrographics storage.

In general, the linkage operates in both directions. Systems have now been developed to enable the transfer of data from a computer to micrographic media. There are also systems that can digitize the information stored on microforms so that a computer can use it.

Over the last ten years technological advancements in digital storage media have made computers the most cost-effective devices for interactive information storage and retrieval. Because microfilm is the cheapest alternative for storing large volumes of information, it is only natural that systems have been developed to integrate computers and micrographics.

7.2 COMPUTER OUTPUT MICROFILM (COM)

Until recently, if the records manager wanted to transfer active records from a computerized data base to archival storage on microfilm, the process required two steps. First, the computer operator would have to generate a printed version of the records on paper. Second, the micrographics department would have to photograph the computer-generated printout and then print the photo on microfilm. In short, this process would require an intermediate step involving the use of paper. If the volume of data for transfer were large, the cost of this process could get quite high.

COM writes digital data—a stream of bits which represent either text data or graphic images as they are stored on a computer—directly onto microfilm. Traditionally, COM recorders used a CRT or video image as the input source. Once a page of alphanumeric or graphic data has been gathered and displayed on the terminal, the COM unit takes a picture of it and develops the picture at a high speed on either 16mm, 35mm, or 105mm film. This process could be performed either on-line or off-line. The on-line process requires the computer to compose the video screens for photography during the filming process. When performed off-line, the computer generates a magnetic tape that contains all the data to be put on microfilm. The tape serves as input to the COM device, which has a logic section to format the page for photography the way it will look on the microfilm frame. The camera unit is mounted directly in front of the CRT screen where the formatted page is displayed. In both the on-line and off-line processes, the camera is synchronized so that it only takes pictures when a complete form has been displayed.

The newer COM recorders have progressed to the extent that the video screen and the camera have been eliminated completely. The digital input to the new state-of-the-art COM device controls a laser beam which burns the image directly into the microfilm. Digital impulses are interpreted as commands to focus and aim the laser to a specific location on the surface of the film. The light from the laser exposes the film and creates the image. This COM process is dry in the sense that the film must not be placed in a bath to be developed. The dry COM process enables the production of microfilmed documents from any sort of computer-based information-processing system. Because paper documents are relatively expensive to produce, transmit, and store, the COM process reduces the cost of producing microfilm images of computer-generated documents. Because digital data may be transmitted electronically, computers at multiple sites can make use of the same COM hardware. Thus, remote sites distributed throughout a large complex can be tied to a central records base.

How can COM assist the records manager? Because of the digital nature of data input to the COM device, the source material can come from any digital media. For example, the sources available for production of documents on COM include magnetic disk or magnetic tape, direct channel connection from an optical character reader, data transfer lines in local area networks or direct satellite broadcasts, and even optical disks.

The production and storage costs of COM are much lower than the equivalent paper costs. Especially when a high number of copies are needed, COM usage can save from 80 percent to 90 percent of printed page costs. When linked with CAR systems, the storage and usage cost savings can be even greater. For example, the cost of producing a photocopy of a 200-page report is today between $6 and $10, while the cost to capture that report on microfilm is below $2.

Another reason for the expanded use of COM is that it can be used not only as a paper replacement medium but also as an adjacent or backup copy to an on-line data base. COM systems replace the paper generation of computer system output such as operations logs, program documents, and memory dumps. Tied in with dynamic disk indexing, microfilm storage systems can be used to back up database management systems. In this way, updated information can be reproduced with COM software and automatically integrated into the backup microformed data base. At periodic intervals the backup must be rewritten in its entirety. With a high-speed COM system, the complete on-line data base may be reconstructed on microfilm, and the old backup data base may be discarded.

The emergence of COM has made microforms useful in a myriad of new ways and for the foreseeable future. The versatility and long life of microfilm and the economics and simplicity of COM devices suggest that COM will maintain its presence in the office for years to come.

7.3 COMPUTER-ASSISTED RETRIEVAL (CAR)

Approximately ten years ago when CAR first emerged as a viable technology for document and information management, its use was limited to very large standardized institutional settings. Banking, insurance and financial services, utilities, military, and health industries were typical corporate users. Several factors limited application of CAR to institutions with large-scale homogeneous data bases.

The CAR software was not yet standardized; customized programs were very expensive to install and maintain; and the programs required a large memory capacity. Additionally, the systems were not particularly user friendly, were limited in what they could do, and required considerable expertise on the part of the operator. All of the foregoing factors caused high associated personnel costs. Finally, CAR systems were not evolving with the other office systems. CAR systems did not incorporate and use new technologies.

Fortunately for the records manager, equipment manufacturers have learned from the past, and today's CAR systems are greatly improved. At the root of the improvements in the "new breed" of CAR systems is the widespread availability of inexpensive processing in the form of microcomputers. This has not only made large-scale CAR systems much more satisfactory for rapid data retrieval in a high-volume setting, but has made them economically feasible for smaller offices and satellite operations.

CAR systems combine the computer with micrographics and utilize the strengths of each while minimizing their weaknesses. The computer uses on-line magnetic memory to store a description and location of each image stored on microfilm. The microfilm or microfiche store the documents at greatly reduced costs and minimal space requirements when compared with paper.

This relatively low-cost, efficient, and rapid document retrieval ability has resulted in a host of applications. Among companies which use microforms, accounting departments are the greatest users, followed by finance, personnel, and DP/MIS departments. The growth rates of CAR systems sales have also placed it toward the head of the pack when it comes to office automation.

To gain a clear understanding of how a CAR system functions and how it can be used in an effective records-management program, let's take a closer look at a generic CAR system and follow a document through each of its stages. This description is not meant to be exhaustive or all-inclusive; certain systems may have additional features or capabilities. This is especially true of systems designed for a specific user group such as the legal, medical, or accounting profession. These systems satisfy particular needs with storage and access characteristics targeted for fairly specific demands.

The first stage in the CAR process consists of capturing the document image. Depending on the volume and nature of the document stream, this could be performed with a step-and-repeat camera, a planetary camera, or a COM device. While the document image is being filmed, a sequence number is attached. This number, along with the roll or fiche number, becomes the document address in the computer-based retrieval system. Either during the image filming or after film development when the images are checked, a data-entry operator keys the document sequence number into the computer along with any other descriptors desired to form an index. The descriptors included will depend on the type of indexing format being utilized and the number of search and retrieval fields established. Today's computers and database software allow for extensive index specification to take place. Additionally, cross-field searches and multi-user access are available features on the larger systems. Such features are the current state of the art in office automation and provide considerable flexibility for the records manager.

With the document safely stored and indexed, a number of additional pieces of equipment are used to retrieve a document. To begin the search, the user would provide the index information on a CRT attached to the computer-based retrieval system. Employing search parameters, the desired document and its address description would be determined. The terminal then prompts the user to have the correct film reel or fiche cartridge loaded by the microform storage and retrieval device. This is a computer-controlled electromechanical device which allows for image storage and retrieval without human intervention. It can be on location or at a remote site to which the user is tied in by a LAN link.

Once loaded, the microfilm reader automatically locates and scans the document image, and the image appears on the user's CRT. If desired, a hard copy can be generated by a variety of types of printers. When access is completed, the storage unit automatically rewinds or disengages the storage file and replaces it in the library.

This example is straightforward and simplified. There is a great variety of small, medium, and large-scale CAR systems. Exhibit 7.1 lists some of the major companies that produce CAR systems. The smaller stand-alone CAR systems are microprocessor-driven and can range in price from $10,000 to $40,000. Of course, these systems have limited index and search and storage capacity, and their software flexibility cannot match that of higher-scale systems.

Exhibit 7.1
Some Companies Producing Computer-Aided Retrieval Systems

• Access Corporation	• Infodetecs
• Bell & Howell	• Information Designator
• Canon	• Minolta
• Consolidated Micrographics	• Philips
• Eastman Kodak Co.	• 3M
• Fuji Film	• Visual Systems Corp
• Fujitsu	

Complementing this hardware improvement and cost reduction in CAR systems, a number of software programs have become available which can link micrographics hardware and PCs. In fact, CAR applications are starting to become just one more facet of the integrated electronic office network.

New standalone CAR systems are available on a turnkey basis from various vendors for prices ranging from $10,000 to $100,000. Some of the latest features on these systems include the ability to use a variety of search parameters, unlimited data entry and retrieval fields, and various indexing formats which allow for image retrieval across many search fields. These systems also have the ability to collect and produce various database reports, perform complex audits covering data entry, and offer a number of index sorting options.

Medium-scale CAR units have multiple interfaces, more automated functions, and greater software flexibility and storage capacity. Their prices can range from $40,000 to $75,000. Some of them also offer modular add-on capacity and additional features such as electronic mail or word-processing ability. Additionally, these systems begin to take advantage of optical character readers and high-speed digitization.

The high-end CAR systems start at prices of several hundred thousand dollars and can range up to the millions. They are generally customized and offer high speed, high capacity, multiple local and remote access ports, and multiple-display technologies. They also offer modular formats where additional capacity or alternate storage technologies such as optical disks can later be integrated. In these systems, various media can be merged and controlled, offering truly automated information management.

The selection of the right CAR system must be based on a thorough and realistic assessment of the company's needs in order to allow for immediate records-management benefits. If the process is well thought out, future requirements can be anticipated or provided for with as little disruption as possible. CAR is already here and will continue to be with us in the future.

7.4 OPTICAL CHARACTER RECOGNITION (OCR)

One more technology deserves mention while we are on the subject of data conversion between digital and image formats. Optical character recognition (OCR) technology enables an input document written on paper to be converted onto some type of digital media. OCR is different from CAR because the digitized output is not a picture of the page; rather it is a digital encoding of each character on the page. In other words, a textual document may be written to a disk and later accessed for further word processing. In principle, OCR scanning technology could be used in conjunction with microfilm to make changes to text that is stored on micrographic media. Text on microfilm could be transformed to a computer-readable format, edited on a word processor, and then returned to micrographic storage by means of a COM device. This is not a typical application of OCR technology, however. More often, OCR devices are used by the word-processing department to save time in rekeying large volumes of text.

OCR scanners include three basic functions. A paper transport device separates a sheet from the paper stack, pulls it through the machine, and deposits it on the output hopper. The transport function is similar to that found in a reprographic device or copier. The scanning mechanism employs some sort of directed light that scans the page line by line and "reads" the page. A photoelectric cell senses whether the spot on which the light is focused is black or white. The scanner sends this signal to the recognition logic unit which identifies the character based on the signal pattern. The character as identified is then converted into its standard digital representation and written to the magnetic disk.

In order for the OCR scanner to function correctly, it must have a high-quality source copy. If the scanner cannot recognize a character, it may send the wrong digital code to the disk. Many scanners will rescan a character if it cannot be recognized, and if the machine fails again, it will display the character to the operator to be typed in manually.

A typical OCR scanner can transfer anywhere from three to forty pages per minute onto a digital storage medium. Most OCR scanners can recognize characters from a number of different type fonts, especially when they are designed to analyze features instead of simply matching features one-to-one. The cost of an OCR unit can range from $6,000 to $75,000.

Although an OCR unit may be of limited use in the records-management environment, it can be invaluable for a firm that must maintain and update a large quantity of paper records, particularly when information is tabular or textual.

7.5 CURRENT OPTICAL DISK TECHNOLOGY

Whenever a new technology is introduced, misconceptions arise over what it can and cannot do. Optical disk (OD) technology is no exception. For many years, records managers have heard of OD storage systems and each time have heard how they were about to break forth on the scene and revolutionize document storage and handling. Several years passed, and still the breakthrough did not occur. Understandably, skepticism arose about the viability of optical disk technology.

In the interim, however, all has not been quiet in the laboratories and manufacturing facilities of the firms struggling to perfect the optical disk. Among these firms are some of the biggest names in high-tech electronic gear in the United States, Japan, and Europe (see Exhibit 7.2). One development is the spread of compact disks (CD) for music storage and playback. The CD market has grown beyond even manufacturers' projections. As volume continues to climb, costs are dropping steadily. This industry has proved to be a vast laboratory and testing ground for advancements in the state of the art in OD information storage.

Exhibit 7.2
Some Companies Developing Optical Disk Media and Hardware

• AT&T	• Optical Storage Int'l
• DEC	• Philips
• Filenet Corp.	• RCA
• Fujitsu	• Reference Technology
• Hitachi	• Sharp
• IBM	• Sony
• Kodak	• Storage Technology
• Laser Data	• TAB
• Matsushita	• 3M
• Mitsubishi	• Xerox

It finally looks as if OD systems are here to stay. The technological, economic, and legal obstacles, if not already overcome, are close to falling. Optical storage is probably the best means to date of image processing, and these images can be anything from forms to x-rays to computer-generated designs. Once this information is digitized, a requirement in any OD system, the power of the computer can be harnessed for processing, indexing, retrieving, and communicating. Before proceeding to a closer look at optical storage in records management today, a review of the basic technical aspects of optical disks is required.

7.5.1 What Is an Optical Disk?

Current optical technology uses a laser to record data on a flat disk-shaped medium. The compact disks now available for recording music also use this new technology. In the recording process, a mark made by the laser onto the surface medium of the disk represents a binary one, and the absence of a mark a binary zero. This allows a stream of digitized data to be recorded and later played back. Because the process utilizes a focused laser beam of very narrow proportions, fractions of a hair's width, large quantities of data can be recorded in a small space.

A number of differing physical processes are used to preserve data on the disk surface, depending on the type of system being employed.

Although a majority of the OD systems released to date are of the non-erasable type (characterized as being either read-only or write once read many), an intense effort is currently underway by a number of both American and non-American companies, principally Japanese, to develop erasable technologies that would allow the disks to be updated or reused. Once such erasable systems are developed, OD technology will really take off.

7.5.2 Three Optical Disk Systems

Currently, there are three major types of optical disk technologies. The first two are non-erasable and are available today. The third is still in development and features the ability to erase and update disks.

Non-erasable media. Read-only memory (ROM) optical technology allows access to information already encoded by a manufacturer or publisher. Users cannot record their own data. In this system a laser beam is used to etch pits one micron wide onto a master disk, which is then used to make prerecorded copies. This method is an ideal one for mass applications of either text or digitized graphics that require wide distribution and no alteration. It allows fast random access of information, and the disks are inexpensive to produce.

Write once and read many (WORM) optical technology allows a user to write once on a disk and permanently store data, which can then be accessed repeatedly. Letters, forms, and contracts, for example, can be digitally encoded as a document image and recorded. But once they are recorded, they cannot be changed.

WORM technology utilizes one of two techniques for data storage. In ablative recording, a laser burns a series of small pits in the surface of the medium, which exposes a reflective underlayer or substrate. In the bubble-forming technique, laser light applied to a sensitive metal layer heats an underlying polymer layer, causing it to generate gases. These gases push up on the thin metal sheath and create bubbles. In both techniques the reading task is accomplished by using a low-power laser to illuminate the disk and measure the distortion created in the reflected light by the pattern of pits or bubbles.

Erasable media. As in WORM technology, two differing methods are under investigation and development by the industry in the erasable medium area. Magneto-optical recording makes use of a low-power laser to alter the surface magnetic characteristics of a disk by means of temperature changes. In the playback mode these magnetic differences affect the polarity of the reflected light and distinguish the ones and zeroes of digital data.

The second technique, called phase change, uses a brief laser heating pulse to convert low-reflecting amorphous material to higher reflecting crystalline material. Once again changes in the reflected light during playback create an information stream. To alter the disk, a long-lasting, less intense heating pulse is used to convert the crystalline material back to its original amorphous state.

7.5.3 Today's Integrated Systems

Many of today's state-of-the-art data-processing and document control systems utilize COM and CAR. If such systems are planned and developed with care, OD technology can be gradually introduced to complement advanced micrographic systems. In the same fashion, optical storage can be linked with magnetic storage and disk drives to increase the overall capacity of a system.

OD technology is simply not going to supplant existing micrographics and magnetic media. In fact, some predict that expanding OD usage will increase the use of magnetic drives because new information storage and manipulation techniques will be developed. On-line magnetic drives will be used to store, manipulate, and enhance data. When the final stage is reached, the document or file can be transferred to other locations over a LAN or other inter-office communication line. It would then be downloaded to an optical disk storage system, whose characteristics of speed and data compaction are ideal for mass storage and retrieval.

Most managers are intrigued by the potential of the OD technology to store and retrieve vast amounts of information in a very compact format at low cost. The technology can store more than a billion letters or numbers—one gigabyte of data—on each side of a 12-inch disk. This is equivalent to more than 25 file drawers of paper, or the complete *Encyclopedia Britannica*, photographs included. With 60 to 120 times more data than a similar sized magnetic disk can retain, the optical disk has a capacity equivalent to more than 3,000 diskettes. The savings in storage over other media are impressive and are now approaching the pennies-per-megabyte level on multiple disk systems. Combined with their high speed and random-access abilities, OD systems are the records-management tool of the future that is already here today.

Current uses of optical disks can be divided into two main categories. The first, using ROM technology, is practiced in situations where wide availability of a large static data base is desired, such as in reference materials, codified regulations, or periodically updated catalogues. These applications require a very high level of compaction and image as well as text storage and retrieval. Unlike magnetic media, which require sequential input of data during duplication, an OD can be stamped with data during the manufacturing process at a very low cost. This allows for electronic publishing. The quality of ROM data is also high, since optical disks do not suffer from deterioration associated with repeated magnetic or microform media usage. Its storage life of ten years places it between magnetic's three-year life and film's span of 50 to 100 years. Therefore, at this stage, at least, long-term archival needs are still better satisfied with film than optical disks.

With optical disks that incorporate WORM technology, the user has the ability to input information. In addition to keyboards, other input devices such as OCR scanners allow a wide range of documents to be electronically encoded digitally and captured.

Because OD storage and retrieval systems are seldom standalone units, most applications require the integration of disks into existing document and image handling systems. Alternatively, such disk systems are major components of hybrid systems becoming available from a variety of vendors. These systems combine a number of new technologies including OD, laser printers, document scanners, high-resolution displays, multifunction workstations and high performance LANs. These hybrid systems are the topic of the next section.

7.6 HYBRID SYSTEMS

A number of manufacturers have recently announced products that are labeled image or document management systems. Generally, these systems offer fully integrated information-management capabilities by wedding advanced computer database, electronic image processing, and state-of-the-art communications technologies. This union allows these hybrid systems to capture, store, manipulate, and deliver both source document information and images, and computer-based data to local or remote users at multifunction workstations.

An example of such a system from a major name is Kodak's new KIMS (TM) (Kodak Image Management System), slated for commercial availability in 1986. A good example of a smaller company's entry into this field is the Filenet (TM) Document-Image Processor offered by the Filenet Corporation.

Both of these systems integrate different media to increase productivity in document management activities. For the records manager they represent an entirely new approach to all phases of document handling. By integrating a number of systems—COM and CAR, magnetic data bases, OD technology and high-capacity LAN networks—a total document control system is created.

In these integrated systems there are four basic functions: input, storage, processing, and output. Corresponding to these different data manipulation functions are four types of hardware. Although different manufacturers may vary in their approach to integration, generally the following elements can be distinguished.

Input. Every information or document processing system requires some means of entering data. These advanced systems handle data electronically and therefore utilize image scanning equipment to transform hardcopy paper-based documents to digital data. High-resolution optical scanners, or optical character readers (OCRs), capture 200 to 400 dots per inch and transform a document page into 4 to 16 million bits of data. OCRs are available in both automatic and manual modes. A middle-of-the-line automatic OCR can handle 15 pages per minute. Manual scanners are hand-fed and are best suited for low volumes or situations where automatic feed is not suitable, for example, graphics, maps, engineering drawings, and the like. Many forms of documents can be recorded with scanners; in the medical field, for example, x-rays are now frequently being scanned. Additionally, keyboards can be used to enter text, data, or index information into the system.

Image storage. Once information is digitally encoded, this component stores and manages it so that it can be accessed and integrated with other information. Here is where software such as the master filing system is applied. This software element applies modern database management techniques to the stored information. In hybrid systems three storage media—magnetic tape or disk, micrographics, and optical disks—are integrated. The mix of each of these media and their role in the system varies from manufacturer to manufacturer.

Magnetic media are generally used to store the indexing and operating software and an on-line and backup copy of the document or documents being worked on. It thus ties together all of the system's elements.

Microfilm or WORM optical technology is used to store the "library" of information. OD technology offers the benefits of very rapid random access and high-density data compaction.

Microfilm offers the benefits of its tried and true technology, long storage life, and the capabilities of CAR and COM technology. An electromechanical or robotic device locates and loads the desired microfilm magazine or optical disk. Data may be accessed within seconds and 1 to 20 million pages of image information can be stored in only a few square feet of floor space, on microfilm or on optical disks, in a "jukebox" arrangement.

Processing. This component allows for the accessing, manipulation and processing, and restorage of information by the user. It can range from a simple keyboard and screen to a more complex multifunction workstation with its own OCR printer and other peripheral devices. End-user needs determine its design.

Output. This component disseminates the final information product. The output component consists of a printer station such as a laser printer or a combination of daisy-wheel and line-plot printers. Information in digital form can also be distributed via a LAN or, for further distances, dedicated wire or satellite service. Thus, an entire organization with remote locations can be tied into a comprehensive information and data-processing system.

The new hybrid systems represented are today's top-of-the-line information handling and office automation equipment. They blend all the elements of technology which can be applied to each stage of a record's life cycle and allow for the integration of future upgrades. The system should be designed dynamically so that add-ons and improvements can be accommodated. Unprecedented access and manipulation abilities are made available to modern offices in these systems, and the records manager plays a vital role in how they are selected, introduced, and utilized.

QUESTIONS AND ANSWERS

Q. What does a computer output microfilm (COM) device do?

A. From digital data—a stream of bits which represent either text data or graphic images—COM devices create a microform record without an intervening paper stage. Because an electronic information stream is the source, cameras can also be eliminated in the dry microfilm process.

Q. What are the benefits of COM?

A. Compared to paper, the costs of microfilm production and storage are much lower. Because COM creates a record directly from a digital data stream, no photographing of a paper document is necessary. COM allows documents from any digital source to be transferred to microfilm. Magnetic disks, magnetic tape, optical disks, data transfer lines, and direct channel connection are all valid sources for the COM device.

Q. What is computer-assisted retrieval (CAR)?

A. Computer-assisted retrieval (CAR) is a process that combines the strengths and capabilities of a computer with the benefits of non-paper-based records storage media in a single system. In such a system the on-line magnetic memory of a computer is used to store the description and location of an image captured on microform or optical disk. A robotic library contains the disks, fiche, or roll film. Following directions from the computer, the system retrieves individual documents, displays them, and replaces them in the proper location automatically.

Q. What are optical disks?

A. Optical disks are the newest form of information and disk storage technology on the market. They get their name from the method by which data are read from and written to the disk surface—namely, by means of an optical laser beam. The laser beam is used to record data by marking the surface of a flat disk-shaped metal and plastic composite medium. To read the disk, a low-powered laser is focused on the surface, and distortions in the reflected light are measured for their data content.

Q. Why aren't optical disks more widely used?

A. Currently the two biggest problems with optical disks are high costs and their lack of erasability. Because of the latter factor, disks may not be modified or updated. Nevertheless, a number of determined manufacturers are now pursuing technological solutions to these shortcomings. Because optical disks are not widely used, they are not yet considered acceptable for the storage of evidence. In fact, no one has developed a standard optical disk operating system. But, as optical disks penetrate the market in greater numbers, some of these problems will disappear.

PART 3
PERFORMING A NEEDS ASSESSMENT

Initiating a Records Program

8.1 LOCATING THE RECORDS-MANAGEMENT FUNCTION

Every firm has a records system, whether it consists of a few filing cabinets or a computer-assisted storage and retrieval system, but not every company has a records-management department. Although it is older than data processing, records management is still a relatively recent arrival on the corporate scene. Many smaller businesses have no assigned records manager, and an office manager or administrator takes on records management among other tasks. Before any records programs can be implemented or revised, responsibility for the task must be clearly delegated.

When managed by the administrative services department, records management is grouped with other support functions like the mail room, micrographics, reprographics, and word processing. By combining all of these services under the auspices of administrative services, user needs become the primary focus instead of technical expertise. Another advantage of the linkage of user support functions is that the technological capacity to integrate all of these information functions now exists. For this reason some firms have recently renamed their records-management departments, calling them information resource management departments. For example, data entered into a PC can be electronically transmitted to a copier-printer or produced directly as microfiche with no intervening paper stage. Given the current potential for linking systems electronically, it now makes sense to link the management of these systems organizationally.

The automation of the traditional service functions, however, has also made the organizational question more complicated. It can be argued that records management should be located in the data-processing or MIS department. Because MIS handles the collection, storage, and retrieval of electronic data and information, its functions may overlap with those of the records manager. MIS can also provide considerable technical expertise on the operation of computer-based automated storage and retrieval systems.

But records management involves more than control of automated systems. It is concerned with the entire life cycle of many types of documents stored on a variety of media. MIS usually does not have much experience in regulating manual filing systems or paper production. In addition, it is not equipped to research the legal or regulatory issues involved in records retention and storage. Perhaps the most serious drawback of locating records management in an existing MIS department is that MIS is often more adept at dealing with technical problems than with user needs. Records management is however a function whose effectiveness depends on user satisfaction. The problem of integrating a service mentality with technical expertise may be solved by the creation of a new information services department.

8.2 GETTING MANAGEMENT SUPPORT

A records program consists of the human and technical resources required to monitor, maintain, and control the organization's records. As such, it will include the inventory of existing records, the development and administration of regulations and procedures, and the writing of a records manual. To institute such a formal program or to overhaul an existing one, top management has to be actively supportive. Unfortunately, convincing the top decision-makers that information management is a high budget priority is not always easy. Often the records manager's most challenging job is not implementing a new system but convincing both management and end users that such a system is desirable.

Records management doesn't receive the kind of media coverage given to other areas of office management. Thus, it is often difficult to raise corporate awareness about new developments in the field, unless problems involving record security, storage, or production are readily apparent. In addition, implementing changes in records programs is neither cheap nor easy. As a result, many executives choose not to face squarely their information needs.

Records management often becomes a priority only after a disaster traced to faulty storage or retrieval has occurred. For example, the president of a major California insurance company admitted that he never considered the issue of records security until an aircraft crashed into the office building next to his. He explained to a consultant, "The business implications were tremendous. If our company suffered a similar catastrophe, we might never be able to reconstruct our business. It made me realize that our records are fundamental to our business."

Records managers should begin their programs with a campaign to educate corporate executives and gain their support. They can target areas of concern to management and gather documentation which backs up their position. Articles from trade journals and business magazines can be scoured for their relevant contributions. The thrust of this collection of articles should be to discover the major weaknesses of records-management programs and the remedies that have been successfully employed.

Articles should focus on three major areas of concern: general business problems, litigation, and records automation. The first category will show how inadequate records management has resulted in financial loss or administrative difficulties. The second category of articles should remind executives of the legal implications of inaccessible or lost documents. And finally, information on records automation can educate executives about technological solutions to records-management problems.

As part of a promotional campaign, records managers should attempt to educate management about their profession and the scope of their responsibilities. For this task, they can use publications of the Association of Records Managers and Administrators (ARMA) or even bring executives to an ARMA meeting. These contacts should provide illustrations of well-run records programs at other companies, perhaps even those of competitors.

With general information in hand, records managers can proceed to define the liabilities of their own firms' systems and to assess their future records-management needs. This task can be broken into several steps, with top management approval required between completion of the various phases. The first step should consist of a general overview of the current situation and the selection of a pilot area for implementation. Only after a target project is successfully implemented will management be likely to approve substantial changes on a corporate level. The result of this preliminary process should be a presentation or white paper which outlines a records work plan and estimates the budget and staff which are required to carry it out. This chapter is designed to help you prepare such a document.

After this presentation has been approved, and a budget and staff have been allocated, the records-management team can undertake a full-scale examination and analysis of the company's records control. These steps, from conducting an inventory, to assessing user needs, to designing a new system, are the subject of the next four chapters.

8.3 ASSESSING THE CURRENT SITUATION

The initial survey is designed to help the records manager sell the work plan to management. It should provide an overview of the control, security, utility, and cost of the existing records program. It should be only a brief review of the records situation that pinpoints the types of records the company holds, where they are stored, what media they are stored on, and finally, an estimate of how many records are currently in the firm's possession.

To accomplish this task, some preliminary data must be collected. If the necessary figures have already been compiled, this step will be a simple one. If not, an interview or questionnaire is probably the quickest way to gather accurate estimates. Follow-up interviews can be conducted in obvious problem or bottleneck areas. Whether or not the records people decide to interview departmental representatives, the records manager should appoint a liaison in each department to coordinate scheduling, keep records management informed of any procedural changes, and communicate records policies to their own users. The important point to remember at this stage in the planning process, before a full budget is approved and a records-management team is put together, is that the data should be collected with a minimum of time and effort. A full inventory of all company records (a process detailed in Chapter 9) will not be conducted until a corporate records overhaul has been approved.

The following types of data should be targeted in this initial foray:

1. Location
   • Lists and figures on current records stored in divisions or departments
   • On-site and off-site storage facilities
2. Equipment
   • Estimates of the numbers of file drawers currently utilized
3. Quantity
   • Estimates of yearly growth of records
4. Budgets

- Budgets for filing equipment and filing supplies each year
5. Procedures
   - Current assignment of filing responsibility
   - Current problems in access, storage, or retrieval of records
   - Current procedures and how they are documented (indices, instructions, manuals)

Once the background material is compiled, the records manager can formulate strategies for improving the existing program. Part of understanding the problem is having a clear idea of how a system should work. With some hard data in hand and the recommendations of departmental users in mind, a records manager should be able to compose a set of records-management objectives that will help define the task and set priorities. These objectives should encompass not only specific departmental needs but general corporate information requirements. Thus, pharmaceutical firms and banks differ in the types of information they use and the speed with which it must be accessed. More specifically, this data should give the records manager a sense of how each department should function.

A more detailed analysis of each operating department's information requirements should be conducted after an initial test project has been successfully completed. At that time, the records team will want to do a full-scale needs analysis such as that outlined in Chapter 10.

8.4 CONDUCTING A PILOT STUDY

The initial survey should highlight which department or departments have the most serious records control problems and the most pressing needs. Since such departments are probably wasting a lot of time and money on document retrieval or storage facilities, a records program could achieve dramatic financial results. If there are too many problem areas to focus on immediately, a department that is receptive to the idea of restructuring its records program should be chosen as a pilot area. Obviously, cooperation from departmental employees will significantly raise the test program's chances of success. It is very important that a pilot program show positive, quantifiable results, as it will be one of the tools which will be used to convince top management that such a program should be implemented at the corporate level.

8.5 ORGANIZING A TEAM

The team that the records manager puts together for implementing a pilot project should be the core of the records-management department. For small firms, the records manager and a file clerk may comprise the department, but for larger corporations, records management may be handled by as many as 30 employees. Thus, staffing requirements and qualifications should be carefully considered. The major part of this task is to define the job responsibilities of records-management personnel. Whether records management is centralized or spread throughout various operating divisions, organizing a team for implementing records management should aim to give the records-management function a permanent position in the corporate organizational structure.

In regards to staffing, an entry-level position in records management is a file clerk. This job can probably be performed by an employee with a high school education, as most of the duties are simple and routine. The major task of the file clerk is to sort and file correspondence, invoices, and other documents into alphabetical or numerical order according to their subject matter. To do this effectively, a clerk must be able to grasp the logic of the file classification scheme and be attentive to detail. If these qualifications are met, the clerk should have no trouble retrieving documents as they are requested and keeping a record of those documents which have been checked out. More complex duties include the preparation of company indexes and color-coding schemes and the updating of cross-references. In addition, clerks can be assigned to the classification and disposition of records in accordance with company policies and procedures. Depending on how sophisticated such a decision-making process is, it can be delegated to a higher-level records supervisor.

The records supervisor acts as the link between one or more records clerks and the records manager. As a coordinator, the supervisor must be proficient in personnel and communication skills. In addition, the supervisor should be knowledgeable in records-management techniques and strategies in order to set priorities and help plan and implement new policies. The supervisor will be in direct contact with users and their filing needs and can work closely with the manager to match resources with everyday needs. As an observer of entry-level records-management personnel, the supervisor is also well equipped to organize and run an ongoing training program for new employees. Finally, the records supervisor will provide most of the input for the evaluation of clerks and for developing or re-evaluating their job descriptions.

Specific supervisory duties include complex document classification and enforcement of filing and retention policies. One aspect of this role is controlling access to classified documents. Another is to review document checkout lists to make sure that files are being returned according to schedule. In addition to these functions, the supervisor acts as an advisor to the records manager by recommending equipment purchases and revisions to existing procedures.

To carry out all of these duties effectively, a records supervisor should have at least a couple of years of business experience plus some exposure to records management. In most cases this work experience should be accompanied by some college-level courses in management and office administration.

8.5.1 Training the Records-Management Staff

Where a records staff already exists, on-the-job training for new employees will give most low-level employees the requisite filing skills. Nevertheless, a training program will be helpful for any company that plans to undergo a major records-management overhaul. Instruction in short- and long-term records-management objectives can give everyone from file clerks to supervisors a broader perspective of their roles in the company. Periodic training sessions can be used to communicate updated records goals and to receive staff input on existing procedures. Training can and should be personalized to meet the skill levels and requirements of all employees and to help them achieve the records-management goals.

Training programs that achieve the best results are usually those in which the teaching methods and formats are varied. For example, in addition to sponsoring lectures, trainers should reserve some sessions for open staff discussion and staff originating problem-solving ideas. Many times greatly improved methods of performing tasks can be discovered by merely getting the input of those who regularly do the task. Technical or procedural training can be augmented by sessions which spotlight various areas of records management. And finally, as a spur to staff members' personal advancement, they should be encouraged to add to their skills by taking outside courses. If possible, part of the budget should be allocated for reimbursing tuition costs in such relevant courses as data processing, office management, office equipment, and personnel management.

Besides offering educational reimbursement, a training program can provide worker incentive by structuring channels for worker advancement. If possible, the records manager should begin by upgrading job classifications and salaries. Because the entry-level jobs are considered menial and are paid accordingly, turnover in these jobs is high. However routine the tasks these clerks perform, mistakes are costly, and constant retraining is time-consuming. Salaries should at least be competitive with comparable jobs in other companies. Job titles, accompanied by pay raises, can be structured to provide career paths for every level of employee.

Fancy titles, however, will not relieve the boredom of doing a single filing task for eight hours. Although many people would argue that extreme specialization is the most efficient way to run a business, job diversification can improve morale and thus performance. Again, a training program can work to expand the skills of employees from clerks to supervisors and to provide job enrichment. For example, file clerks can be trained to operate microfilm cameras, and copyists can staff a records center.

8.6 WRITING AND SUBMITTING A PROPOSAL TO MANAGEMENT

The proposal that the records manager will submit to management is a sales pitch. It is not a complete catalogue of all the findings to date, but a critical overview of the current records situation. Without going into detail about the status of records management in each department, the proposal should pinpoint the problem areas and outline a method for improving records services. The focus of the report will be a work plan that explains how these improvements can be implemented. A good way to combine both short- and long-term projects is to divide the work plan into phases. This approach allows management to approve a program in stages. It also gives the records manager more flexibility in revising the details of each phase as the process unfolds. The first phase will consist of detailed implementation steps for the pilot project. The second phase would outline a proposed schedule for a companywide needs assessment. The third would deal with developing new records policies and systems. The final phase would address the implementation and maintenance of a records-management program.

After sketching the work plan phases, the proposal should be sure to enumerate the benefits that the completion of each stage of the work plan will bring to the company. These deliverables should include improvements in storage costs, record retrieval speed, and record security. The benefits should be as specific and quantifiable as possible, as this section may be the records manager's main selling point in getting management approval.

Benefits can best be quantified by formulating a cost-justified budget. The budget request should thus demonstrate how savings from program implementation would outweigh the expense of the program itself. That is, it must show management what to expect for a return on its investment. The prospects for such a return can be measured in several ways. One of the most common is break-even analysis, which finds the point at which the accumulated savings equal the initial conversion investment. In the case of records storage, for example, such a calculation would divide the net cost of the conversion by the annual value of freed floor space. To supplement this analysis, a multi-year comparison can follow the expected costs of the system as is, and the system as proposed, for a ten-year period. This method of cost justification should reveal a more substantial savings than the break-even calculation.

Finally, the proposal should include a request for a records-management staff or a temporary team to carry out the project. While the manager needn't include the detailed job descriptions which were drawn up, the proposal will state clearly how many employees must be hired, what their qualifications will be, and how much money is needed to pay their salaries.

To summarize the information which a presentation should include, it may be helpful to see it in the form of a possible table of contents:

1. An Overview of the Current Situation
2. The Work Plan:

   Phase I: Implementing a Pilot Project

   Phase II: Assessing Corporate Records-Management Needs

   Phase III: Designing a New System

   Phase IV: Implementing and Maintaining the Records Program
3. Anticipated Benefits
4. Budget and Staffing

When the proposal paper has been prepared, the records manager should arrange a meeting to present it to top management representatives. During the presentation, management will have the opportunity to explore any questions they may have about the project and will have the option of offering comments and criticisms. If the program does not get immediate approval, the records manager should take the objections and either formulate convincing answers or revise the work plan accordingly. In this manner a records program can be initiated.

QUESTIONS AND ANSWERS

Q. Who is responsible for records management?

A. Although every company has a record system, not every company has a records-management department. A dedicated records-management department is a fairly recent arrival on the corporate scene, and recent changes in the scope and tools of records management have changed its reporting relationship in many companies.

Q. Why have some companies decided to have records management report to MIS?

A. The argument for locating records management in DP/MIS usually centers on the technical expertise in that department. Records management is, however, more than the control of automated systems. It is concerned with the entire life cycle of many types of documents stored on a variety of media. It is also based on user needs, and its effectiveness rests on user satisfaction. Technical expertise is necessary, but it should not be the primary concern.

Q. What steps can records managers take to gain management support to implement new programs?

A. The first step in a campaign to gain support from top management should be an effort to educate them in the need for effective information resource management. The next step is an assessment of a company's present system and the selection of a pilot area for implementation of a new program. Preparing a white paper or outline of a new system with a corresponding budget is the next step to gain support.

Q. What is the argument for doing a pilot study before conducting a companywide evaluation?

A. A pilot program allows quantifiable results to be demonstrated in an actual work setting. These results are an important tool in convincing top management to implement a new program at the corporate level. It also allows the records manager to lab test and fine tune the proposed program.

Q. Who should be on the pilot program team?

A. The team that the records manager puts together should be the core of the records-management department. One aim of organizing this team to implement new programs is to give the records-management function a permanent position in the corporate organizational structure.

Q. What should a proposal to management accomplish?

A. A good proposal will pinpoint problem areas, delineate future plans, and outline a method for improving records services. The focus of the report will be a work plan that explains how these improvements can be implemented. Additionally, anticipated costs and savings should be clearly presented.

9

Conducting an Inventory

Once you are equipped with a management mandate and a budget for renovating records management, the first task is to figure out what records exist and how they are managed. Then you can move on to how they should be managed, and finally to how the present program can be brought up to where it should be. The automated tools, which were discussed in the previous section of this book, have the potential to streamline your firm's information flow for greater efficiency and accessibility. But tools are useless unless they are applied to specific jobs. The rest of Part 3 will be devoted to uncovering the state of records management in your own company and defining and charting the changes which must be made. This chapter will concentrate on conducting an inventory and an appraisal of all existing records, whether paper-based, micro-photographic, electronic, or audio-visual.

9.1 OBJECTIVES OF THE RECORDS INVENTORY

The scope of a thorough inventory is more than simply counting documents. Basically an inventory is a tool to maintain or achieve control over a firm's records through standardization, central management, and cost-effective storage. Establishing an inventory control system is a crucial step toward the effective use of automated tools and the development of an automated records-management storage and retrieval system. As such, an inventory seeks to determine the location, value, and status of each record and to provide a means for evaluating its function.

The primary objective of a records inventory is to identify the type or function of each document. Existing functional categories will provide the framework for how records are grouped into series. Thus, documents will be inventoried as either correspondence, reports, forms, invoices, and so forth. If a significant number of documents do not fit into any of the existing divisions, it will be clear that the company's present system of categories is inadequate. The identification of duplicate or multiple titles will provide the basis for a relative file index and for an appropriate uniform filing classification system if it does not already exist.

As an aid to establishing a filing system, an inventory can also track the way in which records series are classified for retrieval. As described in Chapter 4, filing schemes can be based on either numerical or alphabetical ordering. As with other inventory objectives, the goal should be to describe the existing classification scheme as a prelude to prescribing any necessary changes.

Another basic inventory goal is to determine the quantity of documents that the company possesses. Assessing numbers of units can give different clues as to how the present system functions. Regular inventories can chart the growth of one type of record over another, making it easier to plan the expansion of storage facilities.

In addition to counting documents according to function, an inventory must locate where they are housed. In general this process means identifying on-site and off-site storage centers. But further, the inventory should be designed to pinpoint where particular records series are held, whether in a central records room or in an individual desk file. Storage facilities themselves must be included in the inventory, with a full account of how many and what kind of file cabinets exist, as well as the extent of electronic storage means. A map of document storage centers can also provide information for conducting a cost analysis of storage space utilization. Traffic patterns and access needs can often be improved resulting in time and cost savings. Thus, an inventory can help determine the convenience/cost ratio of storing records in-house as opposed to situating them in an off-site facility. Such a map will also illustrate if the storage layout fits company policies regarding the centralization or decentralization of records, but this question will be dealt with more fully in Chapter 13.

Another inventory task is to determine record status—that is, whether the series is actively used, kept only for occasional reference, or stored as vital to the firm's identity. Record status dictates appropriate location as well as the length of time for which a record should be saved. Thus, vital records are stored in a locked vault; inactive records are located in a special facility; and active records should be within reach of their users. An index of how often and for what purpose a file is used can also assist the records-management team in evaluating company records retention policies for the destruction of document series. Setting up such a schedule will be dealt with in detail in Chapter 13. At any rate, part of the short-term task of an inventory is to target records series which can be immediately destroyed or moved to inactive storage, and to indicate those records which still merit active management.

The last inventory objective concerns the general value of the records to the organization. Besides performing a variety of other functions, all company records have a definable value in at least one of the following areas: administrative, an area which covers company organization; financial, which involves fiscal operations; legal, that is, the domain of government policies and business law; and historical or archival, which documents the company's existence.

9.2 CHOOSING AN INVENTORY PLAN

There are two basic approaches to conducting a companywide inventory: physical and survey inventories. In either case, counting records does not mean going through each individual document. Inventories only attempt to verify series of documents, such as a year's worth of purchase orders from the sales department or of the CEO's personal correspondence. Not everyone agrees on which type of inventory is the most effective, but each certainly has advantages and disadvantages.

Some would argue that surveys produce the quickest, most accurate information, because the questionnaires are completed by department heads who are familiar with the classification systems and storage facilities in their particular area. In addition, survey inventories are less costly and probably less disruptive precisely because they rely on departmental employees. Others would counter by pointing out that department heads rarely have the time to complete a thorough inventory. According to this scenario, surveys will always be plagued by gaps and a lack of adequate detail.

If you decide to use a survey questionnaire, it is imperative that it be carefully designed by personnel trained in records management. Survey forms should be personalized to address specific departmental needs and should be clearly and concisely worded. Care must be taken to simplify instructions or confusing terminology and to explain the purpose of the inventory.

Even with these precautions, surveys cannot provide the in-depth information that a physical inventory can. They can be most successful in locating records and equipment and in revealing departmental classification systems. But they are limited when it comes to assessing records status or value, as departmental heads lack the broader vision to make such judgments. For example, it is impossible for each department to know whether its records are duplicated in other units. While this can be checked by a coordinating team after the surveys have been compiled, the cost and the effort would probably cancel the benefits of doing a rapid survey inventory.

If you are conducting an inventory for the purpose of a wholesale records-management overhaul, a physical inventory is still probably the best bet, whether you use an in-house team or an outside consultant or service. Therefore, it should be useful to take the time to outline the steps for completing such a process. Two types of inventory forms are essential for gathering data. Included here are examples of a records inventory form (Exhibit 9.1) and an equipment inventory form (see Appendix A) to guide you, but forms like these are most successful when they are personalized to fit the needs of a large corporation with numerous departments, or a small business with one or more operating units.

The inventory team should select standard forms to be used throughout the company. Forms such as those exhibited track all the elements of records storage as outlined above. They have the additional advantage of requiring a minimum of writing effort while providing a maximum of data for both the inventory and the subsequent analysis of the records. For convenience, these forms can either be printed on cheaper full-sized sheets of typing paper or reduced to fit on more durable 5-inch by 7-inch cards.

9.3 PREPARING A SCHEDULE

After a survey team has been appointed to conduct the inventory, the first step should be to develop a work plan. In order to do this, floor plans of each department must be drawn so that basic storage units can be mapped out. For doing a physical inventory, each department and location site should be designated by an identification number. Individuals on the inventory team can then be assigned specific areas to cover within a given time frame.

When actually setting the schedule, several factors should be taken into account. First and foremost, the inventory team must coordinate its actions with all departments and concerned employees. Optimally, the inventory should be scheduled for each department, with completion dates and sequences set before the first document is counted. It is important to be as nondisruptive as possible to normal operating activities, and the timetable should be designed to avoid peak work-load periods.

Exhibit 9.1
Records Inventory Worksheet

Date:

Inventoried By: (1)

Dept. Name (2)

Series No. (3)

Record Series Name (4)

DATES		FILE ORDER & LIMITS			LOCATION			Equip. Type (13)	Records Inches (14)	CUBIC FEET (15)	REFERENCE		AC-TION (18)	SERIES SPAN	
From (5)	To (6)	Seq. (7)	By (8)	Range (9)	Bank (10)	Cab. (11)	Dr. (12)				(16)	Mo/Cu Ft (17)		Year Started	Year Ended

MICROFILM APPLICATION

Eligible After   System

ACTION

Transferred   Destroyed

Cu. Ft.   Cu. Ft.

SAVINGS

Equipment   Space

DESCRIPTION/USE: (19)

COPY: (20)
☐ Record
☐ Duplicate
☐ Information

FORMS: (21)

TYPE: (22)
☐ Transaction
☐ Subject
☐ Reports
☐ Graphic
☐ Other:

MEDIUM: (23)
☐ Paper
☐ Microfilm
  ☐ Roll
  ☐ Jacket
  ☐ Fiche
  ☐ Com
  ☐ Aperature
☐ Magnetic Media
  ☐ Card
  ☐ Tape
  ☐ Disk

SIZE: (25)
☐ Letter 8½ x 11
☐ Legal 8½ x 14
☐ Tab/Check 3 x 7⅞
☐ EDP 14 x 17
☐ Other:

HOUSING: (26)
☐ Folders
☐ Binders
  ☐ Ring
  ☐ Post
☐ Loose
☐ Other

USE: (24)
☐ Intra-Dept.
☐ Inter-Dept.
☐

RECOMMENDED POLICY

	Storage	Total
Office		

POLICY REVIEW

	Signed	Dat
Operating		
Legal		
Tax		
Audit		
Records Mgmt.		

APPROVED POLICY

	Storage	Total
Office		

Another reason to schedule in advance is to make sure that the employees responsible for retrieving files are present. Staff members can answer questions about file particulars and also verify the accuracy of the inventory. Having departmental employees present can prevent resentment and misunderstandings from developing over lost or misfiled records or nonstandard storage methods.

In order to draw departmental employees into the process, some type of questionnaire for gathering their input on scheduling and inventory priorities should be circulated. This step can be included whether you are making a survey or conducting a physical inventory. At a later stage in the records-management overhaul, you will want to do a more detailed evaluation of what departmental users expect and need out of a records policy (see Chapter 10), but this step will follow the inventory procedure.

In terms of a general time frame, over half of the effort should be spent on collecting the information: the numbers, types, and location of existing documents. But time must also be allotted for appraising the data gathered from each department or unit. By assigning record status and value, this stage of the inventory process leads directly into recommendations for reorganizing files, for purchasing new equipment or systems, for training new personnel, and for setting new policies and procedures for records management.

In determining time frames, it can be surprising how quickly records are inventoried once a methodology is developed. For each department, when using in-house employees familiar with the records, one or two days should suffice. On the average, one individual is able to inventory 1,000 cubic feet of records in a week.

A work plan must also be concerned with more than a time frame. Exhibit 9.2 illustrates the four phases of the inventory process. First, the team must review current records policies. Second, it must adopt or create a records audit methodology which is appropriate for classifying records stored in a variety of media: electronic, micrographic, paper, voice, and video. Third, the work plan must account for man-days allocated to the staff for conducting the inventory. Finally, a summary report must be produced to be submitted to management with the records team's recommendations. Such a report is a crucial means of maintaining management support. If it is given by the inventory team in the form of a presentation, direct feedback can speed the records evaluation process.

If the team encounters a large volume of records that seems to pose an obstacle to conducting a complete inventory, then the project can be divided into manageable parts. These divisions can be assigned priority according to how fast records accumulate, with rapidly multiplying series given top priority. At any rate, overwhelming volume is probably

Exhibit 9.2
Four Stages of the Inventory Process

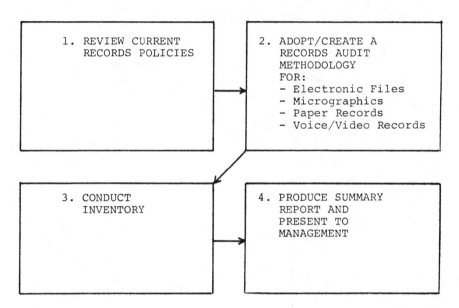

a sign that records retention policies are law. Many firms who complete records audits report that up to half their existing documents can be destroyed as the result of an inventory. Of course, the impact such a determination can have on storage costs is enormous.

9.4 CONDUCTING THE INVENTORY

One records inventory form (see Exhibit 9.1) should be completed for each record series in your office files. Separate forms should be filled out even if the series is a copy whose original is held in another department. This process will aid in the eventual destruction of unnecessary duplicates. Instructions should also be provided which clearly explain the steps for getting complete data on each series. Basically, however, the worksheet covers the following points:

- name of department
- time span of records series
- file location
- file volume
- file medium
- retention policy

- records titles and descriptions
- file classification and range
- file equipment
- file origin
- file use/description

Exhibit 9.3
Illustration of Equipment Addressing

(Numbers are assigned from bottom to top in a
clockwise fashion according to floor plans.)

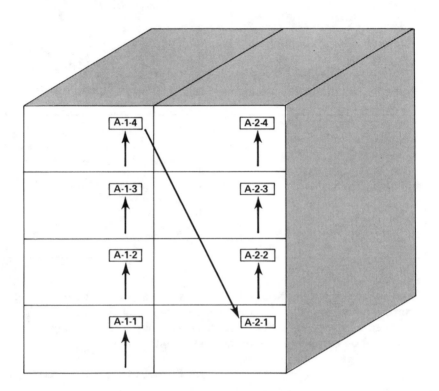

The first step to conducting an equipment inventory is to obtain a
department or unit floor plan printed on graph paper. The plan should
illustrate entrances, window banks, posts, or unique features that will
help identify the area. If an up-to-date floor plan is not available, have
one sketched. Next, take the sketch and draw in all records storage
equipment. Identify the individual upright file cabinets, lateral file cabinets, shelves, bookcases, overfiles, table tops, boxes, desks, and other
equipment used to store records. Be sure to differentiate among sizes
of letter, card, and legal file cabinets. The drawing does not have to be
scaled but should show apparent differences in equipment types.

Once the floor plan is filled in, assign symbols to each piece of equipment which indicate their location. First, define your record banks. A
bank can be one file cabinet standing alone, a group of file cabinets
clustered together, or a combination of file cabinets, tables, or bookcases
in one location. Then, letter each bank of equipment in alphabetical

order. Proceed clockwise from the main entrance to the department and identify every piece of filing equipment. Within each bank, number sequentially from left to right when facing the equipment, as demonstrated in Exhibit 9.3. For example, A–1 will be the first cabinet from the left in the "A" bank, and B–7 is the seventh cabinet from the left in the "B" bank.

Once filing equipment has been labeled, you can then count and measure the various kinds of equipment used to house records, coding each receptacle according to an equipment code such as the one in Exhibit 9.4. Included on the inventory forms should be a reference to equipment size, in linear inches and cubic foot capacity (Exhibit 9.5). One drawer in a letter-size upright file cabinet holds approximately 1.6 cubic feet when full; therefore, a five-drawer letter-size cabinet will hold 8 cubic feet of records. Similarly, a legal-size upright drawer holds 2 cubic feet of records, and a five-drawer cabinet holds 10 cubic feet. Capacities of other nonstandardized pieces of equipment can simply be measured. Finally, use the information gathered to make and affix labels to each piece of equipment. Working from the floor plan, number each by location, equipment, and drawer, starting from the bottom drawer or opening and working up to the topmost drawer or opening. Then apply removable stickers to each cabinet opening or drawer and make sure that the labels correspond to the information recorded on the inventory forms.

Exhibit 9.4
Equipment Codes

Vertical Letter	L
Vertical Legal	LS
Lateral Letter	LL
Lateral Legal	LLG
Card	C
Binder (14 × 18)	B
Plan-Flat	FP
Plan-Hanging	HP
Plan-Roll	RP
Microfilm	M
Supply Cabinet	SC
Shelves	SH
Voucher (8 × 10)	V
Storage Box	ST
Transfer Case	TR

	Drawer	Cu. Ft./drawer
Exhibit 9.5		
Determining Cubic Footage of Records		
For Vertical Files:		
Letter size	24"	1.6
Legal size	24"	2.0
For Lateral Files:		
Letter size	30"	1.8
	36"	2.2
	42"	2.6
Legal size	30"	2.2
	36"	2.6
	42"	3.0
For Card Files:		
3 × 5	24"	0.2
Tab file	24"	0.35
5 × 8	24"	0.6

FOR ALL OTHER RECORDS, USE THE FOLLOWING FORMULA:

Width × Height × Filing Depth × 0.0058 = cubic feet

9.5 ASSIGNING RECORD VALUE

After the physical inventory has been finished, records series must be appraised according to their value to the organization. As mentioned before, the four categories are administrative, legal, fiscal, and historical or archival. Determining record value is an essential preliminary to setting a retention schedule—an important part of records-management control which is discussed in detail in Chapter 11. As with other inventory information, it can be included on the records inventory form as an aid to evaluating the future status of each series.

Administrative value refers to the time in which the record may be used for the firm's internal and external business. This type of value can usually be determined by the department heads who hold original or primary copies of each series. Of course, if multiple copies exist, other departments' needs must be taken into account. The same managers should be able to break down administrative value into active and inactive time periods. Briefly, series classified as active are filed for greatest and most rapid accessibility, while inactive records are stored in cheaper areas with greater storage capacity. How to set these values and how to transfer them to new locations or equipment will be discussed in Chapter 11, but it is safe to say that few administrative files will remain active for more than two years. An exception to this rule would be something like an employee's payroll account, which would remain active as long as he or she were employed.

The difference between a firm's evaluation of a record's value and the government's is called the record's legal value. A myriad of federal, state, and local statutes cover records retention policies and procedures. As with other laws, ignorance is never an excuse for not meeting standards. One possible way of setting a value system which takes legal demands into account is to use a vendor's or a consultant's suggested retention schedule. Unfortunately, however, companies are not all responsible to the same regulatory agencies. An identical document could therefore be kept for two years at one firm and for four years at another. Some companies, like pharmaceutical firms for instance, also have particular types of documents which are unique to their industry. Thus, the regulations governing drug research documentation set by the Food and Drug Administration have little application to other industries. To make things even more complicated, state and local regulations vary, so that off-the-shelf retention schedules are likely to apply only to federal statutes.

In order to take full precautions, it is best for a legal consultant or a corporation's own legal department to individually examine the records series to determine if they have any legal value, and, if so, what retention period should be assigned. Evaluation can be aided by the Office of the Federal Register's yearly publication: *Guide to Record Retention Requirements*. This summary of the 1,000 or more federal regulations can be purchased for a small fee by simply writing to the Superintendent of Documents, U.S. Government Printing Office, Washington, DC 20402. As to be expected, similar state and local publications must be procured by querying the appropriate records offices or archives.

For both, retention periods can be confusing, as there is no centralized or standardized schedule which links the various regulatory agencies. Presumably, five agencies could require five different retention periods, some of them as vague as "as long as seems appropriate." In general, you are required to meet the most stringent standards. If this turns out to be an "appropriate" period, it is acceptable to merge a record's legal value with the firm's own administrative value.

Before moving on to a record's fiscal value, we should issue one word of warning. Although the confusion of legal requirements can be overwhelming, it is to your financial advantage not to fall back on a fail-safe, all-inclusive retention policy. Besides wasting valuable storage space, keeping all records indefinitely slows the retrieval process considerably. In addition, if a company is actually required to produce some document for a legal action, it is more likely that it will not be found at all or recovered at great cost and effort. Therefore, every effort should be made to evaluate each series carefully during the inventory process. Time spent at this stage of the inventory will be more than repaid in future savings of space, time, and money.

Fiscal value refers to a record's monetary or tax value. As such, fiscal record retention must meet both company use and audit requirements and the regulations of agencies like the Securities and Exchange Commission or the Internal Revenue Service. To determine the fiscal value of any records series, you should assign a qualified person from the firm's financial or accounting department or, if one is unavailable, an outside financial consultant.

Historical significance often cannot be quantified in financial terms, but most companies retain an interest in saving documents that have no direct administrative, legal, or fiscal value. Company publications, like in-house newsletters or product catalogues, can be useful as a gauge of the firm's changing face or development. There has also been a recent trend in writing corporate histories, and more firms are seeing such a document as a useful tool in staff orientation and morale building. If the firm already has an archivist or a librarian, that individual should be given the responsibility of determining historical value. If not, the records manager can take on the task, but only under a set of definite corporate guidelines approved by top management.

Having completed the inventory and appraisal process, you should have a good idea of the scope of the existing records and equipment and of the records program which regulates them. Before you move on to the substantive task of improving the system, with or without automated support, it is now imperative that you take stock of the expressed records needs of the company's users. The next chapter deals with formulating and carrying out a user needs analysis.

QUESTIONS AND ANSWERS

Q. Why conduct a records inventory?

A. An inventory is a means for maintaining or achieving control over a company's records through standardization, central management, and cost-effective storage. An inventory should therefore be designed to provide current information about the types, functions, series, quantity, location, status, and value of the records held by your company.

Q. What are the approaches to conducting a companywide inventory?

A. There are two basic approaches to conducting such an inventory—survey and physical. Survey inventories are designed to delegate the responsibility for monitoring current records practices to department or section heads. Physical inventories, on the other hand, are those in which a team physically examines the company's records base and records the results.

Q. What is the advantage of a physical inventory?

A. More complete confirmation, not only of quantity, but status and value of the records can usually be obtained. This will aid the later process of records evaluation and new systems or plan formulation.

Q. What are the stages of a physical inventory?

A. Once the inventory team has been established, the inventory project can be divided into four phases. First, the team must review current records policies. Second, it must adopt or create a records audit methodology which is appropriate for monitoring records stored in a variety of media formats. Third, the team conducts the inventory. Fourth, the team produces a summary report which will be presented to top management along with a set of recommendations for a new records system.

Q. What tools are available to conduct such an inventory?

A. Various standardized records inventory forms should be employed. Such forms gather data not only on the records base itself, but also on such factors as the present equipment (along with its location and capacity), and the access rates and locations of various document categories.

10

Conducting a User Needs Analysis

10.1 OBJECTIVES OF THE USER NEEDS ANALYSIS

The primary reason to survey users is to ensure that filing requirements are being met. With the results of the records inventory in hand, the records team is already aware of the kinds of records kept by the corporation and how they are stored. Before any decisions can be made about what to do with the firm's documents, the records team must determine what the users' requirements are for information retrieval and storage. A needs analysis can define how records are used in each department, how much time is spent performing records functions, and what complaints, if any, users have about the operation of the existing records program. Exhibit 10.1 is a work flowchart of such a study. It includes the steps outlined in Chapter 9, this chapter, and Chapter 11. Since the records-management function is traditionally oriented toward providing a service, it makes no sense to design a new records program without the input of those who are serviced.

The result of an in-depth needs analysis should be a more efficient records service. It can help to achieve this goal by providing valuable information highlighting problem areas. It can point out ways in which waste—in terms of time, storage space, and lost or inaccessible docu-

Exhibit 10.1

Records Management: Study Methodology

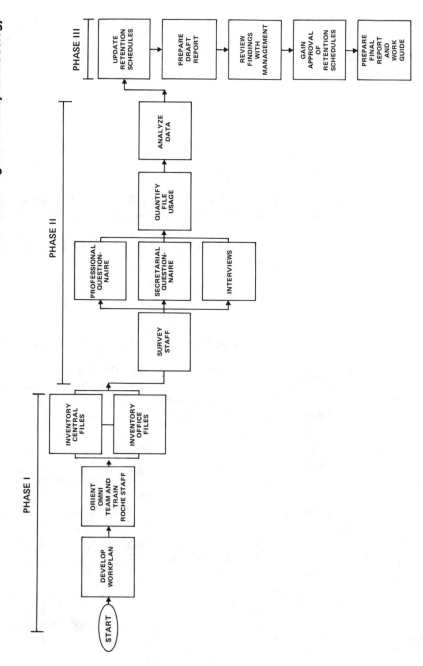

ments—can be alleviated. And the needs analysis reinforces the records-management team's commitment to satisfying the company's information needs.

The needs of end users vary greatly according to job. The most obvious distinction in information requirements is between professionals and support staff. Supervisors require access to tracking data which can match employee performance against corporate and department objectives. Middle managers, such as plant managers, district sales managers, and bank branch managers, are primary suppliers of business data and records. Lawyers, researchers, and systems analysts are users of specialized and sometimes classified information. And finally, top managers rely on a variety of sources to carry out their roles as business leaders and decision-makers.

Support staff, on the other hand, are charged with meeting these managerial information requirements with speed and accuracy. Their needs can be met by making it easier to organize, retrieve, and store the documents required by their business roles.

With the existence of competing and conflicting information needs, users tend to arrive at their own individual solutions to accessing records. As a result, resources do not always get shared, and document copies proliferate. An electronic storage and retrieval system may be tailored to one department's requirements but be incompatible with the neighboring department's filing scheme.

The records-management team's task is to reconcile these needs with efficient records storage and retrieval. This chapter deals with the first half of the equation: how to investigate and document user needs.

10.2 CONDUCTING AN ORIENTATION SESSION

Before the records team initiates data collection in user departments, it should make an effort to prepare them for the process. An orientation meeting can serve this purpose and ensure that the study will run as smoothly as possible. Orienting support staff and principals should be separate enterprises. Although the basic orientation goals are similar, the information would be differently weighted. All meetings would cover issues such as why the needs analysis is being performed, a short history of records management at the firm, what potential benefits may derive from the study, and the methodology of the study, including an explanation of forms and scheduling.

Support staff orientations are designed to educate these workers on why the study is being done, what the survey schedule is, and how to complete the survey forms. Staff questionnaires can actually be distributed and completed in 35 to 40 minutes during the orientation session. In addition to the practical instruction, the team will introduce themselves and the project. When staff members understand why it must be done, they are going to be more cooperative during the study. Orientation should be scheduled immediately before the data collection process commences, so that procedures are fresh in people's minds.

Principal orientation, on the other hand, should be more conceptual than the support staff orientation, with greater emphasis placed on the expected corporate benefits of the needs analysis and the records-management program. These workers must also be instructed on practical matters, such as how to fill out their questionnaires and whom to call if they have any problems or questions. Professionals should be exposed to the entire needs analysis process, since it will be disturbing the normal work routine of their departments. Without their bosses' active cooperation, support staff are going to be less eager to carry out their responsibilities for accurate data collection.

10.3 DESIGNING SURVEY TOOLS

A needs assessment survey can be as simple as a series of interviews or as complex as a systems audit. Whatever level of detail you strive for, it is essential that the data be accurate. Since the key to the collection effort is the survey tools, they should be carefully designed for ease of use, accuracy, and thoroughness. At times these objectives may clash, but the best possible balance must be strived for.

If a questionnaire or task log is not easy to use, respondents may either put off completing the forms or make mistakes filling them out. It must be remembered that users have their hands filled with their job responsibilities, and any form which the records team gives them is an additional headache. Conducting a survey during normal work hours is disruptive and inconvenient, but it is up to the team to work on fostering cooperation rather than hostility.

Like inventory forms, needs analysis questionnaires should be simple in format and require as little writing as possible. Questions should be structured to avoid misinterpretation, with instructions either clearly printed on the form or stapled on the back. If there are any special codes or marks which could confuse a reader, they can be easily explained on the form itself.

The easier the forms are to use, the more likely they will be filled in accurately. For example, multiple-choice questions are easy to fill out as long as all possible responses have been anticipated. Otherwise, users should be given space to fill out a more detailed or unanticipated response. In addition to well-designed questions, forms should provide users with a "hot-line" number which offers immediate assistance. Finally, any data collection process should set aside a couple of days at the beginning for users to try out the survey tools and correct any problems.

The completeness of the collected data is always relative, as no survey can ever be exhaustive. It is necessary, therefore, to achieve an appropriate balance between thoroughness and the proportional costs of collection and analysis. A complex office organization requires more time to analyze, but the effort may well pay off in long-term savings. This is the trade-off which must be assessed before attempting to convince management to approve the study's budget.

To help you achieve all of these data collection goals, we have included a sample group of study tools. Because of their length, the secretarial and professional questionnaires are included as Appendixes B and C. The remaining exhibits in this chapter are useful examples of some of the information gathering and analysis which can be done. However, they are meant only to serve as guides and will need to be tailored to fit the specific needs of a department or firm. For example, questions may have to be added or deleted depending on whether the filing system is centralized, if there is a records library, or if the company has an off-site storage facility.

10.3.1 Questionnaires

Two types of questionnaires must be designed, one for support staff (see Appendix B) and one for managers and professionals (see Appendix C). The staff and professional responses should provide valuable insight into how well employees at all levels think the filing system works. Points of incongruence make it easy to locate problems and areas of dissatisfaction. All questionnaires should be anonymous but coded by department or division. If time allows, it is preferable that they be completed and analyzed before any other data collection takes place.

The principal or professional questionnaire should probe managerial satisfaction with the quality of existing file services. In addition, it should reveal the extent of professional knowledge of, and involvement with, the records function, that is, how much do principals delegate filing tasks and how often do they use the equipment themselves. The support staff questionnaire is intended to get secretaries and file clerks to comment on their work routines, the nature of the information requests they receive, and the problems they perceive in the way documents are organized and distributed.

10.3.2 Daily Task Logs

Support staff can monitor records activity on a daily task log (see Exhibit 10.2). A task log should be completed by each staff member

Exhibit 10.2
Daily Task Log

Participant   Department   Date

Time	Code	Vol.	Time	Code	Vol.	Time	Code	Vol.	Time	Code	Vol.	Time	Code	Vol.	Time	Code	Vol.	Time	Code	Vol.
7:30			9:00			10:30			12:00			1:30			3:00			4:30		
32			2			32			2			32			2			32		
34			4			34			4			34			4			34		
36			6			36			6			36			6			36		
38			8			38			8			38			8			38		
40			10			40			10			40			10			40		
42			12			42			12			42			12			42		
44			14			44			14			44			14			44		
46			16			46			16			46			16			46		
48			18			48			18			48			18			48		
50			20			50			20			50			20			50		
52			22			52			22			52			22			52		
54			24			54			24			54			24			54		
56			26			56			26			56			26			56		
58			28			58			28			58			28			58		
8:00			9:30			11:00			12:30			2:00			3:30			5:00		
2			32			2			32			2			32			2		
4			34			4			34			4			34			4		
6			36			6			36			6			36			6		
8			38			8			38			8			38			8		
10			40			10			40			10			40			10		
12			42			12			42			12			42			12		
14			44			14			44			14			44			14		
16			46			16			46			16			46			16		
18			48			18			48			18			48			18		
20			50			20			50			20			50			20		
22			52			22			52			22			52			22		
24			54			24			54			24			54			24		
26			56			26			56			26			56			26		
28			58			28			58			28			58			28		
8:30			10:00			11:30			1:00			2:30			4:00			5:30		
32			2			32			2			32			2			32		
34			4			34			4			34			4			34		
36			6			36			6			36			6			36		
38			8			38			8			38			8			38		
40			10			40			10			40			10			40		
42			12			42			12			42			12			42		
44			14			44			14			44			14			44		
46			16			46			16			46			16			46		
48			18			48			18			48			18			48		
50			20			50			20			50			20			50		
52			22			52			22			52			22			52		
54			24			54			24			54			24			54		
56			26			56			26			56			26			56		
58			28			58			28			58			28			58		
9:00			10:30			12:00			1:30			3:00			4:30			6:00		

Exhibit 10.2—Continued

Instructions: 1. When you stop doing one task and start another, draw a line across the column.
2. Enter the proper task code and any applicable volumes of task units in the columns indicated.
3. Please provide explanations in the space provided on the back of this form.

CODE	TASK DESCRIPTION	VOLUME
AB	ABSENCE [Including partial absences for Dr.'s appts., etc.]	
ARR	ARRANGING TRAVEL/CONFERENCE	
CL	COLLATING MANUALLY	PAGES
COM	COMPUTATIONS	
CON	CONFERENCE WITH FELLOW EMPLOYEE	
DE	DATA ENTRY	
E	ERRAND [Explain on back of this form]	
ER	WORKING ON EXPENSE REPORT	
F	FILING	UNITS
FB	BURSTING OF DATA FORMS	
FM	FILES MAINTENANCE OR ORGANIZATION	
FP	FORMS PROCESSING MANUALLY [Explain on back of this form]	
I	INTERRUPTION [Over 2 minutes]	
L	LOGGING OR POSTING INFORMATION	
LU	LUNCH	
M	MAIL SORTING OR DELIVERY OR PICKUP	PIECES
MS	MISCELLANEOUS [Explain on back of this form]	
OP	OPERATING EQUIPMENT [Not typing or copying] [Explain on back of this form]	
P	PERSONAL TIME	
PC	PHOTOCOPYING	COPIES
PR	PROOFREADING	PAGES
R	RESEARCH	
S	STENOGRAPHY	
SP	SPECIAL PROJECT [Explain on back of this form]	
SF	SURVEY FORM	
T	TELEPHONE	EACH CALL
TY	TYPING	PAGES
WB	WORKING ON BUDGETS	
WR	WRITING OR COMPOSING CORRESPONDENCE	
WW	WAITING FOR WORK	

NOTE: Very brief (less than 2 minutes) interruptions may be indicated by a check (✓) within another major activity's time frame. The only exception is a brief telephone call, which should be indicated by a mark (x) within another major activity's time frame.

every day for the duration of the study, usually from five days to three weeks. These logs are designed to capture the amount of time which is spent performing records functions. As demonstrated in the exhibit, the log catalogues both time spent and activities pursued. Records activities should be listed and coded for ease of completion. For example, retrieving a document from a department file, color-coding files, microfilming documents, or obtaining a record from a central files location are all discrete activities which would be identified by letter or number. The time ladder format involves very little writing and therefore takes only a few minutes to complete.

Task logs should be collected at the end of each day and reviewed by the records-management team. In the initial trial period, they should be checked carefully for common errors, like miscoding or blank slots. Part of the team's job will be to communicate these errors to staff liaisons and discuss ways in which they can be corrected.

10.3.3 Observation Sheets

Observation sheets provide a cross check for the information gathered from daily logs and questionnaires (see Exhibit 10.3). Records team members should observe file areas and support staff workstations five times daily for the duration of the study period. Team members should be careful to stagger these observation periods, so staff members cannot predict a regular pattern and alter their activities accordingly. However, observations should only be scheduled at peak work hours and not during the first or last half hours of the day or through the lunch break. As with the task logs, data collected the first couple of days would be regarded only as trial material. The sheets should be coded by zone and include a list of all employees who work in the observed area.

The observation sheet itself can be designed along the parameters of the task log with activity codes and time slots. The observer's name should be recorded on the top of the sheet along with a list of staff members with their corresponding activities and time slots. With such a format, the sheet can be quickly filled out in the course of a normal walk through the designated zones.

The results of the observations can then be compared to the task logs completed by the observed staff. Any major discrepancies should then be rechecked. If examiners find any daily logs that prove to be largely unreliable, they should disqualify them from the analysis.

10.3.4 Interview Guides

Interviews complete the data collection process (see Exhibit 10.4). They are not meant to be exhaustive but rather serve to fill in gaps in the data

Exhibit 10.3
Observation Sheet

Observation Sheet

Observer: _____ / _____ / _____
Date: _____ / _____
Time: _____

Participant	Absent	Away from Desk	Idle	Collating	Conference	Data Entry (workington terminals)	Filing	Logging/Posting	Mail Handling	Photocopying	Preparing Form	Proofreading	Reading	Steno	Survey (filling out forms)	Telephone	Typing	Miscellaneous	Comments
	A	AW	ID	CL	CF	DP	F	LP	MH	PH	PF	PR	R	S	SF	T	TP	MI	
	A	AW	ID	CL	CF	DP	F	LP	MH	PH	PF	PR	R	S	SF	T	TP	MI	
	A	AW	ID	CL	CF	DP	F	LP	MH	PH	PF	PR	R	S	SF	T	TP	MI	
	A	AW	ID	CL	CF	DP	F	LP	MH	PH	PF	PR	R	S	SF	T	TP	MI	
	A	AW	ID	CL	CF	DP	F	LP	MH	PH	PF	PR	R	S	SF	T	TP	MI	
	A	AW	ID	CL	CF	DP	F	LP	MH	PH	PF	PR	R	S	SF	T	TP	MI	
	A	AW	ID	CL	CF	DP	F	LP	MH	PH	PF	PR	R	S	SF	T	TP	MI	
	A	AW	ID	CL	CF	DP	F	LP	MH	PH	PF	PR	R	S	SF	T	TP	MI	
	A	AW	ID	CL	CF	DP	F	LP	MH	PH	PF	PR	R	S	SF	T	TP	MI	
	A	AW	ID	CL	CF	DP	F	LP	MH	PH	PF	PR	R	S	SF	T	TP	MI	

Task Codes (Circle One for Each Participant)

Exhibit 10.4
Secretarial Interview Guide

Name: _____

Date: _____

Department: _____

I. Interviewer introduces self, explains the purpose of the interview and the purpose of the study.

II. Whom do you work for and what do you do? What is your current job title?

_____

Title: _____

III. Is your work load usually even or unbalanced? Why?

_____

Do you often work overtime? Why? When?

_____

When you have more work to do than you can handle by yourself, can you get help? How? Does this approach usually work?

_____

Do you feel that too many different types of jobs are requested at once, or are the demands reasonable and manageable? (Get respondents to elaborate.)

_____

IV. How appropriate is the typing equipment you now use for your applications? (Ask for specific examples, if any, where equipment is inappropriate for applications.)

_____

Are there good applications for advanced word processing equipment in your department? Could you be specific?

_____

Do you now type work that has a lot of reused material such as stock paragraphs; very long, heavily revised documents; repetitive letters; or form letters? Please be specific.

_____

Do most things get retyped or revised? (If so, why?)

V. What about photocopying? How long do you have to wait on line? Is the equipment conveniently located? Is there much down time?

_____

Exhibit 10.4—Continued

VI. What kinds of job opportunities interest you?

_____

What do you like most about your job? What things do you feel you do particularly well?

_____

What do you like least about your job?

_____

VII. Do you have any suggestions for improving secretarial jobs?

_____

Do you have any questions you would like to ask me?

Interviewer thanks participant for his/her help.

collection, clarify ambiguous answer forms, and provide greater detail in problem areas. The guides should be designed to follow up questions resulting from data collection forms analysis. Thus all other survey data must be collected and analyzed before interviews are scheduled. Ideally, interviews should target no more than 10 to 15 percent of those surveyed. Team members who perform interviews should make it clear at the outset what the interview's objectives are and try to keep it focused accordingly. Interviewers should also be instructed to summarize and submit the responses as soon as possible in order to avoid undue confusion in reconstructing the interview after it has taken place.

10.4 FORMS ANALYSIS

Forms management may be part of the records team's responsibility or may be entrusted to a special forms manager who reports to the corporate records manager. The most likely scenario, however, is that forms analysis is left to each department. In this case, form control is probably loose, with duplicate and outdated forms proliferating. A forms analysis attempts to attack the problem of self-perpetuating unnecessary forms by determining what forms users need and why.

Business forms are important tools for communicating with clients, employees, governmental agencies, and suppliers. Forms include payroll checks, billings, purchase orders, employment applications, invoices, and tax forms.

The first step in conducting a forms analysis is to collect all of the existing forms. This process is simpler than a records inventory because you can simply send out a memo requesting the submission of all business forms. The department head should identify each form with the department's name, the form's origin, who or what machine completes it, the amount of money the department spends on its purchase, and how many copies are consumed annually.

Once the forms have been gathered (in triplicate), the forms analysts will classify and sort copies of them within each of three different file categories. First, a numeric file simply orders all the forms according to a designated numbering system. This file would include all general information on the form's generation, cost, and design.

Second, the functional file sorts the forms by their purpose, or what they are supposed to do. Setting up this file is more complex and probably requires two or three subdivisions. For example, a file name might begin by describing the subject of the form—anything from accounts payable to customers to equipment. This subject classification would be followed by the object of the form—such as payment, inventory, or repair.

Third, the specifications file classifies forms according to their physical properties and is used to consolidate the ordering of different types of forms. Examples of specification files would be envelopes, letterheads, labels, or carbon forms.

Once the forms have been sorted, a forms analyst can pinpoint functional overlaps and cases in which similar forms might be consolidated. The analyst can also pick out those forms whose use or value is unclear. Any form which is targeted as problematic by the forms team should be brought back to the users for their input. This can be done in a series of interviews which probes users on the value of the information provided, how frequently it is used, and the appropriateness of the form's design. When a forms management policy has been established, interviews can be scheduled with department heads who request a new or revised form.

10.5 REPORT ANALYSIS

Most business reports are written either to communicate important information to other employees, clients, or customers or to fulfill legal requirements (such as the annual stockholders' report). Report management, like forms management, begins with figuring out how much of what is produced is actually used. As with a forms analysis, the report analysis process commences with an inventory of all reports issued. The task of collecting a list of the reports, along with information on who requested it, who receives a copy, and what the production costs were, should be coordinated directly with a liaison from the appropriate department. Reports analysts can figure out manual report production costs by multiplying employee hours by wage rates.

Once all the report data has been collected, the reports must be sorted. Unlike forms, which are classified by subject matter and size, reports should be ranked according to how much they cost to produce. The major reason to control report generation is to save money. Since determining a report's usefulness or cost-effectiveness is time-consuming, it is not feasible to analyze every report for possible revision. Thus, reports which consume the most resources should be evaluated first. One may even establish a cut-off dollar value, below which reports are not worth revising.

The most costly reports will be the subject of a needs analysis conducted by a reports analyst. This process consists primarily of interviewing the recipients of the designated reports. Interview guides for conducting the survey will not be as specialized as those used for the complete records-management program. It is likely, however, that some professionals will be on the distribution lists of several reports. It is necessary in these cases to tailor the interview by recording responses to different reports on separate forms. Basically, the interview should reveal how each recipient uses the report. Questions can include how often the report is received versus how often it is needed, and how the report could be improved or condensed. The most important questions, however, will deal with the report's specific value to the reader.

One of the advantages of conducting interviews is that alternative report formats or distribution schedules can be discussed on the spot. If a recipient has no clear need for a report besides to "review" it, the interviewer might suggest that he or she share a copy or have access to a library copy. Likewise, if weekly reports are only glanced at monthly, a less frequent distribution can be recommended. And of course, if no one expresses a concrete need for the report, it can be eliminated entirely. If needs and changes in procedure are discussed candidly, there will be less resentment when someone is dropped from a distribution list.

10.6 ANALYZING SURVEY FINDINGS

By this point in the data collection process, the records team will have collected a vast quantity of information. Before it can be used, it has to be systematically organized and evaluated. Obviously, every firm will approach such an analysis with different objectives. However, some guidelines can help to simplify the process.

The process of data analysis is twofold. First, all the information, both quantifiable and nonquantifiable, must be summarized for display. Second, the summarized results must be evaluated. The first step involves tabulating survey data, perhaps on a computer, and then presenting the summary in a readable form, such as a series of graphs or charts. A findings report would probably intersperse data tables with summaries of nonquantifiable responses such as user complaints or suggestions for improvement. Organizing these responses can be more difficult than data tabulation, but the records manager should be able to design categories which will highlight the important information. The categories might include satisfaction with filing systems, frequently requested changes, or professional-secretarial relationships. Tabulation can be standardized and simplified by using summary sheets for each data collection tool.

Questionnaire summary sheets should list the survey questions and provide space for recording responses. This process is fairly elementary but can be time-consuming depending on the length of the questionnaire.

Task log summary sheets are more complex to design and to complete (see Exhibit 10.5). Records analysts should keep one sheet for each department. Along the vertical axis, the sheet should list the support staff who completed task logs. Along the horizontal axis, the various activities should be sorted into categories of records functions, like filing, classifying, or retrieving documents. To expedite the summary of several days of task recording, task logs should be transferred to a summary sheet daily. Thus at the end of the study period, you should have a series of daily totals on how much time was spent on which activities and by whom. These can be quickly transferred to a cumulative summary sheet for easy reference.

Observation data can also be calculated daily by using a simple summary sheet (see Exhibit 10.6). List the observed activities across the top of the page and the staff who are performing them along the vertical axis. Each day you can derive a total of activities performed by each individual and a total of activities performed by the entire group. When the observations have been completed, cumulative charts for each worker and each work group can be easily compiled.

After all the summary sheets have been compiled, the most complex form for organizing data can be completed: the data analysis worksheet (see Exhibit 10.7). This form serves the important function of integrating data from all collection tools so that a cross-analysis can be done. The data analysis worksheet collects activities statistics from each group or zone. It also adds a calculation of activity time translated into dollar (or labor) value.

The second step in data analysis is the evaluation of the summarized results. At this point you should be able to determine what works and what doesn't work in the present records-management program. In order to determine these parameters, the analysis of data will refer to the original objectives of a records-management study, as outlined in Chapter 8. Thus, you will want to compare what a records-management

Exhibit 10.5
Daily Task Log Summary Sheet

Day _____

Telephone

Secretary	ARR	CON	EC	ER	FM	R	SP	Min.	Vol.	WB	WR	TOTAL	AB	I	LU	MS	P	SF	WW	x	✓	TOTAL
1																						
2																						
3																						
4																						
5																						
6																						
7																						
8																						
9																						
10																						
11																						
12																						
13																						
14																						
15																						
16																						
17																						

Exhibit 10.5—Continued

Secretary	Collating		Filing							Mail		Photocopy			Proofreading			Typing			
	Min.	Vol.	COM	DE	E	Min.	Vol.	FB	FP	L	Min.	Vol.	OP	Min.	Vol.	TOTAL	Min.	Vol.	S	Min.	Vol.	TOTAL
1																						
2																						
3																						
4																						
5																						
6																						
7																						
8																						
9																						
10																						
11																						
12																						
13																						
14																						
15																						
16																						
17																						

Exhibit 10.6

Observation Summary Sheet

Observation Date	Absent	Away from Desk	Idle	Collating	Conference	Data Processing (working on terminals)	Filing	Logging/Posting	Mail Handling	Photocopying	Preparing Form	Proofreading	Reading	Steno	Survey (filling out forms)	Telephone	Typing	Miscellaneous								

Task Codes

Exhibit 10.7
Data Analysis Sheet

Code	Task Description	Net Min.	Staff Equivalent	Dollar Equivalent	% Total	Prof. Questionnaire % Total	Diff.	Secretarial Estimate % Total	Diff.	Observation Sheet % Total	Diff.		
AD	Administrative												
ARR													
CON													
EC													
ER													
FM													
R													
SP													
T													
WB													
WR													
DP	Document Production												
PR													
S													
TY													
CLE	Clerical												
CL													
COM													

Exhibit 10.7—Continued

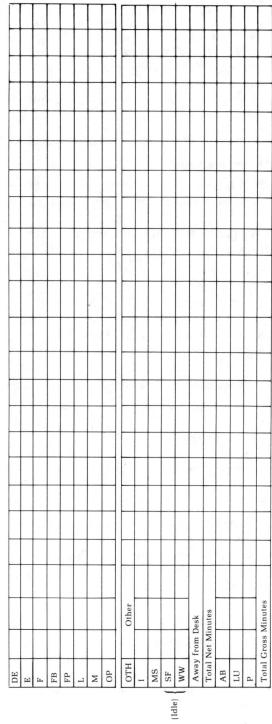

DE																				
E																				
F																				
FB																				
FP																				
L																				
M																				
OP																				

OTH Other																				
I																				
MS																				
(Idle) SF																				
WW																				
Away from Desk																				
Total Net Minutes																				
AB																				
LU																				
P																				
Total Gross Minutes																				

program should achieve with what it is actually doing and costing the company. Important categories of analysis include records security, storage space, staff productivity, filing system efficiency, ease of access, and user confidence with the filing system. From here, you will move on to developing recommendations to improve or replace your records-management program—a process we will examine in the next two chapters.

QUESTIONS AND ANSWERS

Q. Why conduct a needs analysis?

A. A needs analysis is conducted to determine how records are used in each department, how much time is spent performing records functions, and what complaints or suggestions users have about the operation of the existing records program. It must be kept in mind that records management exists to serve the users.

Q. What is the first step in conducting a needs analysis?

A. In order to correctly assess user needs, the first step in this process should be an orientation session in which users are informed of the data collection process before it commences. This will help the study run as smoothly as possible and improve the quality of the data gathered.

Q. What are the tools available in conducting a user needs analysis?

A. A variety of tools can be used in gathering data. The survey can be as simple as a series of interviews or as complex as a complete systems audit. The types of tools used depend in part on the level of the survey. Questionnaires, interviews, and observation periods are some of the principal tools commonly used.

Q. What about the records generation phase—is this also studied?

A. Any needs analysis should also examine the various forms currently being used and also the creation, use, and destruction phases of the various reports generated by a company. When quantified, the total costs related to reports and all their aspects can be surprising, for both records managers and top management alike.

Q. How are the results of the survey used?

A. Before the gathered information can be useful, it must first be systematically organized and, second, evaluated in light of the specific objectives of your individual company. There are two stages in the evaluation process. The first is to determine what is currently taking place with the existing records systems, and the second is to use this data to formulate a new system which better meets the needs and demands of the organization.

Q. What are the steps in making a forms analysis?

A. The first step in conducting a forms analysis is collecting all of the existing forms. When this is done, data such as the form's origin (department, branch, section), how it is processed, number of copies used annually, and total cost should also be gathered. The various forms are then classified into three categories or files: numeric, functional, and specification. At this point, with all the relevant information laid out, the forms analyst can make informed recommendations and changes.

Q. What are the steps in a reports analysis?

A. Reports analysis, like forms analysis, begins with determining what is produced and what amount of that is actually used. Toward this end, a complete list of all the reports produced along with all ancillary information such as distribution and total cost is made. Reports are then ranked according to cost, and an evaluation is made of each report utilizing input from users and recipients. Informed recommendations are then made by the analyst.

Q. How are the various findings of users' needs analyzed so that they may be applied?

A. In the process of data analysis, first, all the information must be summarized for display. Second, an evaluation process takes place. Both quantifiable and nonquantifiable input and responses must be taken into consideration. Various worksheets and tools are also available to the analyst or records manager at this stage of the process, and examples of these are included in this chapter to assist him or her in the effort.

11

Achieving Records Control

11.1 THE RECORDS LIFE CYCLE

At this point in the records evaluation, you have gathered and analyzed a tremendous amount of data. It is now time to translate recommendations into concrete policy revision or development. This chapter will deal with setting records control policies which cover all four phases of a document's life cycle (see Exhibit 11.1).

The first phase of a record's life cycle is generation, or creation. In this phase, documents are produced in the form of letters, reports, forms, or statistics. They are stored on a variety of media, either electronic, paper, voice/video, or microform. And finally, they are copied and distributed to one or more individuals in the firm.

After the document has reached its first destination, it enters the second phase, that of active use. When it is received or produced by the department that will use it, it has to be classified and filed to ensure easy access. The information it carries should be up-to-date. Therefore, retrieval is the key concern for active records.

The third phase is semi-active or archival use, initiated when frequent access to a document is no longer required. The chief concern for these records is cheap storage for large volumes of documents. An additional

Exhibit 11.1
Records Life Cycle

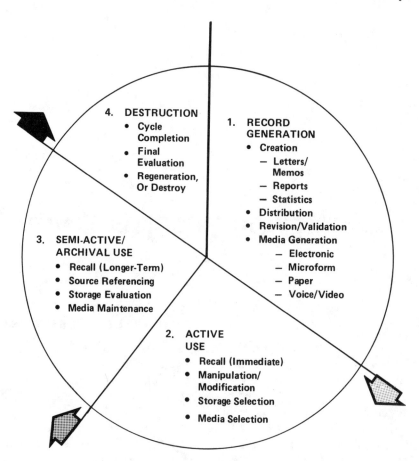

worry is the preservation of these older records and the possible transfer of records from unstable to more stable media.

The final phase of the business records' life cycle is document destruction. One of the primary responsibilities of the records-management team is to determine when a document has become useless to the company. A strict records retention schedule, which defines when each group of records should complete its life cycle, can be one of the most important contributions to controlling a firm's records.

In order for a firm to achieve records control, it must monitor all of the phases above. Neglect in any one area could jeopardize the success of policies in others. When revising or designing new methods of document control, therefore, be sure to cover all categories systematically.

11.2 FORMS MANAGEMENT

The goal of forms management is to make the design, production, and distribution of business forms as efficient as possible. Forms are an important tool for creating documents because they often determine what information is to be collected and saved. Thus, managing forms is a good way to control the generation of records at the source. Assuming that the forms analyst has already completed a forms inventory and analysis (described in Chapter 10), he or she should have a good sense of where overlapping information, poor forms design, and forms duplication waste money. At this point, the goal should be to eliminate the waste and institute controls which prevent future inefficiency. To this end, the forms analyst should

- revise forms, delete irrelevant questions, and reformat forms for clarity,
- terminate forms which are no longer used,
- consolidate forms that gather similar information,
- monitor new forms to prevent duplication of effort, and
- control ordering and distribution of forms to prevent unnecessary stocks.

To carry out and meet these objectives, the immediate creation of a uniform and centrally monitored forms program is preferable to taking piecemeal actions in different parts of the corporation. If resources are not available for such a major effort, however, policies can be introduced step-by-step. The centralized approach probably suits small to medium-sized firms which do not already have a forms management program. Large firms which have controls in place, however inadequate, may be more reluctant to undergo a complete restructuring.

11.2.1 Forms Design

The first step to controlling forms production is to design forms that meet users' needs. With the results of the forms analysis in hand, the forms designer should have all the information needed to create effective forms. The basic elements of forms design are size, layout, and readability. The specification of each of these elements depends on the form's content and on how it is used.

For example, several considerations affect the form's physical appearance. If the form will be eventually microfilmed, it should be created on white paper for clearer reproduction. The requirements of microfilm cameras can also limit the form's size and the weight of the paper it is printed on. If the document is not to be microfilmed, paper weight may still be a concern. The longer a form will be in active use, the heavier the paper it should be printed on. Likewise, the form's size will be affected by how it is to be used, for example, whether it has to fit into a briefcase, a coat pocket, or a business-sized envelope. Margins and spacing will vary according to the need for visibility versus compactness.

The sorting and arrangement of information on a form also relies on the results of the needs analysis. The data that the form is designed to collect can dictate the format, such as multiple choice or fill in the blank. The importance of each piece of information can determine where it should be placed on the form. Finally, knowing who will fill in the form affects how the questions are laid out and how explicit the instructions for completing the form must be.

All of these considerations must be fit into a cost-effective product. Some features may have to be traded off against each other to arrive at such a goal. For example, odd-size forms will be much more expensive to order than forms printed on standard-sized paper. It may be worthwhile to revise the margins or spacing on odd-size forms so that the information fits on one of the standard paper sizes. Storage costs are another consideration. If many copies of a form are stored by the company, it is less costly to maintain paper or microfilmed card files than 8-and-a-half-inch by 14-inch filing cabinets.

11.2.2 Forms Control

Controlling the production of forms involves more than the supervision of their design. The forms manager has to coordinate the printing, shipping, ordering, and stocking of forms in order to prevent unnecessary forms generation.

The decision on where to have the forms printed depends first on the existence of an in-house printer. If the firm has printing equipment, it will probably accommodate most of the smaller printing jobs. In this way, production, shipping, and handling costs can be minimized. For printing tasks which exceed what the in-house machinery can economically produce, a printing house should be engaged. Some firms may find it cost-effective to hire a printing house to design, print, and stock all its forms. The program will be professionally monitored but perhaps not tailored to your firm's specific needs. In all cases, a balance between control and cost must be worked out. Whether or not printing is sent out, the forms manager must monitor the work closely.

The ordering of forms is often left to the purchasing department, which simply processes requests for additional copies. There are obvious disadvantages to decentralized and unsystematic purchasing. Often, forms are automatically restocked without being periodically evaluated.

Further, piecemeal ordering costs more than large volume purchase. If ordering is centralized, then the purchasing department can negotiate an advantageous contract with one or more printers which is likely to reduce per-form costs.

The only way for a forms manager to run a centralized management program is to have an efficient inventory control system. It is simple to keep a running inventory of how many forms are ordered, received, and dispensed. This information can be stored on inventory control cards and filed in a central forms file. The central file can be a useful way to monitor all form activity and ensure that adequate supplies of each corporate form are kept. If the central form file is organized by subject or form purpose, the file can illustrate where overlaps occur. Thus, it can be an important tool to reduce waste as well as to regulate supply.

The final task of the forms manager is to make sure that forms that are no longer needed are destroyed. This is not as simple as it may sound. Some forms, such as IRS tax forms, have clear expiration dates. The status of others may alter as a result of organizational changes. These modifications may not automatically filter back to the records or forms department. Forms may thus continue to collect unnecessary information long after they have become obsolete or outlived their usefulness.

A management program would prevent the perpetuation of obsolete forms through a periodic evaluation of forms as they come up for reordering. Once a form has been officially dropped, the forms manager should notify everyone involved in the form's production and distribution. Even printing plates should be destroyed to avoid accidental printing runs.

11.3 REPORT MANAGEMENT

The production of reports has significantly contributed to the paper glut in today's office. The ease with which computers can generate lengthy documents has made the data-processing department the source of many of today's corporate reports.

The objectives of a report-management program are similar to those of a forms-management program: to control unnecessary paper production and to save money. The actions which may achieve these objectives are also similar:

• consolidate departmental reports,

• cut distribution lists and reduce copies,

• delete useless reports,

• investigate COM (computer output microfilm),

- look for applications for inexpensive production (see Chapter 7), and
- recommend less frequent production where appropriate.

Report analysis provides the information you will need to set priorities. At this point, reports have already been ranked according to what they cost to produce. The most obvious approach is to simply begin with the most costly report and work down.

Redesigning reports for greater cost-efficiency is more complicated than reworking forms. In some cases you may want to condense a 50-page report into a three-page summary. The best place to start is with results gathered from the user survey. These should contain references to what is important about each report and what should be deleted. When the reports analyst has completed a draft of a newly formatted report, it can be submitted to the report's recipients for approval. Then, if the report is computer-generated, the data-processing department should determine the production feasibility of the alterations.

Another way to reduce production costs is to delegate responsibility for researching and writing a report, thus reducing labor costs. The task of preparing the report can be divided into research and writing phases and delegated to two or more employees competent in each area. To make the task easier to perform, standardized report formats can be provided as models. The savings produced by such a reassignment are easy and impressive to display. Calculations of necessary labor time prior to the change can be derived from user surveys and can be compared to calculations made based on the new format to show cost improvements.

Since many business reports are now churned out by the data-processing department, reports analysts should investigate the possibility of replacing paper output with microfilm. Computer output microfilm (COM) produces documents directly onto a microfilm medium without ever generating a paper copy. The advantages of this option for storage and cost reduction are obvious. (For more details of the specific pros and cons of installing a COM system, see Chapter 7.)

Controlling report production is facilitated by maintaining an inventory file on all existing reports, whether on microfilm or paper. Like the forms file, this central report file should be classified according to the report's stated purpose. In this way, the file can help to point out when reports are duplicating information or working at cross-purposes. It can also be useful for maintaining and carrying out a retention schedule for reports and for supervising their destruction.

11.4 IMPROVING THE FILING SYSTEM

When records have entered the second, or active, phase of their life cycle, records managers will be charged with supervising their efficient retrieval. Reorganizing the filing system is one way to make sure that users can reference documents with the least possible effort and delay.

11.4.1 Establishing a Uniform Classification System

The most radical approach to reorganization is to impose a uniform classification system on all of the organization's files. Whether your filing system is centralized or decentralized, such a system can be effective in streamlining retrieval and reducing filing delays. The scheme can either serve as a guide to the central files or be a model after which departments can fashion their own decentralized filing system. In a controlled decentralized system, department file managers would be encouraged to conform to central filing schemes. However, some categories would apply only to certain departments. For example, the R&D department of a manufacturing firm would not contain files on public relations, while the personnel department would not keep specs on new product designs.

The creation and implementation of a uniform classification system is time-consuming. A scheme which fits the company's particular records demands cannot be bought off the shelf. Consequently, the records manager must begin with the results of the records inventory and create a list of all categories of documents which are produced and stored by the firm. Out of this list a functional subject classification system can be developed.

Subjects should be grouped under general headings and then further divided into three or four sub-categories. The example provided in Exhibit 11.2 demonstrates how this might look. ADM, or administration, is a general heading which all businesses would use. The first sub-category is executive travel. Additional sub-categories have been created for all the executives in the firm's law department. Although this task represents a significant time commitment, the effort will pay off in speedy file access. In addition, the creation of detailed sub-categories will make it easier to locate specialized documents which may not fit into a conventional filing scheme.

For ease of use, a subject classification should be accompanied by a relative file index. The index orders all the subject headings alphabetically so they can be easily retrieved. It should be cross-referenced to refer to other related headings or subheadings. For example, a listing under rental cars would refer the reader to transportation—automobiles, or executive travel would refer to administration.

For a functional classification system to be effective, it must be periodically updated to delete or add new sub-categories. But the job of keeping the scheme current involves minimal effort. Once the system has been initiated, improvements in retrieval speed and reduction in misfiling should by far outweigh the time needed to maintain it.

Exhibit 11.2
Subject Classification Procedures

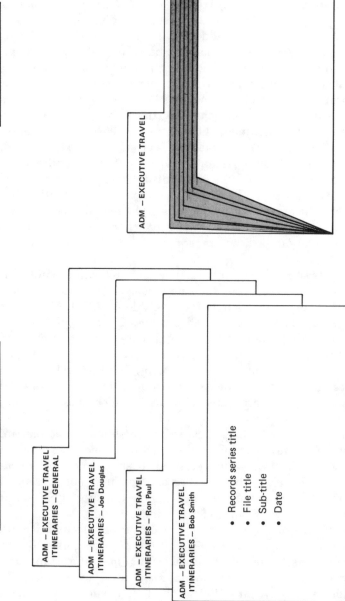

CURRENT PROCEDURE

ADM — EXECUTIVE TRAVEL

RECOMMENDED PROCEDURE (1977)

ADM — EXECUTIVE TRAVEL
ITINERARIES — GENERAL

ADM — EXECUTIVE TRAVEL
ITINERARIES — Joe Douglas

ADM — EXECUTIVE TRAVEL
ITINERARIES — Ron Paul

ADM — EXECUTIVE TRAVEL
ITINERARIES — Bob Smith

- Records series title
- File title
- Sub-title
- Date

As an alternative to implementing a new, corporatewide classification scheme, a firm may decide to work out the bugs in its existing approach. Obviously, this course has the advantage of being less time-consuming. Incremental change also allows staff to be gradually retrained within an environment of continuity. This approach is always acceptable if management refuses to approve any major reorganization. In addition, it may be the best way to improve filing efficiency in a firm which already has a working but imperfect scheme in place.

Getting users to conform to filing schemes can be far more difficult than devising the system. For example, as a member of The Omni Group, I once surveyed the records-management situation in the legal department of a large pharmaceutical firm. Although the system dictated that only one year's worth of records be retained in any file folder, the survey revealed that this policy was not followed. Likewise, a uniform subject classification had been implemented five years previously, but the departments contained office files that were only organized alphabetically or numerically.

An inquiry into these irregularities quickly revealed why policies were not being followed. Because the file folders lacked any sort of color-coding to identify time periods, it was easy for documents to be misfiled. Lack of policy enforcement and inefficiency in the central files permitted office files, which followed their own organization scheme, to exist. These gaps in policy implementation illustrated the problem areas which prevented an otherwise adequate system from functioning effectively.

11.4.2 Organizing the Files

The primary issue in file location is whether files should be centrally located or decentralized. Centralizing the filing system of an organization or a division involves gathering all of the records in one central file room. Decentralizing the system leaves the storage and retrieval of departmental and office records to those who use them directly. Most companies choose to implement a blend of the two approaches. Often the choice is affected by factors other than filing efficiency, as centralization or decentralization may be part of a general corporate attitude or policy. However, there are also strictly practical trade-offs to be made.

11.4.3 Centralized Files

The major advantage of centralized filing is that it regulates direct access to any files. If files are kept in a central location, they will be controlled by trained personnel who are experienced with the classification system and familiar with the retention schedules. This arrangement cuts down on lost, misfiled, and outdated documents. File security is increased by recording when documents are checked out and returned. In addition, access to classified files can be carefully monitored.

A central file room also reduces storage space. By designing an area specifically for filing equipment, space can be more efficiently utilized. In addition, documents that are referenced by more than one department no longer have to be stored in duplicate or triplicate. Central filing is not the solution for every firm, however. Firms with low-volume record storage may not be able to cost justify the transfer to a separate records unit or the staff to operate it. If only a small amount of the support staff's time is spent on filing tasks, there may be no need to hire more employees dedicated only to filing.

On the other hand, large firms with high-volume storage needs may not be able to find a convenient location for a file room. If employees have to walk to the next building or go up eight floors just to get one personnel file, resistance will be high and efficiency will be reduced. If the firm is spread out over a wide area, it may still be feasible to install central file areas in each division, or in each department, if the firm is large enough.

11.4.4 Decentralized Files

If a firm opts for decentralization, it may simply be reaffirming an existing situation or undergoing a change in corporate strategy. Whatever the reason, there are certain advantages in having records at the fingertips of those who need them. Office or departmental records which are kept in their respective offices are well placed for frequent and convenient access. Rather than saving time, the process of daily trips to the central files will only increase aggravation and inefficiency. In small companies where departmental or office files are only used by one or two people who know their content, the advantages of trained central file clerks is less clear. Classified files can be controlled by locked cabinets or can be stored in a separate area.

A decentralized system has obvious limits when it comes to file control. It is impossible to regulate each department's filing system or its policies. Some may work well, and some may not. Duplicate files are more common, because different departments may need access to the same document. Also, it may be difficult to request a document from another department, as filing classification schemes may vary from office to office. And finally, since decentralized files are not the responsibility of any single person or group, it is less likely that strict retention schedules will be met, or that records will be transferred to inactive storage at the appropriate time.

11.4.5 Combination Filing Schemes

Many companies try to benefit from the best of centralization and decentralization by adopting a combination of the two systems. Exhibit 11.3 illustrates how such a compromise took shape in the legal department of a large consumer product firm. Those records which are used only by a single office remain in the possession of its professionals and their secretaries. The general legal records, which are used throughout the department in composing briefs or preparing trial arguments, are retained in a central files area controlled by trained legal records clerks. The library's files contain more general research information not specifically related to the company, as well as subscriptions to relevant journals.

A combination system like this one would be monitored by a records-management department. Its job would be to ensure departmental compliance with companywide classification and retention plans. Those records used infrequently by a few departments can be relegated to the central file area, while those referenced by one office will be kept within their reach. Ideally, this system tries to achieve the most comfortable balance between flexibility and control. Your own firm's priorities will determine which of the filing options you eventually decide to implement.

11.5 CREATING A RECORDS CENTER

When records enter their inactive phase, they are no longer regularly consulted but must be kept for legal reasons or occasional reference. These records must be transferred from the active files in the departments or in the central file area to an inactive storage center. Inactive storage is designed for maximum space utilization and minimum retrieval speed. Each firm must decide where to locate the records center, and as usual the decision involves a series of trade-offs.

The most important trade-off is between convenience and the cost of space. For convenience, on-site options are preferable. A center within the building minimizes the effort of transferring records from active to inactive status. It also facilitates occasional referencing and helps to retain direct control over the firm's records. Usually, an on-site storage facility would be located in the basement of the company's office building. This location reduces both rental costs and the stress on the building caused by such concentrated weight.

However convenient the on-site option is, floor space is not always available or practical. Businesses which are located in expensive urban centers cannot afford to devote costly space to such an enterprise. Large firms with extensive record holdings would be especially burdened by

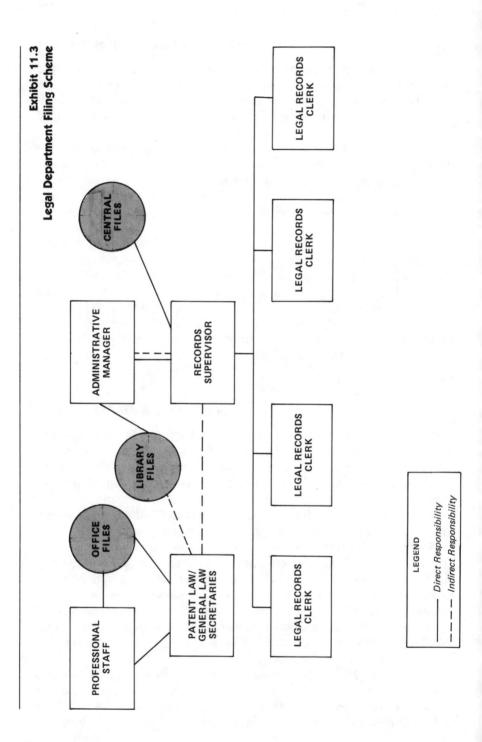

Exhibit 11.3
Legal Department Filing Scheme

CENTRAL FILES

LIBRARY FILES

OFFICE FILES

ADMINISTRATIVE MANAGER

RECORDS SUPERVISOR

PROFESSIONAL STAFF

PATENT LAW/ GENERAL LAW SECRETARIES

LEGAL RECORDS CLERK

LEGAL RECORDS CLERK

LEGAL RECORDS CLERK

LEGAL RECORDS CLERK

LEGEND

——— Direct Responsibility
– – – Indirect Responsibility

such an allocation of space. The on-site center is usually feasible for small to medium-sized firms with underutilized space.

Firms which don't fit this description may want to explore one of the options for off-site storage. Large firms located on spacious suburban plots may want to build an adjacent center to house their records. Although this option may be the most costly of the off-site alternatives, it has the advantage of being directly accessible. The firm can staff the center with records-management people and good phone service to facilitate requests for information. In addition, the facility can be specially designed for record security and preservation.

Smaller firms may not be able to justify the cost of building and operating such a center. An inexpensive alternative is to lease warehouse space in which records can be stored. Although warehouse storage probably represents the cheapest of all options, it is also the most inconvenient to use. Warehouses typically provide no retrieval services. Getting at any document involves notifying the warehouse and sending someone from the firm to dig out the record.

The last off-site option is the commercial records center. Using such a center involves a considerable, perpetual investment, but the money entitles your firm to a variety of services, from document search to destruction. The level of services provided does vary from center to center, so it's best to check carefully into the schedule of charges and services provided. For instance, some centers will only retrieve entire boxes of records, while others will search specific documents. Again, some will deliver requests, while others require that you pick them up. In addition to services, the facilities should be fully evaluated, as some have better fire protection or climate control for records preservation. A cost comparison with a custom-built site would depend on the size of your firm and its records holdings, the availability of company property, and the nature of your retrieval needs.

11.6 TRANSFERRING RECORDS

Records should be transferred to the storage center in a methodical and systematic way. Many firms schedule records transfers once a year, after the fiscal year has ended. The moving process is disruptive and costly, especially if the storage area is off-site. It is most cost-effective to consolidate the transfer process and to coordinate it centrally. The records manager can facilitate the process by providing the documents and procedures which regulate the process. A conversion table can help staff figure out how many files fit in one box. A list of procedures, including regulations for packing, marking, and shipping records, will ensure consistency. And a records transfer document can help to keep track of all the transactions.

The records storage card (see Exhibit 11.4) should record each series which is to be moved. This card can be filled out by either those who are sending the series or the storage staff who receive it. The cards create an index of all records stored in the center. In addition, the card only displays file numbers on the outside of the storage box. In this way, unauthorized access to documents without the card index file is made much more difficult. Finally, the index card serves as a certificate of destruction, once the record series has been destroyed. Legal regulations often require that this proof be held permanently, long after the record series has completed its life cycle.

Most correspondence files and some financial records are only kept in active files for one year. There will be some overlap, however, so that 1985 correspondence will probably not be moved until February or March of 1986. A system of rotating files could reserve the top two drawers of a filing cabinet for the current year's files. The bottom drawers would contain the previous year's files, which would be moved to the storage area at some designated point during the year.

Other files may complete their active status according to another, independent time frame. For example, documents referring to a specific legal case or a student will enter inactive status when the case is settled or the student graduates. In these cases, the organization may want to schedule periodic or continuous transfer dates, but costs of additional transfers must be carefully justified.

11.7 SETTING RETENTION SCHEDULES

The document that orchestrates the records' life cycles is the retention schedule. It is essentially a contract on records disposition, agreed to by those who produce records, those who use them, and those who control them (that is, the records-management team). The schedule specifies both the final retention period and the time which the record spends in active or inactive storage. Most important, it indicates when a record series may be destroyed.

The setting of final retention schedules should come directly out of the inventory appraisal. At that time, documents are appraised for their administrative, legal, fiscal, and archival value. As discussed in Chapter 10, each of these values may impose certain restrictions on retention. Before any individual retention schedule can be developed, these restrictions must be set. Of course, retention schedules for different types of records, ranging from bank to university records, can be purchased off the shelf. Even if this option is chosen, however, the firm should hire a legal expert to customize the schedule to take account of local, state, and company regulations.

Once these policies have been set, the records manager can begin

Exhibit 11.4

Records Storage Data Sheet

Record Title							Dept. Received From		
			Contents						
			Alpha. or Num.		Date				
Date Received	Received By	Box Number	From	To	From	To	Date To Be Destroyed	Date Destroyed	Certified By

setting retention periods for individual records series. Cards should be kept on each records series. They can be organized either by subject or by department (see Exhibit 11.5) and should include each series title, the office where the original copy was generated, the period of active use, and the period of inactive storage. It is important to include the signatures of those who have agreed to the retention contract, as a way of confirming the company's retention policy. Once the series cards have been completed, they should be collected on a master records retention sheet. This sheet can be used to monitor department compliance and to send out periodic reminders for scheduled transfers.

11.8 DESTROYING RECORDS

When the retention period has expired, records must be disposed of in appropriate manner. The regular procedure should be documented and distributed to all departments, so that departmental managers are kept informed. At a specified time before a series of records is scheduled to be destroyed, departmental managers should be notified. This procedure allows for last-minute changes in the schedule and certifies that managers are apprised of the status of all their records. Notification can be accomplished by simply sending the records retention card to the department with the expiration date circled in red. Or special review forms can be circulated, so that managers have a chance to respond and request a stay in the scheduled destruction. When record status has been reviewed and destruction has been approved, the records can be transferred to the disposal area. Whoever performs or witnesses the actual disposal completes the record life cycle by adding his or her signature to the records retention card. This signature documents that the record has been destroyed according to regular company policies and is vital if any destroyed documents are requested for legal purposes.

Records can be disposed of in a number of ways. When the records manager is deciding how documents should be destroyed, several factors must be considered. The most important consideration is the frequency and volume of records to be destroyed. This figure will probably determine whether or not disposal will be done in-house or will be contracted out. Other factors which may influence the decision are regulations governing disposal, the presence of a reliable disposal service, and the in-house facilities available for setting up a disposal center.

If the firm decides not to operate a disposal center, the most economical and ethical alternative for nonconfidential documents is to recycle. Paper which is to be recycled usually must be sorted into recyclable and nonrecyclable items before the recycling house will pick up the records. However, the time spent in this operation is often balanced by the free transport services provided and the small fee which is received for re-

Exhibit 11.5
Records Retention Schedule

Department _____   Division _____   Date: _____   Page _____

Bldg. _____

ITEM NUMBER	RECORD SERIES TITLE	OFFICE OF RECORD COPY	RETENTION PERIOD (Years)				OFFICE PURGE KEY
			Office	Storage	Total	Note/Source	

APPROVAL

DEPARTMENT/SECTION	DATE	LEGAL	DATE	TAX	DATE

cyclable paper. If the alternative is to hire a disposal service to cart the paper away, the cost savings are clear.

Recycling may not be a viable option if there are no recycling plants nearby, or if the volume of paper destroyed each year is not large enough to justify its transport. In addition, it is usually not appropriate for the destruction of confidential records, as the firm has no control over their disposal after they leave the firm's premises. However, some recycling services offer special arrangements for confidential records in which they are sealed in a container for disposal. It is best to check the legal requirements on disposal before pursuing this option.

Confidential records can either be disposed of by a commercial disposal service or by the in-house center. In either case, the records manager or a representative of the records-management staff must monitor and record the disposal.

If records, confidential or otherwise, are to be disposed of in-house, several methods can be used. The most common is shredding. Shredders can be purchased to handle any volume of work, from a few pounds up to 1,000 pounds an hour. The larger shredders accept not only paper but microfilm, clips, staples, and plastic cards. In addition, some models will bundle the paper for easy transport, either to the dump or to the recycling plant.

For larger volumes of records, a pulverizer or disintegrator can be installed. These machines accept material at a rate greater than the largest shredder. They range from several hundred pounds to several thousand pounds an hour. They have the additional advantage of reducing the volume of waste produced by grating it into a fine dust or pulp. This method is sometimes preferred for highly confidential documents which must be completely destroyed.

The final option, that of incineration, is today the least desirable. After the restrictions imposed by the Clean Air Act, incineration became a very clumsy and uneconomical process. Besides, incineration does not ensure even and complete destruction of documents. It is therefore preferable to utilize one of the cleaner, more efficient methods outlined above.

When a record has been destroyed, the records manager's responsibility is satisfied. If the policies which have been set up to guide the record through each phase of the life cycle are effective, the firm should have greater access to the records which it really needs and should have stopped wasting space on those it does not. At this point, the records program is nearly complete. It remains only to choose the equipment and the media which can most effectively enforce and implement the policies of the new records-management program.

QUESTIONS AND ANSWERS

Q. How can records control be achieved?

A. In considering records control, it is helpful to divide the records life cycle into four phases: record generation, active use, inactive or archival use, and destruction. If any records control program is to be successful, the records control policies initiated must cover all four phases of a document's life cycle.

Q. What are some of the specific tools or methods used to improve records control during records generation or creation?

A. For the most part, records are generated in two ways: as forms and as reports. Establishing records control begins with sound techniques of forms management and report management. Forms must be designed to meet user needs with attention to size, layout, and readability. In addition, a workable inventory management system for a company's forms must be established. A process of ongoing forms' review should be incorporated into the ordering procedure to prevent obsolescence. Reports should be redesigned to reduce paper glut. In generating reports it is imperative that the user get only the information he or she needs. Applying this principle by revising production and distribution techniques can save a firm a tremendous amount in labor and resource costs. For example, computer output microfilm (COM) could greatly reduce report production costs in companies using microfilm-compatible equipment.

Q. What tools are available to improve records control in the active phase?

A. Setting up a records classification scheme that is consistent throughout the company is of paramount importance during the active-use phase. Both centralized files and decentralized files have their advantages, and the choice depends largely on the organization of the firm and business goals. Automated filing systems can certainly contribute cost savings for active information files. For files that are regularly updated, magnetic storage media are preferred. For files that are not changed but frequently retrieved, nonpaper media such as microfilm or optical disk technology are beneficial.

Q. Similarly, what tools are available in the inactive and destruction phases?

A. A records center for inactive and archival files is one appropriate solution. The center could be located off-site if the cost/convenience trade-off dictates. Again, microforms and optical disks are useful. In the final phase of a document's life cycle, a company must develop a good retention schedule. Records should be destroyed on schedule to prevent unnecessary expenditures for preserving useless records.

12

Designing a System

12.1 WHAT TO CONSIDER IN DESIGNING A SYSTEM

Assuming the records manager has initiated a program for records control, conducted an inventory of the company's records resources, undertaken a user needs analysis, and arrived at some conclusions about the nature of the new information management system, the manager now faces the difficulty of product selection.

With the recent advances in modern office equipment and in information management technology, more and more firms are choosing to replace time-consuming, labor-intensive manual systems with high-speed, capital-intensive automated systems. In taking this step the traditional records-management task is transformed into a much broader function that falls under the rubric of information management. Along with the increasing penetration of high technology into the office has come the confluence of the records or information management function with data processing and information systems.

Records managers must pay more attention to computer technology, and data-processing and information systems managers (DP/MIS) must educate themselves in the discipline of records management. With this in mind, this chapter assumes that the manager has a clear sense of the existing system for records management and of the user's information needs, and it addresses the complicated question of choosing the best equipment to satisfy the needs of the firm.

No one who has watched the transformation of the office in the last decade can escape the conclusion that advances in office technology have occurred at a bewildering pace. Computing power has moved from the back room to the desktop. The typewriter, an office mainstay for one century, is being replaced by the word processor. Paper, once the sole means of information storage and transmission, now competes with many different media for information. The different products on the market that generate, store, retrieve, and transmit information number in the thousands. Furthermore, new products are being introduced all the time. For vendors to remain competitive in the vigorous market, they must continually develop new products and make enhancements to the old ones. Because of the inherent volatility of the market, products in this chapter will be discussed generically, and references to specific brands will be largely avoided.

In designing a system we will focus on the impact that the company's existing records and the user's current and anticipated requirements will have on the choice between generic categories of information systems and storage media. In addition, each generic category will be considered in terms of its compatibility with other systems, its flexibility, the ease with which it may be upgraded, and its role in the interdepartmental office automation network.

Leading-edge information systems are now virtually defined by the degree to which they incorporate the processing power of the computer. Therefore, the role of the computer, whether it be a mainframe or a personal computer (PC), will be discussed. In addition, we will explore briefly the wide variety of software products that are now available to manage information.

A mandate from top management is absolutely essential to the process of designing an information management system in the modern office environment. The new systems are highly capital-intensive, and, as such, they require a substantial initial outlay for the purchase of new equipment. Management will not approve such an outlay unless it is convinced that an adequate return can be achieved. Thus, it will be necessary for the manager or the information management team to make some projections as to the cost savings and potential benefits that a new system will realize. For this reason we will outline the factors to consider in performing a cost-benefit analysis, paying particularly close attention to human factors.

Finally, we will take a brief look at vendors and suggest some strategies for translating the preference for a general product category into the selection of a particular supplier's equipment line.

12.2 HOW TO COMPARE MEDIA

Today one of the most important decisions the information manager must face relates to the selection of appropriate data storage media. By making a proper choice, a manager can boost the productivity of his or her organization for many years to come. Unfortunately, this decision is also highly confusing.

The media that are currently available for data storage can be divided into four general categories: paper, microfilm, magnetic disks, and optical disks. All recorded information may be characterized as either data, text, or image. What storage medium is most appropriate to what type of information is our present concern.

12.2.1 Paper

One paradox of the office automation revolution has been that the use of paper has actually increased. Many visionaries had made the forecast that with the advent of electronic and magnetic devices, paper would be rendered all but obsolete. Clearly, this has not happened. In the last four years, paper consumption in major companies that have implemented sweeping office automation systems has doubled. Although a skeptic might attribute this phenomenon to custom or to an innate resistance to change, paper does have some fundamental advantages. Of all the media under consideration, paper is the only one that requires no additional machinery to interpret. Paper has a human scale, so it is particularly suitable at the initial stage of the information life cycle, namely, at its moment of creation. Even with word processors being used for the generation of text material, the writer frequently jots down his or her initial thoughts on paper before sitting down at the typewriter or word processor. Similarly, for creating images graphic artists will first render ideas on paper before taking advantage of relatively new and sophisticated graphics software.

Paper is also the lowest common denominator for the transmission of information. Other information storage media can be used for transfers only if both the sender and the receivers all have the necessary equipment to interpret those media. Therefore, it seems unlikely in the foreseeable future that any diminution in paper consumption will occur.

Of course, paper does have its drawbacks. Because of its human scale, it is bulky and occupies a lot of space. One need only compare the huge banks of filing cabinets to a floppy disk library, for instance, to realize the space savings that can result from storing information on other media. Space savings translate immediately into dollar savings, especially given the booming cost of real estate and office space in urban locations. The cost of sending a report through the mail as opposed to transmitting the same information digitally over a telephone line also argues against paper-based information systems.

In the final analysis, paper will remain viable in the most private and the most public realms of information management—that is, at the initial stage of creation and at the widest level of distribution (such as for books, magazines, and newspapers). Between these two extremes, where most business is transacted, it behooves the information manager to examine closely the other alternatives.

12.2.2 Microfilm

Although microfilming has been around for more than a century, widespread commercial use only began after World War II. To produce images on silver halide film, micrographic copiers use special lenses that permit reduction ratios of up to 50 to 1. On a roll of 16mm microfilm, up to 25,000 documents with standard-sized pages may be stored. Typically, businesses place about 10,000 documents on one roll.

Microfilm is, of course, a static medium. Once a microphotograph has been shot, it cannot be changed. For this reason microfilm is an ideal medium for archival storage, and it also may be used during a record's active phase provided that during this phase it does not need to be updated. One of the most common uses of microfilm is to store copies of magazines, newspapers, annual reports, and other publications. It serves this purpose well because it is permanent and space efficient. Micrographics technology has become essential to libraries, and microfilmed source documents have long been admissible as legal evidence.

Microfilm is also ideal for storing information represented by images. Although it has recently become possible to store and transmit images in a digitized format, it is still not nearly as efficient as with micrographics. On the other hand, the ability to digitize microimages provides a gateway to other storage media, thus insuring microfilm a place in the emerging world of digitized office technology. Another advantage of microfilm is the ease and speed with which information may be recorded. Top-of-the-line micrographics equipment can image four business documents per second or over 10,000 per hour.

Although it has many advantages as an archival storage medium, microfilm does have one major drawback. Because it is a serial access medium, information retrieval requires forward and backward searches. This can be a time-consuming process on a roll of microfilm that contains some 10,000 images. Even with a good indexing system, the retrieval process would not be as fast as with information stored on a magnetic disk on a drive with read-write heads. The good news is that robotics and similar technology will speed the microfilm document retrieval process.

Whereas microfilm does not provide the ideal solution to all data storage needs, new hardware developments are encouraging. Computer output microfilm (COM) devices provide the vehicle for translating computer-generated data, stored digitally on disk, to storage for the long term on microfilm. COM units write images on microfilm with laser light that is controlled by digital input. Thus, data stored on disk during its active life may be transferred to the cheaper, more permanent medium for archival storage.

12.2.3 Magnetic Disks

In conjunction with computers, magnetic disks are the most widely used data storage device. Mainframes and minicomputers use disk packs, stacks of 14-inch magnetic disks, which offer large storage capacity and rapid data access. Microcomputers such as personal computers use compact, permanently loaded Winchester disks and, of course, the popular floppy disks. Floppy disks are much smaller than Winchester disks. Today's standard floppy disk holds the equivalent of about 150 double-spaced, typed pages. Also, floppies are convenient to mount and dismount from the PC, and when not in use, they can be shelved in users' local libraries.

Magnetic storage media have several major advantages. First, they are randomly accessible. The user can jump directly to the desired records without reading every piece of information from the initial position to the destination. This is possible because disk-drive heads are stepped into position by carriage assemblies. A precise positioning device places the read-write head directly over the desired disk track. Information is recorded in discrete blocks on these tracks. The disk drive configuration permits fast, random access to data and represents an ideal on-line storage medium.

Second, magnetically stored information may be updated. This characteristic really sets magnetic disks apart. Because information can be added, removed, or corrected at any time, magnetic disks are ideal for the active-use phase of the records life cycle. In a local information network, a disk file server can provide hundreds of megabytes of mass storage capacity. Protection schemes are relatively easy to implement, making it virtually impossible for unauthorized personnel to tamper with restricted information. Because magnetic media are erasable, they are the lowest-cost choice for transient information. The same physical disk may be used repeatedly. On the other hand, accidental erasures of information have been known to occur, so careful attention should be paid to ensure adequate security backup procedures.

The storage density of magnetic technology is improving constantly. In 1970 an 8-inch magnetic disk could hold 200 kilobytes. Now, research is underway on 5-and-a-quarter-inch disks that can hold up to 50 megabytes, a 500-fold increase in storage capacity. Even with these magnificent strides, magnetic media are still not the most efficient means to store images and graphic information. Microfilm can still compact an image in all its detail into a smaller physical space than the digitized representation on a magnetic disk. Modern computer graphics systems, however, are beginning to make inroads into the image creation and storage function.

Magnetic disks are the natural storage media for on-line data bases, word-processing applications, and temporary storage and information transfer applications. Erasable magnetic disks make sense for working files. They are not, however, the best choice for archival storage of source material and documents. Because information on magnetic disks may be manipulated, information stored on disk cannot be used as evidence in legal proceedings.

12.2.4 Optical Disks

Optical disks are the newest form of disk storage technology on the market. Also known as videodisks, they have several attractive characteristics. Optical disks have a very high storage density and are quite inexpensive for the amount of information they can hold. Optical disks are similar in shape to magnetic disks, but they operate on a different principle.

The optical disk gets its name from the method by which data is read from and written to the disk surface—namely, by means of an optical laser beam. A laser beam is focused onto the acrylic, light-sensitive surface. The beam burns pits into the surface to record information. The pits represent the binary digits that are the fundamental elements of digital data storage. After the data have been recorded, a reflective coating of aluminum is layered over the disk. To read the disk, a low-powered laser is focused on the surface, and the digital information is retrieved based on the pattern of reflection. Thus, many mechanical problems associated with magnetic disks are avoided. There are no read-write heads making close contact with the disk, so its longevity is greater than that of the magnetic disk.

Unlike the magnetic disk, optical disks may be written on only once. The recording surface cannot be erased. For this reason, optical disks are frequently touted for their archival storage capacity. A single side of a 12-inch optical disk can store over one gigabyte of information, equivalent to about 400,000 pages of double-spaced typescript.

Typically, the time it takes to access data on optical disks is longer than for magnetic disks, so they are less suitable for any application that requires frequent read access. However, data may be written to optical disks at a very high speed, like microfilm. Although many claims have been made about the longevity of optical disks, microfilm has greater longevity. The low-powered laser used to read the disks acts like an abrasive, albeit a very mild one.

Because track-to-track spacing on the optical disk is limited only by the wavelength of the laser used to read it, there is a trade-off between longevity and data density. Still, in the long run, optical disks will offer a persistent packing-density advantage over magnetic disks. Like magnetic disks, optical disks are randomly accessible.

Given these characteristics, the optical disk has been cited as ideal for archival storage and quite adequate during the record's active-use phase so long as the data in active-use need not be updated. Given their high packing density, optical disks are already more economical than traditional microfilm and microfiche systems. Since data are digitized before being written to the disk, optical disks cannot be used to image source documents that are needed for legal proof. Interestingly, optical disks are also an economical storage medium for audio recording, and stringent signal-to-noise quality standards are already being met.

12.3 USER REQUIREMENTS

Having performed the user needs analysis outlined in Chapter 10, the records or information manager must now incorporate the information that has been gathered into the process of designing the new information system. There are no hard and fast rules to guide the manager throughout this process, no recipe to guarantee the ideal result. In all likelihood, the results of the user questionnaires and the records inventory may be outright contradictory. Therefore, the process of designing a system will include everything from logical analysis to blind intuition and will require a great deal of sound judgment based on less-than-perfect information. Now that the task has been stated, we can construct some guidelines for its completion.

12.3.1 Examining the Results of the User Survey

The user survey provides information about the human factors associated with the filing system. It reveals the quantity of human resources measured in worker hours devoted to maintaining and operating the filing system. It also shows what personnel are engaged in managing the system, in what capacity, and with what devices. Perhaps most important, the survey provides a general index of the trouble spots in the filing system as seen through the eyes of its users.

Translating this information into a concrete recommendation for the design of a new system may be direct or circuitous. For instance, if the survey shows that five members of the secretarial staff are responsible for retrieving files from a certain system, that the average time required to retrieve a file is at least five minutes, and that no one makes decisions as to how the material shall be filed, the recommendation is clear enough: A system should be organized, a supervisor designated, and the responsibility for accessing files should be divided among the staff to minimize the time spent. In fact, if the filing system contains mostly active files that pertain to the work of a localized department, it may make sense to automate the system. Several personal computers could be set up and a central floppy disk library organized. This would reduce the space occupied by the manual system and speed the process of updating information on file.

Suppose, on the other hand, that the survey covers all the users of a large, centralized filing system that contains a wide variety of different file series and caters to a number of user departments throughout the organization. If the user survey reveals general satisfaction in some departments, dissatisfaction in others, or that parts of the system are overburdened while other parts are underutilized, and that more than one person believes he or she has managerial responsibility over the same series of files, no single, clear recommendation for a new system will be immediately apparent. Some users will demand change; others will resist any sort of change. At first, decentralization may appear to be the only answer, but upon re-examination it may be determined that decentralization will be more costly in the long run. When no clear alternative presents itself, it is necessary to seek further information or to begin evaluating checks and balances.

12.3.2 Incorporating the Results of the Records Inventory

The user needs analysis is not the only source of information available to the system planner. The records inventory provides a detailed analysis of the information stored for use by the organization. Although the user needs survey reveals staff requirements, the inventory gives the systems planner a fix on the volume of information held by the firm overall, the variety of that information given by the number of different file series and the use of each, the storage requirements in terms of the storage medium used for each file and the length of time it must be preserved, the time taken to access information, and the frequency with which different records are retrieved.

In a sense, the user needs analysis only scratches the surface. The needs expressed by the users apply directly to the user interface of the information management system: the terminals, the microfilm scanners, the CAR systems, and so on. The records inventory sheds light directly on the internal mechanisms. From the inventory it is possible to tell how much information is in the active phase, how much is archival, and even how much should be destroyed, either because it is no longer useful or because it is outdated. Furthermore, the inventory reveals how the information is related. For instance, does information in active use become archival after some time or are the active and archival information bases completely independent of one another? The answer to this question will have a direct impact on the design of the new system. If an on-line database management system is chosen for active files, and microfilm is chosen for archives, the former example would dictate the need for a COM device, whereas the latter would not.

Similarly, if information in the active-use phase is regularly updated, magnetic disk storage would be desirable because it is erasable. But if active data are not changed, but rather only written once and then retrieved, then optical disk storage would be better because it has a higher density and a reasonably fast response time. The optical disk would also be ideal for active information that becomes archival after some time has elapsed, since it would be unnecessary to transfer the data from one medium to another.

It is important to remember that such considerations ultimately have an impact on the users. From a user standpoint, response time is one of the most important considerations. Choosing the proper storage medium may reduce the cost not only of the physical resources but also of the human resources both in terms of time and stress.

For example, in an archival application, users may complain about some microfilm facilities where they must repeatedly run back and forth between the files and the display machinery. In this case, a good solution might be to set up a multi-user optical disk system with a file server and several attached terminals. On the other hand, the archival staff may complain that with an automated optical disk system they have little control over which disk is loaded onto the system at a given time or that because archival material is largely image data, the terminal representation is harder on the eyes. Contrary sentiments such as these do not admit one solution that will be popular with everyone.

12.3.3 Balancing Contradictory Information

Frequently, the results of the records inventory will suggest one course of action, and the user needs survey will demand action which runs counter to the first. When this happens, it is important to remember several things. First, user claims may be self-contradictory. User responses are often matters of taste, and tastes do change. Sometimes dissatisfaction may be expressed simply because the user is not yet familiar with the system. Such difficulties may be remedied without changing the system but merely by providing some guidance and instruction. Second, what may be expressed as dissatisfaction with a system component itself may only be a complaint as to its location or its availability. Such complaints need not be resolved by purchasing an entirely new system; they may be alleviated simply by rethinking the user procedures or by moving components around.

When evaluating the inventory against the user needs, it is important to remember that user needs often address the end nodes of the information system, whereas the inventory concerns the internal storage devices. Sometimes user needs can be addressed by choosing appropriate peripherals, and inventory requirements will dictate the choice of central processors, file servers, or CAR devices. Provided the hardware chosen is compatible with a wide variety of alternative devices, product choices can be made to reconcile user needs with inventory requirements. Of course, such a radical independence of peripheral devices from central file storage media is rare in a system. The choice of media will limit the available devices at the user end. Similarly, selecting devices based on user friendliness will have implications on the structure of the system as a whole.

Finally, the system planner must remember that the ultimate goal of undertaking an inventory and polling the users is to design a proposal for an information system. Cost-effectiveness in the broadest sense is the key. Therefore, when it comes to resolving competing claims, the planner will have to decide which alternative will be the most cost-effective in the long run. If the user needs analysis points to some sort of distributed information system, and the inventory suggests that a centralized information management system is preferred, the systems planner must weigh the two alternatives, reconcile differences where possible, and choose the cost-effective solution.

12.4 CONFIGURATION REQUIREMENTS

Typically, at the time the firm may be considering an overhaul of the records-management system, it may have already developed some sort of automated office system for other tasks necessary to the business. In this case, it makes sense to take advantage of the configuration that is already in place and to build on it. Similarly, the firm may not yet have any automated systems in place but may have a future plan to automate much more than the information management system. With this in mind, this section will focus on systems configurations and how different configurations can solve problems associated with different information management needs.

12.4.1 System Configurations

For the sake of simplicity, we will divide configurations into five general categories and briefly discuss each one. First, the records-management system can be set up on personal computers that operate the same file management or database management software. For example, an organization's budget planning process would be well suited to such a configuration. Each department would have a different information base appropriate to its specific functions, but the form that the final budget projection takes would be similar for all departments. When it comes time to aggregate the budget for the entire organization, all the data are in a similar form, and it may be processed with the same software. Obviously, this configuration is appropriate for a solution where data are different from department to department, data are often updated, and the volume of information is not huge. Typically, a PC-based system uses magnetic storage media. PCs may or may not be linked to one another by a data communications network, but information can be shared via transferable floppy disks.

A second alternative would be a minicomputer-based local area network that supports some sort of records-management or database management software. This configuration is ideal for a high-volume, interactive records-management system. For example, a firm in the service sector of the economy could use such a system to maintain a data base on the activity of its customer accounts. Terminals are linked to the central minicomputer and distributed throughout the customer service department so that sales and account management personnel within the firm can have immediate access to customer data. Data can be updated instantaneously, and information backup and archival procedures may be easily worked into the system. If the system is well designed, it can remain operational 24 hours a day, and peripheral devices such as optical disk drives and COM units can be attached to permit regular archiving.

A third possibility that has emerged only recently is the integrated office system (IOS). A number of established vendors have designed integrated office systems (IOS) that provide a wide range of office funtions including word processing, electronic mail, database management, decision support, and graphics. The major advantage of such systems lies in their modular design. The user may acquire new hardware and software as it is needed with full confidence that all the system components are fully compatible with one another. Among the vendors that have introduced integrated office systems are IBM, Data General, Hewlett-Packard, Digital Equipment Corporation, Wang, and Lanier. With an IOS, a firm can customize a system to fulfill its records-management needs.

So far, we have considered systems which are entirely computer-based, and we have ignored the other information storage alternatives. One of these is micrographics. A wide variety of data is still suited for storage on microfilm. CAR and COM systems enable micrographics to be combined with computer technology. CAR systems permit the automated retrieval of information stored on microfilm, and COM systems permit data that are stored digitally to be written directly to microfilm. These systems provide a natural bridge between active and archival data storage.

The final alternative involves constructing a hybrid system which incorporates features from all the types of records-management systems outlined above. In practice, the large firm will almost inevitably end up with some sort of hybrid system since its data storage needs are likely to vary widely. There may be several completely independent records-management systems within one firm where the functions have no overlap. For instance, payroll and personnel records have no relation to customer service information. Depending on the breadth and scope of the system design project, hybrid systems may provide the only way to satisfy the needs of individual user groups that share a common information base.

12.4.2 Upgrading the Configuration

If the business in which your organization is involved is by nature volatile or highly service-oriented, the potential to upgrade your records-management system will be critically important. Service-oriented businesses depend on the rapid retrieval of information, and advances in computer technology are cutting access time by orders of magnitude. Thus, when designing a system for customer service, components should be chosen to allow for upgrades while retaining full system compatibility. IOS configurations are designed with exactly this issue in mind. In other configurations compatibility is not ensured.

In a PC-based system, compatibility can be ensured fairly easily by purchasing the same PCs and the same operating software. This would allow information to be passed freely among users without any cumbersome data conversion procedures. Another dimension is introduced to the problem, however, if data that are used actively today need to be stored archivally tomorrow. It would then be necessary to design some sort of interface to permit the transfer of data stored on magnetic media to either optical disks or microfilm. The need for compatibility would obviously restrict the product choice. Similarly, a LAN-based microcomputer system deals quite well with active files, but compatibility issues might be introduced by the need to transfer old active records into archival storage.

Compatibility issues are of much broader concern when considering hybrid systems. A far-reaching hybrid system may require the integration of a centralized database management system, a number of localized data-processing centers, communication cables and transfer devices, distributed system access nodes, and nondigital information reproduction devices such as COM recorders and printers. Pulling all of these devices together into one integrated system requires a number of individuals with expertise in different areas including data processing, systems analysis, communications, micrographics, and, of course, records management. Fortunately, such a large systems planning task will be undertaken only in firms that are likely to staff personnel in all these areas of expertise. In smaller organizations, the issue of system compatibility should not have as many variables, and one manager charged with proposing a system design should find the problem tractable.

12.4.3 The Main Components within Any System Configuration

At the center of any records-management system will be the storage media and the devices that operate those media. For magnetically stored data, there are disk controllers and I/O servers. Tape drives also permit data to be written magnetically to tape. Laser readers scan optical disks. Of course, there are also a wide variety of micrographics devices. It is essential that these devices be chosen based primarily on the data inventory requirements. The amount of data and the users of the data will be the primary determining factors in selecting the storage medium.

The end-user interface can generally be chosen independently of the medium since most new information management hardware, particularly computerized systems, are designed with an open architecture which gives them a wide range of compatibility. The performance of the end-user hardware will be directly affected by how appropriate the medium chosen is to the nature of the data managed by the system. The one major way in which user needs affect the selection of a storage device will revolve around the network design of a multi-user system. Obviously, in storing information in the active phase, a PC-based system would require a file server or a floppy disk library; whereas a minicomputer-based LAN would employ the standard 12-inch disk drive as the central storage device. In a minicomputer environment, magnetic tapes are commonly used to transfer data from one system to another, for instance, from an interactive data base to an archival information base.

The most common window into an information base in the computer age is naturally the video display terminal. Every computer, from the smallest PC to the largest mainframe, supports terminals as the primary means of human interaction. The technology relating to interconnectivity of terminals is well advanced and dependable. As a result, the system network may be custom-designed both to meet the users' needs and to address the business application.

If the system is dedicated to a particular department, it can be operated from standalone PCs, a multi-user system with controlled access, or a multiple access mode that supports any number of users at the same time. An application dedicated to a particular department may even be set up on a system that serves several departments within the organization. The dedicated system can appear to stand alone, either because the network is designed to permit only certain terminals to communicate, or because the software places limitations on the user's freedom of movement within the larger system by a system of passwords or user identification.

A situation where a number of users may access the system but where application access is restricted is called controlled multiple access (CMA). Under this mode the integrity of the data in one subsystem may be guaranteed by making it accessible only to those familiar with the information base in question. In short, access to the system can be controlled either by the design of the configuration or by the software.

Other peripheral, end-user devices include the COM and CAR units used to generate records and to maintain the microfilm information library. Considerable weight should be given to user needs in selecting these products particularly since such machinery need not be linked by communications hardware. User preferences for reel or slide-type film can dictate the selection of different products for each application.

Similarly, where manual filing systems are still used for paper documents, devices to generate documents (printers, typewriters, and so on) may be selected for their user friendliness. Filing systems which contain archival material could be managed in a standalone manner like a library. In a centralized location, paper filing systems can be designed to satisfy both user needs and business imperatives.

12.5 SOFTWARE CONSIDERATIONS

Systems planners need to consider software as well as hardware when designing a system for today's office. At the moment, the software market is perhaps the most volatile and the most varied in the information management industry. Each year more than $15 billion is spent in the software market. The large Fortune 1000 companies spend over $1,000 per employee on software products, and in smaller firms that figure is even higher. The real challenge in the product selection process is how to choose the right product out of more than 5,000 available packages from over 2,000 companies. The user's choice is further complicated by market volatility. Half of the currently existing programs will be rendered obsolete within two years.

Of course, not all the products on the market are applicable to information management or records management. There are two major categories of software which must be considered in the process of selecting products for information management: operating systems software, and database management software. We shall proceed to discuss each in turn.

12.5.1 Operating Systems

On computers of any size, from mainframes to personal computers, the operating system (OS) is the most basic and essential component. The operating system provides the bridge between the user and the machine. Operating systems are not software tools in their own right. Rather, the OS controls both the hardware and the specific software applications with which the user interacts. The OS ensures that the end-user application directs the computer to perform the correct functions, and the OS provides a suitable operating environment for the user's software application. In a system with many users the OS acts as the "traffic cop" making sure that each user's demand on the system is satisfied.

Typically, the operating system manages the "bootstrapping" of the system—that is, when the user turns on the computer, the OS initializes the system. The OS manages system resources, particularly the allocation of the computer's main memory to different user tasks and the sharing of processor time among the running tasks. The OS also controls all of the peripheral storage devices for data input and output that are attached to the computer. If the computer is tied into a network, the OS may also control the communications protocols. In addition, the OS usually offers user services such as editing, program compiling, user libraries, and file management on the hardware end. Every OS has a command language that allows the user to invoke different applications, manipulate special symbols, and move files and data between different storage devices.

Although every computer requires an operating system, systems vary widely depending on the size of the computer. Mainframe and mini-computer operating systems have become highly complex over the last five or ten years. On the larger computers it is still necessary to have systems specialists and data-processing experts to operate the system. On the other hand, personal computers have operating systems that are relatively easy to use. In some ways, an operating system like PC-DOS shares more characteristics with mainframe OS of the 1960s than with the mainframe OS of the 1980s. The microcomputer operating systems have a relatively limited command language that can be mastered by the end user without too much difficulty. This is one advantage of designing an information system around a distributed configuration of PCs.

One major basis for classification of PC operating systems is the bit size of the microprocessor for which they are designed. There are three categories: 8-bit, 16-bit, and 32-bit. Eight-bit processors have been around for a decade and are well established. The market has settled and the product choice is clear. The same thing may be said, more or less, for 16-bit operating systems. Introduced in the late 1970s for PCs, the major players in the 16-bit OS market are PC-DOS, MS-DOS, CP/M-86, and UNIX systems. Most microcomputer vendors support one of these operating systems. The wave of the future, of course, is now building in the 32-bit market. These systems promise to be much more powerful. The vendors to watch in the development of 32-bit operating systems will be AT&T, Digital Research, IBM, and Microsoft.

Operating systems perform many functions and so they have a wide range of characteristics on which comparisons can be based. Perhaps the most important question is whether the operating system supports the applications software you need. Among personal computer operating systems software, MS-DOS and CP/M-86 support the broadest use of applications packages for records management.

Another key feature of the operating system is whether it permits multi-tasking—that is, can a background task be run simultaneously with a foreground task? Operating systems also handle disk storage, and data access tends to be faster when the system employs multiple data buffers.

In the area of memory management, relocatability is an important feature. A memory segment is relocatable if the operating system permits it to be copied temporarily to disk while it is not being used. Under these circumstances, the system places less stringent restrictions on program size and therefore supports more complex and powerful user applications.

Finally, the OS generates error messages whenever there are hardware errors or software compatibility problems. Clear explanations of error conditions can save the user numerous headaches. In paying attention to such operating system characteristics, the user should be able to make a reasonable choice when it comes to operating system software.

12.5.2 Applications Software

For information and records management, most applications software falls under the general title of database management systems (DBMS). Database management systems have a number of different operating philosophies, but in essence they are designed to handle files. The DBMS creates and manages files, records, and data bases and has become more popular recently as computer usage has increased and spawned data management problems. Such software usually falls into two major categories: file management programs and relational database programs, with the latter currently in greater demand.

File management applications can work with only one file at a time. (A file in this sense is an entire data base of individual records, comparable to the contents of a file cabinet.) A file contains all the retrievable information of a certain type which has been processed. The advantage of database programs is that they let you keep multiple files open at the same time. Some, however, allow simultaneous access to only two files. Others have no limits, and data can be input or edited in any number of files at the same time.

Both types of programs, however, organize data in much the same way: first by files, then by record, then by field. Thus, files can contain a large quantity of information about a fairly broad category. For instance, a file might contain a warehouse inventory. In this case, each separate item in the inventory is represented by a record, which in turn contains fields of specific information, such as quantity, price, and order number, about each item. Although relational data bases view data much like file management programs do, they go one step further. By setting up what is called a "redundant" or "key" data field, relationships between data bases can be described.

As an illustration, think of a relational data base as having two discrete, but connected, records. The first holds the customer name, address information, and a customer number. The second file contains the customer history. The program enables the user to relate customer history to customer addresses by adding the customer number to the history field. This customer number becomes a unique field common to both records, a key field, which can tie them together whenever necessary.

Let's compare the relational data base and the file management program for generating lists. When using a relational data base, only one step is necessary to procure either a list of all of the customer addresses from the first record or the same list and their total outstanding balance from the second record. A file management program would have to sort the data at least twice, and perhaps more, depending on how the files are organized. In order to extract the desired information, one might have to sort initially for customers and orders, and then for outstanding balances. More precisely, if you want to change a name or address, you have to call up the entire database file of records. In a relational system, you can change data held in a specific record without calling up the rest of the file. This speeds up access and cuts the chances of the user inadvertently changing information not intended to be altered.

The virtue of relational data bases is that they allow the user to classify information in whatever manner is most convenient. The user may input and retrieve or edit data at any time and in any order. Because of this capability, Ashton-Tate's user-friendly relational database program dBASE II, one of the first such programs available on the market, has become extremely popular.

Nevertheless, there are some difficulties with relational data bases. Frequently, the link between files is artificially created by adding an extraneous field or, in some cases, three or four. For example, consider a business that requires files to be kept on parts inventory, customer history, names and addresses, and sales personnel. To retrieve data from all those files at once, artificial fields are created containing seller numbers and customer numbers which can be related to sales, seller, inventory, and customer information. These fields are then added to the records in the relational file. Thus, relational files are larger, and records are more cumbersome. In a file management system these fields would not be necessary, so the files and records are more compact. On the other hand, relational information, such as customer and inventory information, would not be accessible.

Most relational data bases can be operated on two levels. The first is the simple command level. Such commands as Create, Append, Edit, and Sort allow the operator to create data bases of records and manipulate them rather simply. Although some file managers can do this, it is an awkward and slow process.

On the second level, the relational data bases have programming languages that allow manipulation of the data base, report generation, graphics, and even interfaces to text-editing programs. This programming language may be a relatively low-level one, like the relational calculus found in IBM's SQL (structured query language), or MicroRIM's R:BASE. These powerful languages are time-consuming to learn and require expertise to use. Although the end user, such as a manager, professional, or secretary, may have neither the time nor the inclination to develop such skill, an effort to learn such applications will pay off in the long run if the user's data structure is relatively complex.

The time involved to get a database management system running is much longer than the few minutes that it takes to figure out simple entry commands. The programming language takes weeks and months to really master. Frequently, the software seller or some other private concern offers training courses in using these languages, but these courses can cost significantly more than the software (not counting the trainees' time). Further, the courses are often inconsistent in quality. In most cases, however, the effort to learn the programming language will pay off.

12.6 PERFORMING A COST-BENEFIT ANALYSIS

Suppose at this point you have conducted a records inventory within your company, performed a user needs analysis, studied the available products and storage media, and decided on a new system design that fits the needs of your firm to a tee. Nevertheless, you have not yet accomplished what is perhaps the most important single task in gaining top management approval to implement a system. To gain approval you will have to justify the system economically. The tried and true method of making the economic case for a new system or plan is to perform a cost-benefit analysis. The goal of the cost-benefit analysis is therefore twofold: to convince management that the new approach is correct, and to persuade management that the new approach will benefit the firm economically.

12.6.1 Comparing Costs

The cost-benefit analysis should justify the new system by comparing current system costs with costs of operating the new system. The precise costs of the current system may not be known at the outset, but they can be determined. After conducting the records inventory, the manager should be able to isolate all the costs, both material and human, of the system. Generally, costs fall into several major categories: personnel, floor space, supplies, and equipment. Personnel costs are by far the largest, hovering between 70 and 80 percent of total costs. In metropolitan areas, floor space may be more costly than either equipment or supplies because rents are likely to be very high. If this is the case, it will be cost-effective to convert space-consuming manual systems to equipment-oriented automated systems. Typically, floor space accounts for about half of the remaining costs not attributable to personnel in a downtown office space.

Costs of space, equipment, and supplies should be relatively easy to determine. To estimate personnel costs, the records manager should interview records personnel and employ studies such as those discussed in Chapter 10. When tallying up current system costs, it would be wise to estimate conservatively to reduce the likelihood that your basic calculations will be challenged. For instance, although many studies have shown that workers perform only four to five hours of "productive" work each day, most cost-benefit analyses assume a full seven hours.

To determine cost savings, it is necessary to balance the expected costs of the new system against the costs calculated for the current system. The costs of the new system may be divided into two categories. The initial cost of the equipment, installation, site preparation, sales tax, and any other start-up expenses which will be incurred comprise the costs of conversion. The other category is the operating cost of the new system once it is installed.

It is important to remember that conversion costs will certainly exceed the cost of new equipment and supplies. Costs of conversion include not only the initial cash outlays for new equipment and office reorganization but also the temporary reduction in productivity engendered by the disruption of the office environment. For instance, the time spent in training personnel to operate the new system will reduce productivity in the short run. During system conversion, a backlog of records for inclusion on the system may accumulate. The firm will incur additional costs in reducing the backlog.

To determine the operating costs of the new system, the records manager will have to make projections. One approach is to determine the amount of time that will be saved in each records operation, assign a dollar value to that time, and multiply it by the frequency with which that operation occurs. As an alternative, one could estimate the amount of time saved per worker per day. The approach one chooses to arrive at an estimate is of secondary importance. It is absolutely necessary, however, to include all the possible costs associated with the new system including operating the flow of supplies, increased electrical costs, maintenance costs, and so on.

12.6.2 Justifying the Costs

Introducing a new system will obviously incur a one-time cost in new equipment, office reorganization, system disruption, and training. Therefore, if the new system is to be cost-justified, the operating costs of the new system must be lower than those of the current system. After a period of time, the cost savings from using the new system instead of the old will accumulate to the point where cost savings equal the initial one-time investment. This point is called the break-even point. Obviously, the sooner the new system pays for itself, the better it is for the company.

One might think that to better justify the system, one ought to estimate the operating costs of the new system to be as low as possible so that the break-even point is achieved more quickly. In practice, this is not advisable. Generally, the break-even point is reached one or two years down the road. Underestimating costs will push the break-even point several months closer at best. It would be better in the cost-justification analysis to overstate the expected costs of operating the new system. Thus, when the new system is actually operating, the firm will reap the benefits of coming in "under cost," and the systems planner will not carry the burden of explaining to top management why the system is not performing as well as it was supposed to.

12.6.3 Capturing Tangible and Intangible Savings

As we have seen, the problem of cost justification reduces to the problem of isolating cost savings. Savings can be grouped into those that are tangible and those that are intangible. Tangible savings can be measured or estimated with a fair degree of precision. By and large, tangible savings can be converted into dollar amounts. Intangible savings, on the other hand, cannot really be quantified or defined precisely. For example, a system which replaces a manual filing system with an automated system would free some quantity of floor space for productive work. This space saving is measurable, can be expressed in a dollar amount, and hence, constitutes a tangible saving.

Intangible savings result in improvements in efficiency or reduced costs in the future, but they may not be translated into dollar savings before such savings are actually observed. For instance, a better information management system might increase the productivity of the existing office staff, might increase job satisfaction, or make the office more comfortable. A system could reduce stress or fatigue and thereby improve morale and the ability of office workers to cooperate. Ultimately, these effects will show measurable results such as higher business volume, shorter turnaround time, reduced personnel turnover, and lower costs for training. Other intangible savings might be the reduction of supervisory involvement. Professionals and managers who spend less time supervising can spend more time making decisions with long-term strategic value. Although savings of this nature cannot be quantified or even accurately predicted, the cost-benefit analysis should make mention of these intangible factors where a reasonable expectation for such results exists.

12.7 VENDOR CONSIDERATIONS

The final step in designing a system will be to pick the specific products and services that will comprise the system. Equipment suppliers, or vendors, provide a variety of products that perform more or less the same function. The process of choosing a vendor is complex at the outset and is only further complicated by sales pitches, promises about product dependability and upgradability, and market volatility. We will study the vendor selection process in depth in Chapter 14; however, at this point we can outline a few general considerations.

If you are contemplating the implementation of a brand new system, one of your primary concerns will be with its longevity. If the system you have selected is rendered obsolete in two years, it could arguably be called a massive waste of time and money. Yet, with the market changing so rapidly, obsolescence is a valid concern. One way around this problem is to choose a vendor with a proven record in the field. Thus, if the state of the art changes within a couple of years, your vendor should be able to offer upgraded equipment that is compatible with machines purchased for the original installation. One key indicator of a vendor's longevity is its financial stability. A quick perusal of a vendor's financial statement by a qualified person could save your implementation team from major embarrassment in the future. Another indicator to consider is the ownership status of the vendor. Some vendors which you may have thought were independently owned have actually been bought by larger conglomerates. Mergers might indicate which companies are going to develop equipment compatible with that of other companies.

Another major consideration in vendor selection will be the type of service and support the vendor can offer once you have purchased their product. One way of determining a vendor's quality of service is to ask other firms that use the vendor's product how well they have been supported. A vendor's geographic proximity to your location will also be important if timely response to a service call is of primary concern to you.

Finally, do you want to purchase all your equipment from one vendor or set up a multi-vendor system? With a single vendor you are likely to get good support and your equipment will be compatible. On the other hand, by shopping around and picking products from different vendors, you may be able to build a system for a lower price or get better performance from each component. The choice you make between a single vendor or a multi-vendor environment will ultimately depend on the specific character of the system you design and on the constraints that your firm must face. In Chapter 14 we will discuss in depth the various selection criteria and how to best balance them against one another.

QUESTIONS AND ANSWERS

Q. What are the major topics to consider when designing an information management system?

A. The information management system must support the information needs of the business. Therefore, when designing the system, the topics under consideration should be the nature and volume of the company's records base, the volatility of those records, and the use to which a firm's records are put. The system designer must also be familiar with the range of products on the market that are built to satisfy the firm's needs. Finally, any sort of equipment purchase must be cost-justified. Because automated systems require a large initial capital outlay, the system designer must make the case to top management that a new information management system will be cost-effective in the long run and will improve the firm's products or service.

Q. What information storage media are available today?

A. A wide variety of products are designed to store information in the modern office. They fall into four broad categories: paper, microfilm, magnetic media, and optical (laser) disks. Some are better for archival storage; others are better for interactive data storage.

Q. What sources of information about the firm are available to the system planner?

A. The system planner has the results of several studies at his or her disposal. The user needs analysis provides data on the number of individuals involved in the records-management function, their location in the firm, and the time they spend managing information. The records inventory provides a complete picture of the data base maintained within the company. Managerial level personnel in different departments can also provide helpful suggestions on how an information management system might best address their needs.

Q. How does one resolve contradictory information or needs from different sources within the firm?

A. One thing to remember is that user needs frequently concern the peripheral devices of a system; whereas the records inventory will impact the design of central components. Some user complaints may be resolved simply by changing usage procedures or by moving components around. Finally, user responses are often matters of taste, and tastes do change.

Q. What various alternatives does the system designer have for configuring the system?

A. Choices are manifold, but they can be divided into five groups. First, the system can be composed of PCs that all operate the same software. Second, the system can be based on a minicomputer with its users connected by terminals in a local area network. Third, the firm can design a comprehensive integrated office system. Fourth, the system can incorporate microfilm into its computer base with CAR and COM technology. Finally, a hybrid system can incorporate a number of different aspects of record management including the traditional paper-based filing system.

Q. What are the main components in any information management system?

A. At the center of any system will be the devices and media for information storage. There is also the end-user interface which typically comprises all video terminals, printers, micrographic displays, PCs, and so on. In addition, if the system is integrated, there will be some sort of data communications network and, of course, a computer.

Q. What considerations enter into the purchase of computer software?

A. Essentially there are two types of software—operating systems and applications programs. Operating systems should be chosen based on their compatibility with particular hardware components and on the various applications that they support. Database management systems (DBMS) are the applications programs most appropriate for information systems. There are two general sub-categories: file management systems and relational data bases.

Q. How does one make the case for a new system to top management?

A. Management must be convinced that the system will be cost-effective and will boost productivity. For this reason the system planner should perform a cost-benefit analysis. This analysis must take into account intangible savings as well as quantifiable cost savings. Costs are best justified by determining how long it will take the system to pay for itself in terms of increased productivity. The time in the future when the system covers its cost is referred to as the break-even point.

Q. Are there any other things to consider in designing a system?

A. The final stage in systems planning is the actual selection of the products. Equipment is generally purchased from vendors, so the system planner must know how to approach the product vendors. The most important factors in vendor selection are product price and performance, vendor support, and product compatibility.

PART 4

IMPLEMENTING A RECORDS-MANAGEMENT SYSTEM

13

Managing Users

13.1 THE IMPACT OF OFFICE SYSTEMS ON HUMAN NETWORKS

When firms decide to implement automated office systems, they are influenced by economic pressures and the desire to cut costs. The impacts of automation, however, are often organizational and social. When planning for technological change, it is often forgotten that organizations are not simply accounting sheets, five-year plans, office buildings, and flowcharts. They are human institutions. An organization's strategies for change must address the human consequences of introducing new information systems.

While the technical problems involved in records management are difficult to address, some tangible output can usually be measured. To solve these problems, there are several business functions whose expertise can be tapped and coordinated: data processing, telecommunications, and administrative management.

The "soft" impact that new tools and work patterns have on human beings does not often receive its share of thoughtful planning. Planners seem to neglect the task of getting the staff to understand, accept, and finally use the new equipment. Too often, office automation is introduced to workers with no conceptual framework and little training beyond pushing the correct button. The result is lower staff morale, decreased productivity, and general confusion. There are enough instances of underutilized or misused systems to assert confidently that an automated office system is only as effective as the people who use it.

The arrangement of the office staff which has been adequate since the 1880s, when the typewriter was first invented, is finally becoming outdated. Professionals who were able to entrust computer responsibility to "techies" are today installing personal computers on their own desktops. The implications of these changes in information technology utilization on staffing and training practices are phenomenal. Some authorities in the field have predicted that up to 80 percent of the white-collar work force will have to be retrained over the next decade. How each firm can handle this challenge, specifically in terms of the records-management function, is the subject of this chapter.

13.2 COMPUTER USE IN THE 1980s

Electronic tools have gained a foothold in the workplace among secretarial and professional workers, and the trend toward automation among both groups will continue. Roughly two-thirds of the support staff in medium-sized and large corporations operate personal computers currently. For managers and professionals the direction of change is also clear. While only about a third of these workers now operate computers, over half are expected to do so within a year. In addition, the number of companies in which only a small proportion of the staff (less than 20 percent) use computers is decreasing swiftly.

Records managers are not isolated from this trend toward computerization. In several hundred Fortune 1000 companies, document managers report that while their receptiveness to automation technologies has increased dramatically over the last two years, many of them reported a lack of knowledge about and familiarity with the new technologies. Over three-fourths of the records managers in both service and industrial firms admitted a need for computer literacy training to enhance their job effectiveness.

While the electronic office is rapidly gaining acceptance in all corners, it is still too early to say what the full organizational ramifications will be. Most advertising for the "office of the future" implies that automation simply makes what we do easier. These advertisements usually display stereotypical workers performing typical roles which have been enhanced by equipment. Few advertisements show professionals performing clerical tasks such as filing, printing, or typing. Most focus on the increase in leisure time and the reduction in stress which will accompany the installation of office systems. No one wants to admit that current work roles and responsibilities have been fundamentally altered by the introduction of office automation tools.

However, the "information age office" has the potential to preserve the positive aspects of the offices of the past and to avoid their failings. Some argue that this will allow a return to people-centered work rather than machine-centered work. The point is that office systems can be used to enhance the quality of work.

The production-line method of office organization, where each employee executes a number of repetitive steps, is no longer necessary to achieve maximum efficiency. One individual with a terminal and access to a data base can handle a complete customer account or personnel file. As yet, businesses have not taken full advantage of this potential to increase both work satisfaction and productivity. Instead, many workers fear that computers will displace them or reduce their jobs to rote button punching. Part of designing a new office system is making sure that advancement opportunities are provided. Part of implementing a new system is convincing users that the new system will provide them with new opportunities.

13.3 MANAGING RESISTANCE

Resistance often surfaces when users are not educated about how work roles are changing. One of the greatest sources of resistance to automation is the threat that it poses to job stability and security. Another fear is that automation will affect the quality of work life. Thus, workers facing screen displays for the first time fear a loss of creativity, the boredom of doing repetitive tasks, or the lack of human interaction. This resistance cannot be addressed by training users simply to operate specific machines.

Education and user participation in the decision-making process, however, can be very effective. In the case of records management, users must be convinced of the benefits of the records-management program. A first step in opening communication lines is to appoint a departmental liaison to coordinate records programs in each department. Obviously, this person should be someone with good communications skills who already knows how the department runs. The liaison should also, however, be open and enthusiastic to the changes which are to be implemented.

Another way of convincing users to accept change is by demonstrating results. One benefit of implementing a pilot program is the positive example it offers. It is hoped that users in the pilot department will testify to the advantages of using computer storage and retrieval systems or to the convenience of consulting microfiche files. Exhibit 13.1 illustrates the reasons users resist technology.

Exhibit 13.1
Sources of User Resistance: Decision-Makers' Perceptions

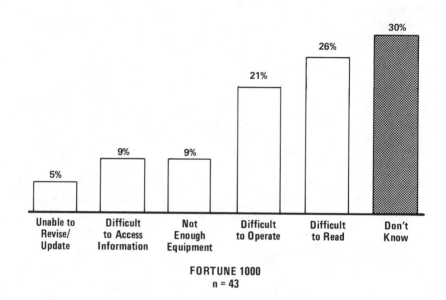

13.4 FACILITIES PLANNING

The records manager can ease the transition to an automated system by making certain that the new environment fits human as well as technological needs. New machines and tasks require new types of work space and furniture design. Although the records manager is not an ergonomics engineer, this person should be aware of some of the factors that will make the altered workplace safer and more comfortable.

Work environment is affected by the office landscaping, lighting, temperature, and sound. For psychological ease, people need adequate and flexible space in which to perform their tasks. For example, when planning the records center, the manager should take into account the need to move up and down aisles and pull out drawers. The center must be adequately ventilated and lit, or employees will experience fatigue and eyestrain.

Computers affect the environment in more specific ways. If your firm is going to install an electronic storage and retrieval system, the building or office must be refitted to accommodate it. Computers generate a great deal of heat. In the winter, heating bills are likely to be lower, but in the summer the office will need a more powerful air conditioning or venting system. Computer terminals also reduce lighting requirements, as the CRT screens catch and reflect light. In addition, terminals cannot be placed near windows where the glare can cause eyestrain. Finally, computers and especially printers create a significant amount of "white noise." None of the office-generated noises have the capacity to damage hearing, but they can disrupt work and increase stress. Acoustical devices and sound-absorbing carpets and drapes can help deal effectively with the noise problem.

Finally, there are questions of employee safety. The effects of long hours in front of a CRT or microfilm reader are controversial. Certainly, many workers complain about fatigue, especially when they are first learning how to operate the new machines. Many studies have been performed to test the impact of prolonged use on work efficiency. Although a clear consensus has not yet emerged from these studies, a significant portion show that no significant long-term decline in work efficiency takes place when screen displays are substituted for paper documents. In addition, many employees should experience a reduction in their initial fatigue after they have become accustomed to using screen displays. However, some screens are easier on the eyes than others, and it is worth paying particular attention to this feature when purchasing readers or screens.

13.5 THE RECORDS MANUAL

The single most important tool which can help users adapt to a new system or effectively use an old one is the records manual. Thus for the records team, one of the most crucial tasks is to create a document that is both informative and readable. If you are not able to communicate how the program works, both to general users and to records-management people, it will be useless.

The purpose of the manual is twofold: to describe the objectives of the records program and to outline standardized procedures that have been created to carry them out. By clearly stating your objectives, results can be measured and compared with original intentions. The primary goal of the manual is to ensure that the records program is implemented in a uniform manner throughout the company.

13.5.1 Who Will Read the Manual?

At some point, nearly every employee, from clerical secretary to departmental manager, will use the manual as a reference tool. Departmental managers will need to consult the manual when setting retention schedules. File clerks may need to clarify classification rules. Administrative secretaries will need to know how to retrieve a document from the records center. And personnel staff must consult records department job descriptions when hiring new workers.

The records manual will be especially valuable for new employees learning how things are done at your firm. The manual can be introduced at an initial training session and later serve as a reference tool. Not all employees, however, need the same amount of detailed information. When designing the manual, therefore, you have the option of creating one all-inclusive manual or two or three versions which are geared to different types of users.

An all-inclusive manual is the simplest and least expensive to prepare. If it is clearly tabbed and indexed, any employee can probably find the required information. But a huge manual is likely to be intimidating to the general user who doesn't need to know the job details of the records staff.

Another option is to create an abridged version of the core manual, specially designed for everyone who is not a member of the records team. A practical introduction like this would be easier to use and cheaper to copy and distribute. The only employees outside of the records department who would receive a complete version are the departmental managers and records liaisons. Any specific questions that go beyond the scope of the abridged version can be directed to them.

13.5.2 The Manual's Content

The core manual should begin with an introductory section which explains the manual's purpose and structure. It should make clear that it has been authorized by top management to standardize records procedures. And it should give credit to those who prepared the manual.

The manual will include an organizational chart which sets clear lines of authority for implementing and maintaining the records program. Following this sketch will be detailed job descriptions for records department personnel, from file clerks to the records manager. Of course, this section of the manual would be deleted from an abridged version designed for general users.

The most important part of the content deals with the policies and procedures which govern the four phases of the records life cycle: generation, active retrieval, storage, and destruction. Regulations concerning the creation of documents deal with forms and reports control (see Chapter 11). Included in the manual will be design specifications for various forms and reports as well as procedures for reproducing and distributing. Firms with large numbers of forms may include procedures for preparing a forms inventory and appraisal.

The section on active retrieval will include explanations of all classification codes, filing systems, and equipment purchasing policies. If a uniform filing system exists, the manual should include an index to the system and how the various classifications are used. If filing is completely decentralized, it is wise to give some general rules, such as how to alphabetize, for departmental filing. If filing is completely centralized, the manual would explain how users submit requests and return files to the central files area. Finally, equipment policies will inform departmental managers of how to obtain purchase approval. If there is not a centralized purchasing department, the manual should include any special vendor agreements or preferred vendor lists which would guide purchasing decisions.

Policies covering the third phase of the records life cycle regulate retention periods and storage facilities. The section can begin with a general explanation of why retention schedules are necessary and what types of regulations—legal, administrative, fiscal, or archival—determine the length of time that a document must be kept. It can then review how specific retention schedules are set and revised. Finally, it should include the complete retention schedule which the records team has created for your firm's records (see Chapter 11).

Some of the policies that govern the operation of the records center are of interest to general users while some will hold interest only for the records staff. General regulations tell departments when and how they should transfer documents to inactive storage, and what procedures they must follow to retrieve them. Operational policies inform the center's staff of how documents are to be maintained, checked out, coded, and retrieved. A special division of inactive storage is the company's vital records program. These records are never referenced and are stored in high-security vaults away from the office. There are procedures for determining whether or not a document is vital, or essential, and a schedule regulating when records lose their vital status. Obviously, most of this information is not useful for the general employee, but everyone should know what the vital records program is, where the records are stored, and who has the responsibility for maintaining them.

The final section of the manual concerns the destruction of records. It should include the method of disposal, whether destruction is performed in-house or externally, and should describe the procedure for final review of the document. Again, most records which are to be disposed of are already in the storage center and thus not of concern to the general staff. However, departmental managers must be made aware of these procedures, in case they want to extend the storage period of a document series. Following the substantive portion of the manual, the records manager should insert a glossary of records terms. The glossary is especially helpful if only one manual, directed at both records personnel and "lay" employees, is used.

13.5.3 Updating the Manual

The task of updating the records manual is almost as important as its initial production. All the effort of creation will be wasted if the manual is not kept current. The records staff should generate updated material through its periodic reviews of the program and the manual itself. One member of the records staff should be entirely responsible for gathering updated material, for example, on retention schedules and legal regulations, and inserting it in the manual. For this purpose, it is best to put the manual in a loose-leaf binder, even though this is a more expensive production method than closed binding.

When the master manual is updated, the records department must make sure that all the departments add the new information to their own. The records staff can send out monthly packets with the updates, but users will not necessarily take the time to insert them. One way of ensuring compliance is to spot-check departmental manuals or, alternatively, to recall the manuals once every few months to be centrally updated.

13.6 TRAINING

However detailed and well-written the records manual is, it must be accompanied by a training program. Most users will respond more readily to verbal instruction and demonstration than they will to printed material. The manual can be used as an instruction and reference tool, but training in records procedures involves more than pointing out where the procedures manual is kept.

If a new records program has just been initiated, or if new equipment has just been installed, the records team should schedule orientation sessions for all staff. Even if the existing program was only modified, it may be wise to conduct seminars to increase the staff's knowledge about records management. Most employees probably have only a rudimentary idea of what records managers do and of what their own responsibilities as records users are. The point of these sessions and seminars is not to provide piecemeal instruction, but to communicate to users the concepts and practices which integrate records management with other business operations.

Separate training sessions should be designed for secretaries and professionals. Although some training objectives will be similar, emphasis will differ. Thus, while it may be a general goal of the corporation to introduce computer literacy, secretaries and professionals will use different software applications and different machines. Similarly, a training agenda should include a segment on the objectives of a records-management program and its relation to general business goals. Managers and support staff, however, will view these goals from different perspectives.

A complete training session should cover four topics. First, the training session offers a perfect opportunity for remedial instruction in basic filing skills. Second, existing records procedures should be reinforced, and workers should be educated about newly created procedures. Third, it should address the role of business and departmental records in the firm's operations. And finally, training must deal with new technology, considering both general computer concepts and specific system or terminal operating instructions.

13.6.1 Secretarial Training

Secretarial training will focus on standardizing office filing. Sessions should begin with a brief explanation of the history and current structure of the filing system. Next, the trainer should go over the major functional categories for filing and list the procedures and policies which determine how documents are classified and how the relative index is updated. Finally the trainer should give a description of the secretary's role in making the system function effectively.

In addition to describing filing procedures, a secretarial training session should outline the steps to be followed to protect vital records in case of an emergency. Also, the trainer should emphasize the importance of following retention schedules and the need to track the generation of paper documents. If the staff are aware of the impact of paper production on the firm's storage costs, they will be less likely to issue unnecessary duplicates. They will also be less resistant to substituting computer-generated microforms for traditional paper copy. When the orientation session has been planned, it should be summarized in a workbook and distributed to all the secretaries for additional reference.

13.6.2 Professional Training

If the support staff have been well prepared to perform in the computer environment while the principals remain ignorant about these new resources, little progress has been made. Professional training should focus less on filing details and more on concepts of records management. Orientation should stress the role of professionals in maintaining an effective storage and retrieval system. The records manager could hold short seminars on various topics such as meeting retention policies, the use of automated tools, effective use of microfilm/microfiche, and effective use of off-site storage.

13.6.3 Corporate Computer Literacy

If the records-management program at your firm includes electronic storage and retrieval systems, a general corporate computer literacy program can be a very useful addition to the training agenda. If your firm is already in the process of implementing an office automation plan, it is likely that such a program has already been developed. A successful computer literacy program would strive to inform workers at all levels and in all information functions about how electronic processing affects both their jobs and the company's mission. In addition, it should be designed to provide the staff with all the skills necessary to fully utilize the system's processing, storing, and retrieving capabilities. If the program is effective, the firm will gain a knowledgeable user community, and the training will more than pay for itself in increased user understanding and compliance.

QUESTIONS AND ANSWERS

Q. How do office systems affect users?

A. Users are affected through a change in the nature of the organization and through an alteration in the social relations of the office. Despite promotional claims to the contrary, users will not find themselves transported to the idyllic office of the twenty-first century. They must adjust their attitudes and thinking to accommodate the new reality.

Q. What can be done to cope with user resistance?

A. Education and user participation in the modernization process can be effective methods for dealing with user resistance. Management must not ignore the issues of job security and stability and the quality of work. Attention to ergonomic considerations can reduce resistance as well.

Q. What is the purpose of a records manual?

A. The purpose of such a manual is twofold: to describe the objectives of a records program and to outline standardized procedures to carry them out. Creation of an informative and readable manual is a crucial task of the records-management team.

Q. What role does training play?

A. Training is a key component of any new records-management system. Users need more than just a well-written manual to effectively use the system. A training program will permit valuable feedback from the user, especially if conducted on an on-going basis.

14

Dealing with Vendors

Records-management equipment ranges from the most basic file cabinet to the most complex electronic storage and retrieval system. Whether you are purchasing manual or automated equipment, however, it is best to follow a consistent plan for choosing and regulating vendors. Only through systematic planning can users match their equipment needs with equipment purchases and avoid the pitfalls of systems incompatibility and unnecessary equipment. It is especially crucial to establish control if computer systems are included in the records-management program. Today's computer market is rapidly changing, with a broad range of vendors competing aggressively for the computer user's business. Sorting out the purchasing options when you are designing a system composed of dozens of components can seem an enormous task indeed. Vendors provide an important information resource for the manager charged with the task of choosing equipment. This chapter will usher you through the steps of the vendor approval process, from making the initial information survey to sealing the final contract.

14.1 VENDORS AS INFORMATION SOURCES

Records managers, caught up in the surge of new technologies and equipment, now face many of the same problems and opportunities that other technical administrators and managers have learned to cope with. The records-management professional must choose from a wide array of systems, some of which were not available even a year or two ago.

Compounding this problem is the fact that many of these systems are offered with slight but important variations by a number of manufacturers. Records managers have always been expected to provide a high level of service at the lowest total cost. Now they are also expected to have sufficient technical knowledge and business skills to select the proper components of an efficient, integrated information resource management system. Often, this means that products and services from various sources must be coordinated. Although this is not an impossible expectation, it does make the task of the manager more difficult.

Vendors and equipment manufacturers are well aware of this situation. As one means of promoting their own products they have long realized that potential customers must be educated to a level of awareness and expertise where the benefits of their products can be fully realized. It is only when a fear of technology or lack of understanding is turned into a desire for technology that a sale can be made.

Toward this end, original equipment manufacturers (OEM) produce large amounts of educational and informational literature. Anyone who wishes to acquire more knowledge about today's technology should take advantage of this important information source. Although this literature is naturally geared toward a particular product or product series, it frequently describes generic qualities of operating systems and technologies common to many products and systems.

In addition to the printed material which is available, the potential buyer should tap the sales force of these OEMs for their expertise. Sales reps, systems specialists, and other service personnel will all provide information if requested. The records managers should be frank in dealing with these representatives and identify what stage of the evaluation or selection process the company is in. Frankness prevents conclusions based on false assumptions and allows each party to portray accurately their needs and desires.

Additionally, several publications specialize in product comparison. Auerbach and Datapro are two subscription services which offer possibly the widest variety of systems evaluation expertise. Both made their reputation in data-processing evaluation but have since expanded into general office systems products.

The Auerbach and Datapro publications offer product-to-product comparisons and some background information on vendors. Basic starter volumes in various areas, such as Auerbach's *Microworld*, are periodically updated with new product information sent to the subscriber. While these volumes do not offer all of the information needed to analyze purchasing options, they provide enough data to get rough comparisons, particularly on price and performance.

Other good sources of information are the records-management trade journals, such as the *Journal of Information and Image Management, Information and Records Management* and *Office Administration & Automation*. Often such journals regularly publish lists of product-specific reference guides for buyers.

Finally, the two major records-management organizations, the Association of Records Managers and Administrators (ARMA) and the Association for Information and Image Management (AIIM), can offer a wealth of information on new technologies and products. ARMA is located in Prairie Village, KS 66208, and AIIM is found at 1100 Wayne Ave., Silver Spring, MD 20910.

These organizations hold regularly scheduled conferences which highlight current records-management issues and problems. They also issue publications which disseminate many types of information and provide company case studies. In terms of evaluating vendor products, AIIM's resources are especially valuable. Its members include both users and vendors, as opposed to ARMA, which comprises only users. Thus, at AIIM's 1985 conference, over 140 vendors exhibited information and image management equipment and held seminars to explain recent product innovations. Perhaps AIIM's most useful resource, however, is an extensive library of image management information sources. Their catalogue can be purchased on microfiche for a reasonable fee.

14.2 ESTABLISHING A PREFERRED-VENDOR LIST

Conscientiously researching product options is only the first step to mastering the vendor environment. Many large companies have approached the multi-vendor problem by establishing a preferred-vendor list. By selecting a small number of vendors to handle all of a firm's business, a company can increase its clout with those vendors and make more informed purchases. Each company creates a list after a systematic elimination process has been completed. During this period, users play the vendor field, and vendors court the users' business. Already, many companies employ the "vendors of choice" list to control purchases, take advantage of volume discounts, and gain some assurance of dependable service.

A preferred-vendor list should include representatives from the four categories of vendor services: hardware manufacturers, software houses, service bureaus, and computer equipment supply companies. The question of product compatibility applies directly to hardware manufacturers. Either pieces of equipment connect, or they don't. Product decisions in the other vendor categories depend primarily on the hardware that has been installed. Software companies design their programs to run only on certain types of hardware. The process of creating user programs to run on a particular computer does not involve the user directly. Computer supply companies provide miscellaneous supplies, such as disks, ribbons, and paper. Thus, software and supply company options will be constrained first and foremost by the hardware you choose. Finally, service bureaus normally process data which has been given to them by a client firm. Output may be a standard payroll, accounts payable, or another business application. It may be microfilmed documents or computer output microfilm. Most service bureaus also provide task support in such areas as media conversion (for example, a one-time conversion of a file series from paper to microfilm).

A majority of large companies have approved-vendor lists, and a sizable portion of smaller firms plan to create lists over the next two years. Already, about three out of every four large users utilize approved-vendor lists for electronic or computer-related equipment purchases.

14.3 SELECTION CRITERIA

The four basic criteria for selection in the multi-vendor environment are performance, price, support, and compatibility. The list may seem short, but actually any of the other detailed criteria which have been proposed can fit into these four categories. In order to judge which trade-offs should be made, the relationships among these factors must be understood.

The first trade-off which most buyers would consider is price and performance. Because better performance is most likely linked to higher prices, it is necessary to do a cost-benefit analysis to measure the options. Costs are fairly easy to identify: hardware, software, personnel, and operation costs. Benefits are trickier. They may be operational, as with the number of documents which can be photographed per hour using one camera instead of another; or they may be intangible, as with worker satisfaction. To maximize the price-performance relationship for every piece of equipment, the prospective buyer would have to perform a case-by-case analysis which considers every available vendor.

It is apparent that optimum decisions cannot be made using only these two criteria. If every option on the market was scrutinized for the most favorable performance-price ratio, the other two criteria, support and compatibility, would be neglected. The firm would be plagued by a proliferation of incompatible machines and would have no assurances about ongoing support. If the firm only considered support and compatibility, on the other hand, it might purchase a lot of expensive equipment which didn't necessarily meet user needs. Unlike the trade-off between price and performance, support and compatibility are two categories which can be simultaneously maximized. When a firm limits its purchases to a select list of vendors to maintain system compatibility, it should gain more leverage with the vendor and thereby get more support.

14.4 WEIGHING THE SELECTION CRITERIA

Companies of all sizes rate vendor support as the most crucial vendor characteristic. Compatibility follows support in all but the smallest companies (that is, those with fewer than 100 employees). Small companies list price as their second major consideration. Interestingly, performance ranks lowest with companies of all sizes.

Firms do not have to sacrifice low prices for good service or compatibility. Often, a firm with an established vendor list is eligible for volume discounts. Vendors competing to get on the approved list offer incentives, such as free service contracts and reduced price package deals. The savings generated in this way will most likely outstrip any savings derived from single purchase bargains for large companies.

Because most users specify support and compatibility as the most important criteria, the vendor list is especially useful in maximizing them throughout the organization. The lack of a centralized purchasing policy has the most serious ramifications in these areas. Users who have to deal with inadequate support and incompatible machines are the first ones to point this out. Sometimes, the only opposition to a centralized mandate comes from top management unwilling to allocate the time and money to establish a list. Needless to say, such a decision can be shortsighted.

14.5 CONDUCTING THE APPROVAL PROCESS

Not all records managers play the same role in the process of selecting vendors. Some firms establish comprehensive vendor lists which include all equipment from office chairs to mainframes. Others have no centralized purchasing policy at all. The rest, of course, fall somewhere in between. If a firm has a complete list or is planning to establish one in the near future, the records manager should be on the approval team. In this case, he or she would be intimately involved in selecting appropriate records-equipment vendors for future purchases of everything from microfilm cameras to COM systems. If no vendor list has been established, the records manager in a medium- to large-sized firm may find it worthwhile to submit a proposal for a records-management vendor list. The success of this list in reducing costs and improving operations might spur management to authorize a more inclusive list. Finally, in small firms with no vendor policy, the records manager may want to pursue vendors on a case-by-case basis.

Whether the records manager is involved in creating a permanent vendor list or simply wants to purchase individual pieces of equipment, he or she should follow a systematic approval and selection process. The first step is to collect information on vendor products. In rating systems and components according to the four criteria outlined above, the many publications which specialize in comparing products are the best places to start.

After using all of these resources to make preliminary product comparisons, direct contact with the vendors in order to make a buying decision can be established. The best way of getting the required details is to request the vendors' technical brochures on products of your choice. At this stage the user should not tip his or her hand that the vendor is under consideration for the approved list. When the brochures have been reviewed, the records manager can create a narrowed list of eligible vendors who will be contacted at length. This contact offers the user the opportunity to scrutinize the vendors in three stages. First, the user will file a request for a vendor proposal (RFP) from each of the finalists, whether they are competing for a slot on a vendor list or pushing for an individual product sale. Second, the vendor proposals and presentations must be critiqued. Finally, the contract will be cut.

14.6 FORMULATING THE RFP

The RFP (request for a proposal) is crucial because it sets the parameters for the information which the vendor will prepare. The vendor's proposal and presentation will be directed toward meeting the needs that the user sets out in the RFP. Also, if a contract is eventually signed, it will build from requirements which were stipulated in the original request. Therefore, the content, form, and submission of the RFP should not be treated lightly.

The content of the RFP should be organized around the four selection criteria: price, performance, compatibility, and support. The vendor's ability to provide support can be assessed by a request for background information about the vendor. A company's questions should focus on the vendor's familiarity with the user's industry as well as the vendor's own solvency and size. Financial information should be readily available in the form of quarterly sales results and annual reports. The firm's position in any pending litigation can give additional clues to its solvency and its operating history.

Automation compatibility is particularly a concern for records managers who are purchasing automated CAR systems. Other types of compatibility issues are not as complex to sort out but must be addressed nonetheless. For example, cassette and cartridge microforms can only be read on specific readers. For researching systems compatibility, the vendor's background information can be helpful. One clue is a firm's ownership of other vendors. A common phenomenon lately is that vendors have been seeking mergers, acquisitions, and joint ventures because they are discovering that end users want complete systems to solve specific applications problems. Not surprisingly, IBM took the lead in this trend by purchasing the telecommunications company, Rolm Corporation. Other large corporations such as Control Data, NCR, and Sperry have followed suit.

Communicating price requirements in the RFP is tricky. Vendors should know that price is an important factor, but the purchaser's specific budget should never be revealed. Computer consultants warn that if figures are quoted, vendors will often fit a system to a budget rather than fit the system to a company's actual needs.

One price decision which can be dealt with directly is the lease versus buy option. The user's particular cash and tax benefit needs will influence the options under consideration, but the particular deal which the vendor can arrange will determine the final decision. Leasing equipment is a viable option for a variety of reasons. Sometimes, a firm has a short-term need for specialized equipment, such as for a one-time microfilm conversion project. Or the records-management department may have an immediate equipment need which cannot wait until the next budget cycle for purchase approval. Finally, leasing can bring in needed equipment with a minimum of cash expenditure and a maximum of tax deductions.

Performance criteria usually make up the bulk of the RFP, as they are the easiest to specify and the simplest for the vendor to respond to. Performance specifications can be divided into three basic categories. First, the user should outline the firm's critical information needs and ask the vendor to list all the products and services it can offer to satisfy those needs. Second, the user should specify a minimum required level of performance in some measurable unit. For instance, the user can request maximum turnaround time for a particular function with the vendor's equipment. Third, the user should request information on the product's dependability, perhaps in terms of average expected "up time" during normal usage.

14.7 WRITING THE RFP

It is generally agreed that the RFP should be a written document, but no standard format has been designed. A written request has clear advantages over a spoken request. First of all, it documents exactly what the user wants. Second, it ensures that all vendors receive identical requests, so that comparisons of their responses can be made systematically.

The tone of the document can vary according to your requirements and experience with the particular vendor. Writing a formal request is obviously an option, but others recommend writing the RFP informally. A formal RFP can end up being long and technical, thereby discouraging vendors from studying it closely or responding to it at all. On the other hand, the request should be formal and detailed enough to elicit all the information you need to make your selection. If the vendor does not trust your intention to buy, you will probably not get a bid.

14.8 CRITIQUING THE VENDOR PROPOSAL AND PRESENTATION

The first vendor screening process comes with the acceptance of the proposals. Consideration should only be given to those vendors who meet the submission deadline specified in the RFP, normally no longer than two weeks. One approach would be to send the first batch of introductory requests and follow up with more detailed letters to those who respond initially. In any case, a delayed response will tell you something about how the company operates, or at least about its interest in your request.

Once all the proposals have been submitted, they must be evaluated according to the firm's records-management priorities, both short-term and long-term. Evaluation can be handled by the records manager or by a team composed of several specialists. For inexpensive purchases with few compatibility implications, a single decision-maker is probably adequate. For more complex purchases, a team is advisable. Those participating could be a technician, an accountant, and an attorney. The technician, who could be the records manager or an outside consultant, would be responsible for matching equipment to user needs. The accountant would be equipped to evaluate various acquisition methods, leasing or buying, new or used equipment. Finally, the attorney would be present to give legal advice and to draft the actual contract.

After the proposals have been examined, vendor sales presentations can be scheduled. Everyone involved in the evaluation process should be present to check the salesperson's claims against the proposal. Responses to questions can uncover important information about vendor support and reliability. Responses such as, "We've got that feature coming out next month," or "It's all clearly explained in the manual" should warn the records manager that the vendor does not approach service seriously.

14.9 CUTTING THE CONTRACT

The final step in selecting either a vendor or a piece of equipment is the cutting of the contract. Without a contract, the value of the approval process is negligible, since the user cannot force the vendor to perform. At the minimum a contract or performance agreement should contain the expectations of both parties, how expectations are to be realized, the consequences for failure to perform, and timetables for performance.

Besides the basic elements of a contract, there are some tricky issues to negotiate. For complicated systems purchases, there may be problems in legally coordinating multiple vendors. Some lawyers contend that each vendor in a multiple-vendor project should be contractually required to warrant the compatibility of its products and to provide general maintenance for those products. For traditional records-management tools, these types of clauses will not really apply, but with new computer-based systems compatibility is a central issue.

Another contract issue that may affect electronic purchases is getting a corporate license for software. Licenses are very difficult to secure, but the money saved often justifies the trouble it takes to negotiate one. A corporate software license might carry a one-time fee of $20,000 for one program. But if the software costs $300 per copy, a large firm that needs 100 copies could save, in this case, $10,000.

Many vendors have standard contracts that they use for all equipment purchases. While this practice may save time and money in drafting an individual contract, it may not best serve the needs of either the vendor or the user. From the user's point of view, obviously, there is a danger of paying for what one doesn't need or of not getting what one wants. Simply because the contract has been used before, there are no assurances that it will fit the special needs of your firm. For this reason, form contracts should not be accepted without a careful reading by legal counsel.

14.10 SOME MAJOR EQUIPMENT MANUFACTURERS

Although dozens of firms sell office automation products, four companies have led the market in image storage and retrieval systems: Kodak, 3M, Bell & Howell, and, more recently, Philips. Not only do the "big four" offer the latest developments in automated storage and retrieval systems or microfilm technology, but they have also been involved in research and development in these areas for some time. All of the leaders in the field share a common vision of an integrated records-management function and have offered an array of equipment which seeks to achieve this aim.

Kodak's product line in image management has grown impressively over the last few years. It offers a variety of micrographics hardware, copiers, and CAR and COM systems. In attempting to establish its niche in the crowded office automation field, Kodak has focused on the problem of systems integration. In terms of records-management applications, it is working on systems that link microfilm, micrographics hardware, and computer equipment. Recently it has introduced two integrated image management systems—KIMS (Kodak Image Management System) and KEEPS (Kodak Ektaprint Electronic Publishing System)—which aim to electronically coordinate document production, filing, retrieving, transmitting, and revising. Kodak installed the first KIMS and KEEPS workstations in 1986.

KEEPS marks Kodak's entry into the in-house publishing field. The components of KEEPS allow user control over the creation of entire documents, from booklets to annual reports. With its electronic publishing functions, it can merge text, headlines, and photographs, and deliver near-typeset-quality output. Furthermore, the same individual can send copies electronically to everyone on a designated distribution list. The implications for report generation and duplication are tremendous.

KIMS builds on Kodak's 50-year participation in the microfilm industry by integrating image and computer database retrieval. It can electronically call up, edit, and then transmit microfilmed information, computer data, or (in the near future) optical-disk-stored information to any location on the network. A worker at any remote terminal could call up a specific document from among up to 3 million images stored in the microfilm autoloader. A robotic device within the autoloader finds the correct microfilm magazine and scans the requested image for transmission to the worker, all in only a few seconds. In this way, paper usage is avoided entirely.

Philips, the Dutch multinational company, is one of the largest electronics manufacturers in the world. Its state-of-the-art contribution to image management is in the field of optical disk technology. In fact, Philips has recently introduced Megadoc, one of the first commercial applications of digital optical recording. Megadoc is a minicomputer-based system for the mass storage of information in virtually any form. It can utilize up to 64 optical disks to store as many as 32 million pages of data in exactly the form it was produced. Documents can be retrieved from anywhere in the system within five seconds by the use of bit-map scanning techniques and laser technology. The system can call up and transmit documents to and from remote terminals.

3M has been perfecting traditional micrographics applications for use in current automated systems. 3M, like the other companies, stresses that all technologies must be integrated if today's information storage and retrieval problems are to be solved. By applying electronic indexing, manipulation, and searching to microfilm retrieval, 3M and others have helped micrographics expand out of its purely archival role and into active file systems. 3M produces a line of computer-assisted micrographic file and retrieval systems called Micrapoint. These systems can electronically index document images on microforms—either cartridges, microfiche, or aperture cards—for automatic and rapid retrieval.

Bell & Howell is another recognized leader in the microimagery industry. It offers a variety of products that integrate microfilm generation with data-processing systems. The Microx system is an updatable imaging system which can instantaneously update and file microfilmed documents. The Data Search series is a group of computer-assisted microfilm storage and retrieval systems. In addition, Bell & Howell produces the Classic family of check microfilmers, an array of new image retrieval devices, and a variety of COM systems.

These four companies are some of the larger players in the records-management and information resources management field. This brief review is not a recommendation or endorsement of their products or systems. Many smaller companies are also active in the field producing high-quality products and systems, especially in the emerging high-tech and custom software areas. What the future will bring cannot be predicted, but users should adopt a long-term approach to their own needs. Users should also expect that vendors will design new systems for information management with similar concern for the long term.

QUESTIONS AND ANSWERS

Q. What should the user keep in mind when dealing with vendors?

A. First, a records or information resource manager should keep in mind that the large majority of vendors want to establish long-term relationships with users of their equipment and that they want any new system to perform up to expectations. Service, while it may vary from one equipment vendor to another, is therefore an important component of the relationship between the equipment supplier and the equipment user.

Q. In the evaluation and selection process, how can vendors help me?

A. Vendors have long realized that records and information resource managers must have sufficient technical knowledge and awareness to make informed rational decisions. As one means of promoting their own products, they produce large amounts of educational and informational literature. This material, along with the expertise of the vendor's sales force, should be tapped and utilized in any good evaluation and selection process.

Q. What are other sources of available information?

A. Numerous trade journals and magazines cover topics of relevance to the records manager in the field of office automation and technology development. Also two major national records-management associations can be accessed for information as well as sponsoring regular conferences on current topics. User groups are also helpful sources of valuable data.

Q. What are the criteria for selection in the multi-vendor environment?

A. There are four basic criteria for selection in the multi-vendor environment. They are performance, price, support, and compatibility. The list may seem short, but actually any of the other detailed criteria which may be proposed can be included in one of these categories. In order to judge which trade-offs should be made, the relationships among these factors and the weight they each are given should be clearly understood.

Q. What are the steps to be taken to determine what vendors will be on a final list?

A. After the field has been narrowed to a small number of qualified candidates, the user will file a request for a vendor proposal (RFP). Next, the written vendor proposals and the oral presentations must be critiqued. Finally, the contract will be drawn up and executed by both parties.

Q. Is there a standard plan to follow in each of these steps?

A. Although there are general rules to be followed in each step of the process, each individual company will have its own perceptions and needs concerning the four principal selection criteria (performance, price, support, and compatibility). This means that customized responses must be formulated by each company equipment and system study team.

15

Dealing with Consultants and Outside Services

In order to plan and implement a successful records-management program, the records manager may have to call upon outside consultants and service bureaus. Before any consulting firm is hired, the records manager should have a clear idea of the services that consultants and bureaus provide and also the services that they are not qualified to perform. Consultants and outside services are tools of the trade. Like any other tools, they can be used effectively or ineffectively. It is imperative that you clarify at the outset of a project that a consulting firm or service bureau is willing and able to fill your particular needs.

15.1 WHAT CONSULTANTS DO

Consultants are usually called in at crisis periods. The client may have a project which must be planned, executed, or audited but has insufficient resources to do the job in-house. Resources could be lacking in any of several areas; among them are expertise, manpower, objectivity, capital or equipment, and time.

Frequently, the client simply lacks the expertise needed to design a program, an office system, or a records center. The appropriate consultant can provide knowledge about equipment, systems, and organizational requirements. Temporarily hiring an "expert" is especially useful if the project concerns a one-time operation, such as a wholesale conversion of records from paper to microfilm. The cost of an outside expert would be justified by the cost of training someone in the company to carry out the conversion. If necessary, the consultant can be instructed to organize training for in-house workers. For example, a consulting firm may set up an inventory schedule and then teach the records-management staff how to execute it. A firm may also need a consultant if an in-house expert has no time to allocate to your particular project.

Bringing in outside consultants can also be useful if the firm lacks the manpower to complete one or more steps in the planning or implementing process. For example, the records manager may not have a team capable of doing a corporatewide inventory or needs analysis. A consulting firm would come equipped with all the necessary staff, specially trained to do a needs analysis in the most nondisruptive and efficient manner. More important, the job or the proposal can usually be finished within a shorter time frame. Unlike in-house staff, consultants can devote full-time effort to formulating a proposal or completing an inventory.

Even if the firm possesses a qualified records-management staff, the records manager may feel the need for the objective analysis that only an outsider can offer. Consultants have no personal reasons for investing in one option as opposed to another. They are outside the web of departmental politics and are more likely to be respected by all involved parties. An objective opinion may be required if several departments or divisions within the firm have proposed conflicting plans for carrying out a project. Soliciting a recommendation from an outside party may be the only way to resolve a conflict. The consultant can simply offer a new perspective as well. Management can get locked into a single way of approaching problems or proposed changes. Sometimes a consultant needs to make only minor suggestions in order to open up new avenues of growth.

15.2 WHAT CONSULTANTS DON'T DO

If consultants are effectively used, they can be a tremendous aid to the records manager; however, consultants cannot do everything. They cannot simply be handed problems with no inside guidance about how the firm operates. Consultants hired to plan a records-management program should be knowledgeable about all facets of the field of records management. However, they will have only a superficial understanding of the firm's records requirements. Usually a consulting team will spend no more than a few weeks observing the firm's operating procedures. A skillful team will make accurate recommendations based on the data it collects. In some cases, however, it may be difficult for consultants to analyze why something does not work. Deciding that a procedure or machine does not meet filing requirements is a fairly simple task. But delving into the origins of an inadequate system can involve more time than a consultant can spend. Thus, consultants' recommendations do not always catch the problem at its root.

In addition, consultants do not automatically save money for the firm. You cannot simply assume that a consultant's recommendations will result in extensive savings. The firm will spend much more in labor costs if it uses consultants as opposed to in-house experts. In order to ensure that a consultant's salary is balanced by the savings that his or her recommendations produce, the records manager must justify the cost of hiring an outside expert against the weight of the expert's knowledge, skills, assignment, and expected benefits.

15.3 SELECTING A CONSULTANT

When you begin your search for a consultant or consulting firm, you should gather a list of leads from various sources. Names on the list could be consultants with whom you have worked before. Or they could be firms that other records managers have recommended. Alternatively, you could decide to investigate consultants whose articles you read in one of the records-management journals, or whose speeches you heard at a records-management conference. Professional journals and information management associations may publish lists of recommended consultants themselves. Finally, you may have met a consultant at a professional or social gathering for those working in your field. Whatever the source of your lead, it is important that you check carefully any consulting group or individual against the requirements of the job.

There are some general attributes which all consultant candidates should possess. In terms of qualifications, the client must look at the consultant's project background and expertise. A good consultant has done more than simply consult. To obtain practical business experience, most will have worked in the operations side of a firm before they became consultants. The records manager should pay special attention to the qualifications of the project manager on the consulting team. A project manager should have a successful record of planning and implementing information management projects.

In order to research the past experience of the consulting firm, as well as of the individual staff members who would be assigned to the job, the client must ask for references and check them carefully. Each reference should be phoned and queried about the consultant's performance, the results achieved, adherence to the agreed-on time frame, and adherence to the budget. In addition, previous clients can tell you if they intend to use the firm again and, if so, why.

A consulting firm must have sufficient technical expertise to analyze your company's problems and offer appropriate solutions. If you are hiring a consultant to design a storage and retrieval system, he or she must be well versed in everything from filing cabinets to optical disks. Records management is a field that mixes automated and manual systems; therefore, it is important to hire a consultant who is prepared to consider both types of systems.

In addition to being knowledgeable, a consulting firm should be distinguished by its objectivity and independence. It is unwise to choose a consulting firm that also sells equipment or software programs. The client should inquire whether or not the consulting firm accepts "finder's fees" from vendors for any equipment they are responsible for selling. Either of these arrangements could severely limit a consultant's objectivity. The most objective firms will be those unburdened by a financial attachment to a particular type of storage and retrieval system. For example, some consultants will be eager to install the latest in automated storage and retrieval equipment without considering whether or not it is justified by the client's records needs. If the consulting firm has published any articles or press releases, you should be able to figure out if it is pushing a single "line" or not.

With these criteria in mind, the records manager should begin the process of selecting a consultant. As with the vendor selection process, each candidate should be asked to submit a written proposal and to give a verbal presentation, usually delivered by the project manager, outlining the plan of action. The evaluation of each proposal should consider the depth of understanding which each one demonstrates for the firm's situation. Obviously, the proposed work plan will be sketchy, as the consultant has not had much time to observe the company's operations. But it should be apparent whether or not the proposal has grasped the heart of the matter. The presentation will give you a further opportunity to probe the depth of the consultant's knowledge.

A presentation will also allow you to meet the individuals you would be working with for several weeks. Although the chemistry of personality conflict or congruence cannot be explicitly measured, it is important. Consultants are professionals trained to levy impersonal criticism, but the whole consulting project will run more smoothly if you can establish a personal rapport with the consultant. A successful relationship between a client and a consultant requires skillful diplomacy. Enough mutual trust and respect must exist to facilitate the exchange of confidential information. Both the records manager and the consultant must be able to respect each other's areas of expertise and to suggest tactfully ways to improve the operation.

15.4 NEGOTIATING A CONTRACT

A contract with a consulting firm can be based either on a flat fee or on a time and materials calculation. The flat fee has the advantage of being simple. If the records manager has a fixed sum of money in the budget which has been allocated for the project, the fixed amount can be the starting point. That is, services can be matched to fit the budget. Often, however, this arrangement is not the most advantageous for the client. Fitting the job to the budget is clearly inferior to fitting the job to the company's needs. Also, consultants who are bidding for flat fees often bid high in order to cover unforeseen delays. As the project matures, it then becomes difficult to determine whether or not a specific task was included in the original estimate. And finally, consultants working on flat fees have less incentive to complete the job as thoroughly as possible.

Despite the many disadvantages of negotiating a flat fee, opting for a per diem schedule can be dangerous if it is not carefully monitored. The consultant should submit a detailed work plan which includes a completion schedule and the activities which will occupy the consultants on a daily basis. The consulting firm will want to stick to this schedule to preserve its own reputation, but often unexpected delays or expenses occur. The contract must specify that the client be notified if such delays occur and why they happened. In turn, the client may be forced to limit the scope of the project if the original time and fees estimate turned out to be unfeasible.

15.5 MONITORING PERFORMANCE

Besides fees and schedules, the contract should negotiate goals that the client can use to monitor the consultant's performance. The deliverables must be specified by the client and agreed upon by the consultant. The method of achieving those results will probably be included in the consultant's proposal, but not necessarily in the contract. Unless the method fails, the client should not have any input into the consultant's methodology.

Whatever the method of completing the project, it should be broken down into manageable phases. At the end of each phase, the consultants have the opportunity to present their work in progress, and the client has a chance to offer comments and suggestions. These client-consultant work sessions should be structured into the work plan. They are an important way to monitor the consultant's performance and compare progress with the original schedule and budget. If the partial results do not meet your expectations, there will still be time to correct operating flaws or re-evaluate expectations.

The exact phases of a consulting project would change depending on whether the product is a plan or an implementation. But there are general phases which make convenient units for evaluation and appraisal. In the first phase, the consulting firm clarifies its understanding of the client's situation. Although consultants may have dealt with similar projects, each firm has its own problems and its own organizational priorities.

The second phase requires the consulting team to delve more deeply into what the firm's records-management needs are, what the strengths and weaknesses of the current records-management program are, and where the opportunities for improvement lie. During this phase the team will collect its data. If the project is a large one, at the end of the first two phases preliminary results may be presented to the client. During this presentation, the client has an opportunity to hear what the consultant's findings have been and help shape the recommendations.

The third phase of the consultant's work is the analysis of the collected data. The consultants will examine alternative technical and organizational solutions to problems revealed by the data. The various options will be measured against the original deliverables to ensure that the solution best fits the client's needs.

The fourth phase consists of the consultant's recommendations on how the firm should proceed. The recommendations will be included in a final study report, which includes results from the previous three phases. The client should insist on a report which is professional, thorough, and formal. It will be used by the records manager to convince top management to adopt the recommendations which it contains.

If all parties, including the consulting team, the records manager, and representatives from top management, agree on the conclusions and recommendations included in the final report, then plans for implementation can proceed. If the consulting team is to participate in the implementation process, it must submit another work plan with schedule and budget. However, the client may have the manpower to carry out the implementation plan. In this case, the consultant has been hired for planning expertise only. The team might finish its project by training company employees to implement its final recommendations. Training can be organized by holding seminars for all the people involved. Staff members may also benefit from participating on the consultant team. The records manager can try to negotiate such participation for a professional in the records-management department. This employee would be in a good position to direct any future projects with similar scope.

15.6 WHEN TO CHOOSE OUTSIDE SERVICES

Service centers and bureaus, like consultants, should be used when your firm lacks the resources to perform the services in-house. Service

centers do not analyze your firm's situation or design solutions to problems. The client who decides to use a bureau or service delegates specialized tasks for which the bureaus have equipment and trained personnel.
The basic advantage of using an outside service is to save the firm from
making an unnecessary investment in capital equipment and manpower.
For example, microfilm services and off-site records centers provide expensive cameras, storage and retrieval equipment, COM systems, and
full-time personnel dedicated to their tasks. On the other side of the
coin, of course, is the cost of hiring such services. In addition, it is often
inconvenient to send work out to be processed, as turnaround time can
be longer than with in-house storage or processing. As with any other
planning decision, the records manager must carefully weigh all the
pros and cons before coming to a conclusion.

Whichever type of service you are investigating, you must undertake
a search process similar to that of choosing a consultant or a vendor.
For sorting out service bureaus, user groups are especially helpful. Other
firms which have used the bureaus can tell you if the quality of the
services provided is satisfactory. Organizations like ARMA and AIIM
also recommend service bureaus. After reviewing all of the recommendations, however, you should scout out the service bureaus in your
area. While other firms' opinions can be enlightening, their requirements
may not exactly match yours. It is thus wise for the records manager to
make the final choice.

Businesses can choose from a variety of automated services to meet
their production needs. Many firms take advantage of word-processing
and data-processing services to process documents and data which are
backlogged in the firm's own data-processing department. These services can often process work as quickly as the firm itself can, especially
if they are conveniently located.

The use of electronic mail also facilitates a rapid turnaround time.
Records managers may need to use data-processing services for analyz-
ing inventory or needs analysis data, if there are no in-house facilities
or resources for managing and manipulating a large data base. But, more
often, the records manager will deal with two types of services: microfilm
bureaus and off-site records centers (see Chapter 11).

15.6.1 Microfilm Service Bureaus

One of the services that the records manager will most commonly use
is a microfilm bureau. Microfilm equipment is expensive and often specialized. If the firm has only sporadic microfilm conversion needs, it may
not be worthwhile to invest in a system. Using a service bureau has
some of the same advantages of employing a consultant. Your firm
benefits from the expertise of personnel trained in a specific field. The

expertise is usually guaranteed in the contract by an assurance of quality, such as the quality of each filmed image. In addition, less time is usually needed to complete a project. Service bureaus have full-time staff dedicated solely to generating microfilm.

Microfilm bureaus provide various types of services, and a firm can take advantage of some or all of them. The most common service is the microfilming of paper documents. If a firm is undergoing a first-time conversion to microfilm for inactive storage, the records manager may have a large quantity of documents to be filmed and stored as quickly as possible. However, once the conversion has been completed, the firm's monthly conversion needs may be too small to justify purchasing and maintaining equipment. In this case, the records manager would want to investigate the service bureau option.

Once you have determined the need for a service bureau, you have several service options to choose from. The service bureau can either film the records at the firm itself or gather them for processing at the bureau. Doing the work off-site may be less disruptive, but probably more time-consuming. If the firm wants to purchase cameras, a bureau can be engaged to develop the film, thus saving the firm all the headaches of processing and guaranteeing the quality of each image.

As a final option, a firm can use a bureau for specialized filming jobs only. For example, you may be able to cost-justify a rotary camera for normal-sized documents, but not a planetary one for oversized drawings. Whenever large or fragile documents need to be microfilmed, a bureau can be engaged to handle the project. Another specialized service is computer output microform (COM). COM systems require a large capital investment, upward of $100,000, so many small to medium-sized firms find it profitable to employ service bureaus for the production of COM. Purchasing your own COM system probably will not be economical unless outside monthly bills for COM services surpass several thousand dollars.

If you decide to hire a bureau to provide microfilming services, it is probably a good idea to have the documents prepared in-house for filming at the bureau. The process of removing staples and paper clips is labor-intensive and requires no expertise or equipment. Therefore, the benefits of having the bureau perform such preparatory services will probably not justify their cost, unless the client is understaffed.

Consultants and service bureaus are two major sources of outside assistance and expertise for the records manager. Their use can make major transitions and projects manageable and increase their level of success. To help ensure the satisfaction of both parties, a judicious and careful selection process should be followed.

QUESTIONS AND ANSWERS

Q. Why are consultants used?

A. Consultants and other outside service bureaus are usually called in at crisis periods. The prospective client may have a project that must be planned, executed, or audited but lacks sufficient resources to perform the job in-house. Most frequently, however, the firm lacks the necessary and sufficient specialized expertise.

Q. What are the limits in terms of using an outside consultant?

A. Consultants cannot be expected to operate in a vacuum. They also cannot be expected to be as intimately knowledgeable about all aspects of a company's operations as its in-house records-management staff. Consultants can bring expertise and knowledge to bear, but only in areas where they have a solid grasp of the conditions.

Q. How is a consultant selected?

A. Working from a list of qualified candidates, the client should investigate the consulting firm's project background and special knowledge. In addition, they should study the project manager's experience. References for the consultant should be obtained, and the client should check the consultant's performance, results achieved, adherence to budgets and schedules, and the overall assessment given by other firms that have used the consultant in the past.

Q. What other special factors should a client keep in mind when looking at prospective consultants?

A. Aside from expertise, experience, and knowledge, the consultant should be independent and objective. Consulting firms that sell equipment or software or receive fees from other equipment vendors may have a natural bias toward certain systems.

Q. What should a client ask for in the selection process from prospective consulting firms?

A. Besides the references mentioned, a written proposal as well as a face-to-face presentation should be requested. Both of these steps should establish additional factors that could be used to reach a decision.

Q. Are fees negotiable?

A. The schedule of fees as well as the scope of the work plan and related schedules are all negotiable. Each phase of the project may be separately negotiated to fit the firm's objectives and its budget. The client and the consultant can therefore work together regularly to fine tune or redirect the project.

16

Preparing for Tomorrow

At this point the records manager (or the information resources manager) has mastered a large amount of both technical knowledge and organizational knowledge. This knowledge should assist records managers to design and implement cost-effective and efficient systems of information management. The task, however, does not stop here. Both the changing nature of technology and the changing needs of the company as it responds to the forces of its environment require the records manager to be flexible and adaptive. The maxim "adapt or be superseded" applies in the modern world of business as well as in the modern world of integrated information management.

This final chapter will point out areas of concern and action for the records of the 1980s and beyond. Even with a records-management system in place, the records manager is still responsible for controlling the creation, processing, storing, retrieving, and use of a company's information base. No small task indeed! To avoid the pitfalls of obsolescence and its negative consequences, which could range from the loss of a company's competitive position to widespread user dissatisfaction, certain steps should be taken on an ongoing basis. Let's examine these more closely so that through better preparation, the benefits of new tools and procedures can be extended as far into the foreseeable future as possible.

The first section of this chapter will examine the need for an ongoing audit within your company to regularly chart performance against goals and improve productivity. The next two sections address sources of information on the industry and some important industry trends. The final section looks at strategies for avoiding obsolescence.

16.1 MONITORING THE SYSTEM: CONDUCTING AN AUDIT

The goal of using new tools and procedures is to gain new or increased benefits. The most commonly cited benefit from automated records systems is increased productivity.

In all likelihood, the case which was presented to top management to gain its support for a new records and information resource management system was twofold. The first point was a claim of higher productivity. Computer based multifunction workstations and digitized image storage and manipulation greatly reduce the human effort needed to handle the same amount of documentation as in a traditional paper-based system.

The second point was that new systems could better aid the company in carrying out its corporate objectives. Greater flexibility, responsiveness, and speed will mark this new era. Entire industries and market segments will be linked by a web of two-way information flow.

To gain top management support for records management, however, everyday concerns such as cost and time savings, space reduction, and increased customer and internal service will be given the most weight. This means that the issue of productivity must be pragmatically dealt with. Quantifiable costs must be compared against estimated and, importantly, quantified benefits.

For a manager to justify following a course of proposed change, he or she must clearly show how the new program and tools are expected to result in improved productivity. This takes place when the project is being sold and before any final decision has taken place. Once the go-ahead has been received and implementation has occurred, the good manager must continue to monitor the system and determine how well it is performing in light of the productivity benchmarks established in the design phase. Performance must be measured to assess how well or poorly the system is functioning compared to these standards.

While quantifying returns in an environment that deals with information as a raw material and decisions as a finished product is more of an art than a science, an effort to do so is necessary. In the classic economic sense, the concept of productivity is defined as the relationship between the output of goods and services and the input of labor, capital, and natural resources. In the more confined range of the office environment, a number of these factors can be eliminated. The office itself can be reviewed as a system for the creation, processing, storage, retrieval, reproduction, and dissemination of information.

To gauge productivity, then, a manager needs the means to measure it and guideposts from which to judge results. Both of these have been presented in Chapter 10. Once new systems have been installed, productivity should be measured on an ongoing basis using these same tools. This is the best means to maintain credibility with top management and insure their continuing support.

16.1.1 The Goal of Continually Improving Productivity

Ongoing education of users at all organizational levels is a key method of continually improving productivity. Additionally, feedback from training and skill improvement sessions allows records managers to target low productivity areas and update their curriculum regularly.

User participation is valuable in these efforts, and many times new solutions or approaches can be gleaned by providing a forum for their expression. When conducted across departments, training sessions allow various user groups to share their information and expertise which can vary significantly from group to group.

The records manager or information resource manager should emphasize his or her role as a source and coordinator of user information and advocacy. In this latter role, he or she can assist users at all levels of the company to fully apply the system which was so carefully designed and selected. The records manager should examine new applications and modifications as well as the reasons for and extent of system underutilization.

This approach is aimed at ensuring that the company gets back the maximum return on its investment in an information network. After installation, a continued concern for user requirements will help ensure that the system performs effectively, efficiently, and economically.

In keeping a close watch on productivity and its fine tuning, adjustments and additions to the system will have to be made. Given the current environment, the records manager can anticipate that the equipment will eventually be superseded by new advances and capabilities. To avoid obsolescence, any well-devised system must be designed to cope with change. The next section will discuss the importance of keeping up with the industry and provide some sources of information for accomplishing this goal.

16.2 KEEPING ABREAST OF THE INDUSTRY

Because records-management technologies continue their relentless march ahead, any good manager involved with records and information management must stay current with these new developments. The best way to accomplish this goal is to continually monitor new information on products and techniques.

16.2.1 Associations, Publications, and Other Sources of Information

Luckily, there are a host of information sources to draw on in the field of office and information systems automation. These include federal government publications, a variety of records-management organizations, industry periodicals, consulting firm publications, and product literature provided by software and hardware vendors. For specific sources, Appendixes D and E provide a list of records-management organizations and related publications.

Other sources of information include the manufacturers and vendors, user groups, and industry-specific associations. Many of them have committees or work groups that cover topics such as office automation and its effect on your particular industry. Particularly in the area of software, specialized programs may have already been developed or modified for your industry-specific needs.

16.3 MAJOR INDUSTRY TRENDS

As difficult as it is to predict the future, some trends in information technology and office automation promise to have substantial impact on tomorrow's modern office and work environment. We shall limit ourselves to the broader trends, as a detailed listing and examination of developments would necessitate its own volume.

16.3.1 Cheaper Processing

Advances in manufacturing techniques, increasing numbers of off-shore producers, and intense competition has driven, and will continue to drive, computer and high-technology equipment prices down. In every product area prices have displayed a sharp downward curve after initial introduction. As market penetration and sales volume increases, economies of scale and new entrants have kept the downward pressure on prices.

Industry developments such as factory automation or CAM—computer-assisted manufacturing—and the increasing use of intelligent or "smart" hardware and software design systems should continue this trend. These techniques drastically reduce the man-hours needed to develop and test prototypes. Improvements are brought to market faster and cheaper.

16.3.2 Faster Processing

Continued improvement in microcircuitry and chip design is speeding up the pace of computation. In fact, electronic engineers are saying that with miniaturization being pushed to its practical limits (this reduces the distance pulses have to travel), it is the speed of electron flow itself through a conducting medium that is the next bottleneck. This barrier to faster computing is already being challenged in innovative ways.

Researchers are currently making important advances in the design of practical light-based switching devices. By way of analogy those can be seen as transistor circuits which use light instead of electricity to process data. The benefit of using light instead of an electron stream is the speed at which it travels, resulting in processing times much faster than previously thought possible. Additionally, the problem of heat generation—a serious concern in today's hardware—is avoided entirely.

16.3.3 Fiber Optics

This new technology is only in its infancy but is expected to grow rapidly. Fiber optics is a new communication technique that uses light transmitted through very thin plastic or glass strands to send and receive messages. Using either light-emitting diodes (LEDs) or injection lasers to convert electrical impulses or signals to light energy, the optical fiber transmits this energy to a receiver. The receivers, in turn, produce an electrical current proportional to the amount of light energy projected onto it, thus completing the cycle.

The use of fiber optics as a communications medium offers a number of superior features and benefits over metallic-twisted pair or co-axial cables. Because fiber optic cables are made from plastic or glass, their cost is usually lower per given length than conventional copper cables. As the usage of fiber optics increases, cable costs as well as the cost of cable terminus equipment are expected to show greater declines. This medium also offers a much wider band width than conventional cables, which means that it can transmit larger amounts of data at faster speeds. It offers greatly enhanced high-speed data transfer.

This light-based system is immune to radio interference and other sources of electrical interference such as power cables, radar, and microwave devices. Along with this signal immunity, it performs very well in harsh environmental conditions which typically degrade its metallic counterparts quite rapidly. Compared with wire-based cables, fiber optics also offer substantial size and weight savings for a comparable transmission capacity. As if these were not sufficient, fiber optic cables also offer higher security levels than their electrical counterparts, as tapping a fiber optic cable is readily detectable. Because of their non-electrical nature, these cables also isolate the equipment they connect. In this way, a common ground is eliminated and inter-system electrical noise is diminished.

A typical fiber optic cable consists of 144 glass fibers, each no thicker than a human hair, yet capable of handling over 4,000 voice channels. For data transmission, fiber optics also offer a much higher, dependable level of transmission.

Today, data transmission accounts for only about 5 to 15 percent of the traffic volume carried by the public telephone networks, but this is expected to increase rapidly. Although fiber optics will find its principal application in public carrier service for years to come, its implications for cutting costs and improving the quality and speed of both voice and data transmission will play a major role in the plans of communications users and those responsible for networking corporate information systems.

16.3.4 The Integrated Digital Network

In both America and Europe the major telecommunications players are beginning to embark on the introduction and trial of a much anticipated service—the integrated digital network (IDN). The main feature of IDN is that it will provide an integrated all-digital network for text, data, graphics, and voice transmission. In the United States, AT&T and the local Bell-operating companies are working together, along with their overseas counterparts, to ensure that there will be a smooth meshing of both national and international networks.

This will accelerate the increasingly international character of telecommunications, especially in fields such as the legal, financial, medical, and military networks. Access to such a global integrated network may even occur through a common interface, similar to the familiar RJ–11 telephone jack, now used to plug a telephone into any standard outlet. This system will make the vision of a unified, fast, and reliable global communication network a much closer reality.

16.4 AVOIDING OBSOLESCENCE

The rapid pace of technological innovation which has marked the last 15 to 20 years in communication and information systems shows no signs of slowing down. Obsolescence or the threat of obsolescence is therefore an unavoidable concern for anyone responsible for overseeing the design, implementation, and operation of records-management systems. Ignoring change only postpones the day of reckoning, making the necessary adjustments that much more difficult.

It is important that records managers recognize and take into account this process of change. There are a number of steps which can be taken to help ease any transitions to be made in the future.

16.4.1 The Modular Concept

An important feature of the advanced records-handling systems that are being introduced today is that the manufacturers have made provisions for the addition of upgraded components and even new technologies. Many producers are designing and constructing their systems with standardized hardware and software requirements so that later additions or substitutions can be easily made. This modular concept means that individual records-management tools, such as OCRs for data entry or CAR units for storage and retrieval, can be replaced with later generation units without disruption or replacement of the entire system.

The large manufacturers, particularly, have adapted this sound tactic after learning from some major mistakes in the past. Under this system, for example, a CAR library which may currently use strip microfilm could be replaced by a new unit with greater speed and storage capacity but which utilizes microfiche cards. Obsolescence would be avoided with the minimum amount of disruption, with improved technology being smoothly incorporated.

16.4.2 Distributed Processing and Records Management: Three Examples

The evolution of data processing from a centralized back-office function to a distributed front-office function is a development which has enormous implications for records management. Distributed processing came about as a means for DP/MIS departments to bring computing power to end users. Having such a system in place allows a variety of records-management functions to be attached at various points or nodes in the network and then be used in conjunction with integrated information systems throughout the organization. Let's go through a few examples of such applications, so that the concept can be more thoroughly understood.

Example 1. When a document is at a point of transition in the records life cycle—for example, from its active to inactive stage—its treatment in a records-management system changes. In a traditional paper-based system all copies but the original are destroyed and the original is then stored (perhaps at an off-site location).

Today, new document or image-handling tools, such as the optical character reader (OCR), allow the records manager to store the inactive document in the company's central data base via the OCR. At this stage, the paper original becomes redundant and can be eliminated.

During its inactive life, which may last from a few months to a few years depending upon your company's needs, this inactive record may be stored on any of a number of media ranging from magnetic to optical disk. In the next example we will look at what could happen when this document reaches the end of its inactive phase.

Example 2. Let us presume that this same document has reached the end of its inactive phase and because of its content or legal status, the document should be archived. A COM unit is utilized to produce a microform record of the document, which is then safely and inexpensively stored off-site in a controlled environment. Efficient document control and records management has taken place with greatly reduced labor and time.

Example 3. In a fully automated information/image management and processing system, records can be stored in all phases of their life cycles. In this scenario, a user equipped with a terminal wishes to access a particular document. With the aid of computer-assisted retrieval, this user can call up any image. This vision of the paperless future is rapidly becoming reality.

16.4.3 The Future

In all of these examples, distributed systems allow for the attachment or addition of records-management functions at discrete points in the system. Users are given great records access and freedom. Additionally, improvements and modifications can be incorporated incrementally without disruption. In fact, changes, such as the substitution of an optical disk library for a microform library, can take place transparently to users. They will only be aware of an improvement in response time. In such a way change can be incorporated and obsolescence avoided. As stated in the beginning of this chapter, provisions for change must be made throughout the design, implementation, and operating phases of the new system.

QUESTIONS AND ANSWERS

Q. What benefits can be expected from using state-of-the-art office automation?

A. First, when used properly, new automated equipment will increase a firm's productivity. Second, new systems may help a company to better fulfill its corporate objectives if those objectives are clearly defined at the outset of the systems' selection process.

Q. How can management insure that the gains in productivity will be achieved?

A. Several methods must be employed. The firm must institute an on-going process of education for the system's users. The records manager should act as a source of information and a coordinator of user needs. The manager should also monitor user performance and stay abreast of new, emerging technology.

Q. What future trends can be expected in the realm of office automation?

A. Computer processing will become still cheaper and faster. Fiber optic technology should speed data communications and enable the integrated digital network of the 1990s.

APPENDICES

EQUIPMENT INVENTORY FORM

	Number	Cubic Feet		Lineal Inches	
		@	TOTAL	@	TOTAL

STANDARD FILE CABINETS

Letter Size

5 drawer	____	____	____	____	____
4 drawer	____	____	____	____	____
3 drawer	____	____	____	____	____
2 drawer	____	____	____	____	____

Legal Size

5 drawer	____	____	____	____	____
4 drawer	____	____	____	____	____
3 drawer	____	____	____	____	____
2 drawer	____	____	____	____	____

LATERAL FILE CABINETS (30" wide)

Letter Size

5 drawer	____	____	____	____	____
4 drawer	____	____	____	____	____
3 drawer	____	____	____	____	____
2 drawer	____	____	____	____	____

Legal Size

5 drawer	____	____	____	____	____
4 drawer	____	____	____	____	____
3 drawer	____	____	____	____	____
2 drawer	____	____	____	____	____

	Number	Cubic Feet		Lineal Inches	
		@	TOTAL	@	TOTAL

LATERAL FILE CABINETS (36" wide)

Letter Size

5 drawer	____	____	____	____	____
4 drawer	____	____	____	____	____
3 drawer	____	____	____	____	____
2 drawer	____	____	____	____	____

Legal Size

5 drawer	____	____	____	____	____
4 drawer	____	____	____	____	____
3 drawer	____	____	____	____	____
2 drawer	____	____	____	____	____

LATERAL FILE CABINETS (42" wide)

Letter Size

5 drawer	____	____	____	____	____
4 drawer	____	____	____	____	____
3 drawer	____	____	____	____	____
2 drawer	____	____	____	____	____

Legal Size

5 drawer	____	____	____	____	____
4 drawer	____	____	____	____	____
3 drawer	____	____	____	____	____
2 drawer	____	____	____	____	____

	Number	Cubic Feet		Lineal Inches	
		@	TOTAL	@	TOTAL

Card Files

3x5 Card Size	____	____	____	____	____
4x6 Card Size	____	____	____	____	____
5x8 Card Size	____	____	____	____	____
Tab Card	____	____	____	____	____

Plan Files

Horizontal 1" drawer	____	____	____	____	____
Horizontal 2 ½" drawer	____	____	____	____	____
Hanging	____	____	____	____	____
Roll Files	____	____	____	____	____
Special	____	____	____	____	____

MISCELLANEOUS

Book Case	____	____	____	____	____
Shelving, Steel	____	____	____	____	____
Shelving, Wooden	____	____	____	____	____
Supply Cabinet	____	____	____	____	____
Tub File	____	____	____	____	____
Voucher File (5 drawer)	____	____	____	____	____
Voucher File (10 drawer)	____	____	____	____	____
Standard Storage Box (Record Center)	____	____	____	____	____
Oversized File Cabinets	____	____	____	____	____
3 Drawer Jumbo	____	____	____	____	____
4 Drawer Jumbo	____	____	____	____	____
Transfer File (Large Corrugated)	____	____	____	____	____

	Number	Cubic Feet		Lineal Inches	
		@	TOTAL	@	TOTAL

OTHER EQUIPMENT

_____	_____	_____	_____	_____	_____
_____	_____	_____	_____	_____	_____
_____	_____	_____	_____	_____	_____
_____	_____	_____	_____	_____	_____
_____	_____	_____	_____	_____	_____
_____	_____	_____	_____	_____	_____
_____	_____	_____	_____	_____	_____
_____	_____	_____	_____	_____	_____
_____	_____	_____	_____	_____	_____
_____	_____	_____	_____	_____	_____
_____	_____	_____	_____	_____	_____
_____	_____	_____	_____	_____	_____
_____	_____	_____	_____	_____	_____
_____	_____	_____	_____	_____	_____
_____	_____	_____	_____	_____	_____
_____	_____	_____	_____	_____	_____
_____	_____	_____	_____	_____	_____
_____	_____	_____	_____	_____	_____
_____	_____	_____	_____	_____	_____
_____	_____	_____	_____	_____	_____
_____	_____	_____	_____	_____	_____
_____	_____	_____	_____	_____	_____
_____	_____	_____	_____	_____	_____

TOTAL   _____   _____   _____   _____   _____

RECORDS-MANAGEMENT STUDY— SECRETARIAL QUESTIONNAIRE

1)   What is your present job title?

_____

2)   What percentage of your day do you spend on filing and files maintenance?

(   )

3)   Do you like to do filing?

Yes (   )   No (   )

4)   In your opinion, which of the following statements most accurately describes your boss's attitude toward secretaries:

He/she values secretaries highly   (   )
He/she values secretaries somewhat   (   )
He/she doesn't value secretaries
  adequately   (   )

5)   What suggestions, if any, do you have to improve secretarial services?

_____

_____

_____

6)   Who handles most of your filing?

I do myself   (   )
Another secretary/clerk   (   )
My boss   (   )
Other   (Explain)_____

7)   Who set up your current filing system?

Self   (   )
Boss   (   )
Someone else in your
  department   (   )
Other Explain_____

8)   Are you familiar enough with your boss's filing system so
     that you could find a file in his absence?

     Yes   ( )
     No   ( )
     Not sure   ( )

9)   Could your boss easily find a file in your absence?

     Yes   ( )
     No   ( )
     Don't Know   ( )

10) What percentage of the time do you not find a file, or it
     takes an inordinate amount of time to find a file?

     _____%

11) Who decides where each document is filed?

     Self   ( )
     Boss   ( )

12) Is secretarial staff in your department trained to protect
     records in the event of an emergency?

     Yes   ( )
     No   ( )

13) Do you feel support staff is provided enough orientation and
     training in the records policies and procedures of a) your
     department, and b) the professional staff member to whom
     they are assigned?

	(a) Department	(b) Exempt Staff
Yes, orientation and training are sufficient	( )	( )
	( )	( )

(14) How are your department's files organized?

     Subject   ( )
     Numerical   ( )
     By color   ( )
     Chronological   ( )
     Don't know   ( )
     Other (Explain) _____

15) Are your files shared by other departments?
    Yes ( )
    No ( )

    a.   Do you access files from other departments?

         Yes ( )
         No ( )

    b.   If yes, do you have difficulty retrieving these re-
         cords?

         Yes ( )
         No ( )

16) Do you have a manual which explains policies and procedures
    for filing?

    Yes ( )
    No ( )

17) Do you think a manual would help you in maintaining your
    files?

    Help substantially   ( )
    Help somewhat   ( )
    Makes no difference   ( )

18) What effect do you think a manual would have on others who
    must access your files?

    Help substantially   ( )
    Help somewhat   ( )
    Makes no difference   ( )

19) Overall, would you rate the current file systems as:

    Excellent   ( )
    Very good   ( )
    Good   ( )
    Fair   ( )
    Poor   ( )

20) Please describe any problems you have with the current
    filing system.

    _____

    _____

    _____

21) Have you any suggestions for improving the filing system at
     your company?

     _____

     _____

     _____

                    THANK YOU FOR YOUR PARTICIPATION!

RECORDS-MANAGEMENT STUDY—
PROFESSIONAL QUESTIONNAIRE

1) Who handles most of your filing in a) the department and b) your personal files?

	Department	Personal
Own secretary	( )	( )
Someone else's secretary	( )	( )
A department clerk	( )	( )
Self	( )	( )
Central files person	( )	( )
Other (Explain)	( )	( )

2) Who set up your current departmental filing system?

Self	( )
Own secretary/clerk	( )
Previous professional staff	( )
Someone else in your department	( )
Other Explain_____	( )

3) Are you familiar enough with your secretary's filing system that you could find a file if she were absent or on vacation?

Yes	( )
No	( )
Not sure	( )

4) Could your secretary easily find a file in your absence?

Yes	(-)
No	( )
Don't Know	( )

5) When retrieving departmental files, what percentage of the time do you not find a file, or think it takes an inordinate amount of time to find a file?

_____ %

6) Is there an index to the files in your department?

Yes	( )
No	( )
Don't know	( )

7)   Who decides where each document is filed? (please indicate
     person)

     _____

8)   When retrieving information, please check which system of
     retrieval would most suit your needs:

     Subject   (   )
     Author   (   )
     Company   (   )
     Document title   (   )
     Keyword   (   )
     Client name   (   )
     Number/date   (   )
     Plaintiff/defendant   (   )
     State   (   )
     Product   (   )
     Other (Explain)   (   )

     _____

     _____

9)   Is your staff trained to protect working records in the
     event of an emergency?

     Yes   (   )
     No   (   )

10) Does your department utilize a corporate records retention
     schedule?

     Yes   (   )
     No   (   )
     Don't Know   (   )

11) In the last three years, have you had records retrieved from
     the off-site Records Center?

     Yes   (   )
     No   (   )

12) How often do you ask the off-site Records Center to retrieve
     records?

     Weekly   (   )
     Monthly   (   )
     Quarterly   (   )
     Semi-annually   (   )
     Other (Explain) (   ) _____

     _____

13) Please indicate the volume of records you have retrieved from the off-site Records Center during the last year.

Number of files   (   )
Number of boxes   (   )

14) Do you feel the existing department filing system is effective when searching for stored records?

Yes   (   )   No   (   )

15) Do you feel that employees are provided with adequate orientation and training in filing policies and procedures?

Yes   (   )   No   (   )

16) Please indicate how your department's files organized?

Subject   (   )
Numerical   (   )
By color   (   )
Chronological   (   )
Don't know   (   )
Other (Explain)   _____

17) Is file information shared by other departments/professionals?

Yes (   )   No   (   )

18) Who determines when records should be transferred to off-site storage or destroyed?

Self   (   )
Retention schedules   (   )
Company policy   (   )
Other (Explain)   (   )

_____

19) Do you have a manual which explains policies and procedures for filing?

Yes (   )
No   (   )

20) Do you think a manual would help you in maintaining your files?

    Help substantially   (   )
    Help somewhat   (   )
    Makes no difference   (   )

21) What effect do you think a manual would have on others who must access your departmental files?

    Help substantially   (   )
    Help somewhat   (   )
    Makes no difference   (   )

22) Do you utilize automated tools to store and retrieve documents?

    Yes   (   )   No   (   )

23) If yes, please list all that apply:

    Computer database   (   )
    Microfiche reader   (   )
    CRT Terminal   (   )
    Other (Explain)   (   )

    _____

    _____

24) Are your files fire protected and/or required to be locked for file integrity?

    Yes   (   )   No   (   )

25) Overall, would you rate the current file systems as:

    Excellent   (   )
    Very good   (   )
    Good   (   )
    Fair   (   )
    Poor   (   )

26) If rated as fair or poor, please explain why: _____

    _____

    _____

27) Are your current departmental files overcrowded?

Yes   ( )
No   ( )
No, but will be soon   ( )

28) Please describe any problems you have with the current
     filing system in your department.

_____

_____

_____

29) Have you any suggestions for improving the filing system at
     your company?

_____

_____

_____

THANK YOU FOR YOUR PARTICIPATION!

RECORDS-MANAGEMENT ORGANIZATIONS

Administrative Management Society
AMS Building
Maryland Road
Willow Grove, PA 19090

American Management Association
135 West Fiftieth Street
New York, NY 10020

Association for Information and Image Management
1100 Wayne Avenue
Silver Spring, MD 20910

Association of Records Managers and Administrators, Inc.
4200 Somerset
Suite 215
Prairie Village, KS 66208

Association for Systems Management
2487 L Street, NW
Washington, DC 20036

Data Management Association
505 Busse Highway
Park Ridge, IL 60068

International Information/Word Processing Association
AMS Building
Maryland Road
Willow Grove, PA 19090

National Business Forms Association
300 North Lee Street
Alexandria, VA 22314

National Office Products Association
301 North Fairfax Street
Alexandria, VA 22314

National Records Management Council
60 East Forty-second Street
New York, NY 10017

Society for Management Information Systems
Illinois Institute of Technology
10 West Thirty-first Street
Chicago, IL 60616

Society of American Archivists Library
P.O. Box 8198 University of Illinois
Chicago Circle
Chicago, IL 60680

PUBLICATIONS FOR RECORDS MANAGERS

Administrative Management
Geyer-McAllister Publications
51 Madison Avenue
New York, NY 10010

American Archivist
The Monumental Printing Co.
3110 Elm Avenue
Baltimore, MD 21211

Business Computer Systems
Cahners Publishing Co.
3381 Ocean Drive
Vero Beach, FL 32963

Business Graphics
Graphic Arts Publishing Company
7373 North Lincoln Avenue
Chicago, IL 60646

Byte
McGraw Hill Inc.
70 Main Street
Peterborough, NH 03458

Computer Decisions
Hayden Publishing Co.
10 Mulholland Drive
Hasbrouck Heights, NJ 07604

Datamation
F.D. Thompson Publications, Inc.
35 Mason Street
Greenwich, CT 06830

Form
National Business Forms Association
300 North Lee Street
Alexandria, VA 22314

Format
Association of Business Forms Manufacturers
19034 Mills Choice Road
Gaithersburg, MD 20760

Information and Records Management
Information and Records Management, Inc.
250 Fulton Road
Hempstead, NY 11550

Infosystems
Hitchcock Publishing Company
Hitchcock Building
Wheaton, IL 60187

Infoworld
CW Communications Inc., Suite C–200
1060 Marsh Road
Menlo Park, CA 94025

Interface Age
McPheters, Wolf & Jones
17000 Marquardt Avenue
Cerritos, CA 90701

Journal of Data Management
Data Management Association
505 Busse Highway
Park Ridge, IL 60068

Journal of Information and Image Management
AIIM
1100 Wayne Avenue
Silver Spring, MD 20910

List
Redgate Publishing Co.
3381 Ocean Drive
Vero Beach, FL 32963

Management Technology
11 Commerce Street
Norwalk, CT 06850

Management World
Administrative Management Society
AMS Building, Maryland Road
Willow Grove, PA 19090

Microfilm Techniques
250 Fulton Avenue
Hempstead, NY 11550

Modern Office Procedures
The Industrial Publishing Co.
614 Superior Avenue West
Cleveland, OH 44113

Personal Computing
Hayden Publishing Co.
10 Mulholland Drive
Hasbrouck Heights, NJ 07604

Popular Computing
McGraw-Hill Inc.
70 Main Street
Peterborough, NH 03458

The Office
Office Publications, Inc.
1200 Summer Street
Stamford, CT 06804

Office Products News
United Technical Publications, Inc.
645 Stewart Avenue
Garden City, NY 11530

Prologue: The Journal of the National Archives
National Archives Building
Washington, DC 20408

Records Management Quarterly
Association of Records Managers and Administrators Inc.
4200 Somerset, Suite 215
Prairie Village, KS 66208

Systems
United Business Publications, Inc.
200 Madison Avenue
New York, NY 10016

Training
Lakewood Publications
50 South Ninth Street
Minneapolis, MN 55402

Training & Development
American Society for Training and Development
600 Maryland Avenue SW
Suite 305
Washington, DC 20024

Word Processing Report
Geyer-McAllister Publications
51 Madison Avenue
New York, NY 10010

Word Processing World
Geyer-McAllister Publications
51 Madison Avenue
New York, NY 10010

Words
International Information Word Processing Association
AMS Building, Maryland Road
Willow Grove, PA 19090

Glossary of Terms

Access time.　(1) The time in which a machine is operating and available for use. (2) The time required to receive information once the computer has been signaled.

Acoustics.　An ergonomic consideration relating to the level of noise within an office and workstation. Noise can be controlled through the engineering and/ or the architecture of the space.

Active files.　Files that contain records that are used frequently.

Active records.　Those records consulted in the performance of current administrative work, or records in working files.

Actuating.　(1) Implementing or starting a process. (2) Putting a process into action.

Administrative support.　The job function of assisting management in performing tasks of a nontyping nature.

Alterable information.　Information in digital form that can regularly undergo deletions, additions, and revisions and is ever changing.

Analog.　Operating by directly measurable quantities from a continuum as opposed to operating in a digital manner.

Analytical staff.　Personnel who collect information and data and analyze and define what is revealed by both statistical data and subjective collection of feelings and thoughts.

Anthropometry. The study of human body measurements for the scaling of sizes, heights, and shapes of furniture and equipment to the dimensions of workers.

Applications software. Sets of instructions used to tell the computer how to do a specific job.

Archival record. Records once considered current files that are now semiactive or inactive and are retained for legal, fiscal, administrative, or historical reasons.

Archive. To store information.

Archives repository. An area established to preserve records for the benefit of posterity.

ASCII (American Standard Code for Information Interchange). A character coding system used for data storage and transmission.

Asynchronous transmission. The mode of transmission between equipment with different protocols, in which a "start" signal precedes and a "stop" signal follows each character to check synchronization, and characters move one at a time along the line.

Back-office processing. Functions associated traditionally with the data-processing group in a firm that concerns the internal functions of a firm. Payroll and large number-crunching applications are typical back-office activities.

Bar graph. A chart that presents information through the use of horizontal or vertical bars.

Baseband. A digital pathway ranging from around 1 million bits per second to 50 million bits per second.

BASIC. This language (Beginner's All Purpose Symbolic Instruction Code) was developed in the mid–1960s at Dartmouth College as a simple, basic interactive language.

Batch stream. A method by which a computer deals with doing a number of tasks. A batch stream is a queue of tasks. The computer takes on one task, finishes it, and moves on to the next.

Batched. Sent in a group; usually refers to the grouping of information and its transmission to an information system.

Baud rate. In telecommunications, the rate of signaling speed. The rate of speed expressed in bauds is equal to the number of signaling elements per second.

Benchmark. A point of reference used in determining a plus or minus accomplishment.

Benchmark position. A job which has been measured; performance criteria have been established that provide a determination as to the worth and value of the position.

Best-guesstimate study. A study in which estimates of work loads and time expended are based on input from the support staff being studied.

Beta site. A site, usually a department within a company, that is used as a test case for an office automation feasibility study.

Bit. A binary digit. The smallest element of binary machine language represented by a magnetized or optical spot on a recording surface. Six to 8 bits are required to form a character or byte.

Bits per second (BPS). A measure of the speed of transmission in information systems.

Black box. An intermediate interpretation device or program used with equipment having different protocols; often called a translator.

Blip. A small opaque mark recorded beneath all or selected microimages in CAR systems. The blips are utilized by readers or reader-printers to advance the film to a specified frame.

Boilerplate. Prewritten and presorted documents that are used repeatedly, such as letters or contracts, to which variable fill-in information can be added via the keyboard.

Broadband. Common-cable TV cable that employs modems and allows multiple streams of data to be transmitted simultaneously.

Bubble memory. A magnetic memory that must be accessed serially but has a higher storage density than many other storage media.

Bus network. A network that consists of a length of co-axial cable (called a bus) along which individual devices tap into the communications cable. There is no centralized hub. Signals from one station move along the bus in both directions to all stations tapped into the cable.

Byte. A sequence of adjacent binary digits that represent a character.

CAD (computer-aided design). The use of the computer's processing capability to generate representations of aesthetic or functional ideas. This capability is often employed by engineers, architects, or artists.

CAI (computer-assisted instruction). The use of electronic equipment as a training tool.

CAR (computer-assisted retrieval). The overall concept of wedding computer-based storage and software ability to the electronic retrieval of non-paper-based document images.

Carbon copy collection. The collection of the copies of all typing accomplished during a set time period.

Cassette. (1) A double-core container enclosing processed microfilm designed to be inserted into readers, reader-printers, and retrieval devices. (2) A light-proof container of rigid metal or plastic containing film for daylight loading in cameras. (3) A container for magnetic tape.

CAT (computer-aided transcription). The capture of keystrokes onto a magnetic media that is then processed through a computer and printed out.

CBMS (computer-based message system). The overall concept of communicating electronically and bypassing the standard paper medium. A system that allows the transmission of text messages to and from the users who are connected to the computer on which the system is based. Electronic mail is one application example.

CBX (computerized branch exchange). A digitally controlled communication switching device.

Centralization. The location of one or more functions at a single site with a central support staff organization.

Checkpointing. The process of shuffling discrete quantities of data in and out of main memory as they are needed by the processor.

CIM (computer input microfilm). A microform based information storage and retrieval system.

COBOL. This acronym stands for Common Business Oriented Language which was developed in the late 1950s, and it is intended for use in the solutions of problems in business data processing.

Cold type. Typesetting on typewriterlike machines or by photocomposition.

COM (computer output microfilm). The overall concept of accessing computer-based information via microfilm. The micrographic form of output whereby microfilm and microfiche are produced directly as computer output, without the intermediate hard-copy and microfilming steps.

Communicating word processor. A text-editing system equipped with electronic circuitry that enables it to transmit data to, or receive data from, a computer, another word processor, or in some cases, a telex or other machine.

Communication processing. The manipulation and distribution of information through video display terminals.

Compaction. A reduction in the number of characters per page achieved by reducing the length of the lines and size of the characters.

Computer graphics. Graph representations produced on the computer.

Computer output mailing system. A mailing system that allows computer-printed continuous forms to be fed into equipment that automatically bursts the forms, inserts them into envelopes, designates zip code breaks, and meter-stamps them for mailing.

Computer teleconferencing. A telecommunications process in which words, data, facsimile images, and voice are transmitted from one geographical location to another.

Conference method. A training session in which trainees are encouraged to express themselves orally and to exchange and compare ideas.

Conventional planning. The designing of office space with many enclosed areas divided by permanent walls.

Cost avoidance. The elimination or reduction of costs in a budget through elimination of the necessity for temporary help, overtime, or additional budgeted personnel.

Cost-benefit. The hard- and soft-dollar savings achieved by implementation of an automated system.

Counting-documents method. A method used to determine the amount of typing produced whereby any completed task (letter, report) is counted as one document and documents are then totaled over a set time period (a day, a week, and so forth).

Counting-lines method. A method of determining the amount of typing by counting the lines produced within a given period of time.

CPU (central processing unit). The information storage area shared by multiple data- or word-processing terminals.

CRM (certified records manager).   A professional classification granted to records managers who have completed prerequisite training and met the accreditation requirements for certification.

CRT (cathode ray tube).   An electronic vacuum tube, similar to a television picture tube, that displays text as it is entered from the keyboard.

Daisy-wheel printer.   In word processing and computer systems, a device which features an interchangeable wheel-shaped print mechanism on which characters are represented by embossed metal slugs at the ends of spokes.

Data base.   The compilation and storage of information consisting of data and text for the purposes of access, retrieval, and printout.

Data-base management.   The management of data via machine storage rather than paper files.

Data processing.   The manipulation of numbers through various computations to deliver meaningful totals and create useful statistical information.

Data retrieval.   The recall of prestored material from a system.

DBMS (data-base management system).   A computer software that handles the storage and retrieval of records stored in direct-access computer data bases.

Decentralization.   The locating of minicomputers and terminals, as well as word processors with standalone intelligence, in the various departments of an organization.

Decision package.   A document that identifies and describes a specific activity in such a manner that management can (1) evaluate it and rank it against other activities competing for limited resources and (2) decide whether to approve or disapprove it.

Decision support system.   Special software that provides significant aids for financial planning, portfolio analysis, tax planning, and market analysis, and for projecting business situations that require mathematical formula calculations.

Desk manual.   A guidebook to particular duties and tasks that remains with the job and the workstation for which it was written.

Determinants of effective leadership.   The situational elements that dictate which type of style will be successful in a given situation (for example, the size of the organization, the amount of interaction, the personalities of leader and group members, the level on which decision-making is encouraged, the organization's health).

Digital.   Data transmission in the form of discrete units; a process that transmits data by translating sound waves into on/off digital pulses.

Disk drive.   The device into which a disk is inserted that reads information, writes information, and physically spins the disk to find information.

Disk pack.   A stack of hard disks that share a spindle, have a standard specification, and a large storage capacity.

Display-oriented text-editing system.   In word processing, a text-editing system that utilizes a CRT display with keyboard for the input of text. Information entered at the keyboard is displayed on the screen and subsequently can be printed or recorded on various media.

Distributed system. A system that provides decentralized memory and storage capacity yet allows network connections and communication over dissimilar peripherals.

Documentary information. Information that is recorded in some kind of permanent form, such as in written or printed materials.

Documentation. (1) A memo that describes an incident clearly and fairly and thus permits a problem to be confronted supportively and with just cause. (2) Observation of a machine in operation, to determine its usefulness to an office.

Dot matrix. An array of points in ink, light, or similar image-forming elements that are used to form alphanumeric characters.

Downtime. Time when equipment cannot be used because of malfunction.

Dry silver microfilm. A type of microfilm used in source document cameras and COM recorders, which is sensitive to light but which is developed by heat without the wet chemicals characteristic of conventional silver halide microfilm.

DSK (Dvorak simplified keyboard). Developed in 1932, this typewriter keyboard makes it possible for 70 percent of the work to be done on the home row and a majority of the stroking to be done by the right hand.

EBCDIC (extended binary coded decimal information code). An eight-bit alphanumeric code used on all IBM computers.

Editing. The correction, refinement, or revision of written material.

Electronic blackboard. A blackboard developed by Bell Laboratories, division of AT&T, that transmits graphics and handwritten communications over telephone lines for viewing on video monitors in distant locations.

Electronic data processing. The manipulation of data through the use of electronic computers.

Electronic file. A logical grouping of information, data, or text that is stored and accessed on a computer as a discrete whole.

Electronic mail. A system of communicating messages electronically to a recipient who receives either a hard copy or a visually displayed message on a CRT screen. The message may be transmitted electronically by facsimile, communicating word processors, computer-based message systems, public-carrier-based systems, public postal services, or private and public teletypes.

Electronic mailbox. A computer-based message system on which messages can be left until the user makes an inquiry.

Electronic proof. Database storage from which information can be recalled and reconstructed by electronic means. Proofing is accomplished by viewing the copy and editing it right at the video display terminal.

Enclosure and access needs. These space design needs may be determined by type of work performed. Space design must also recognize the need to access areas such as restrooms and lunchrooms so as not to contribute to a congested traffic pattern.

Engineering approach. An approach to the analysis of office functions based upon the detailed study of individual jobs, which are broken down into their vital components, to see whether they can be eliminated altogether or combined with other jobs.

Ergonomic concerns. Workstation features designed to promote optimum employee performance.

Ergonomics. Facilities planning focused on the aesthetics of the workstation and its surrounding space, for example, the needs for privacy, a smooth flow of paperwork and communication, balanced territorial and social concerns, adequate access to electrical and communications circuits, and proper lighting, climate, acoustics, and color/decor.

Event schedule. A written timetable of steps to be taken to accomplish a goal (for example, a step-by-step plan to implement office automation).

Evidential-value records. Records that show how an organization came into being, how it developed, how it was organized, what its function has been, and the results of its activities.

External information. Data that originate outside an organization, such as information concerning the products and services of competitors.

Facsimile (also called *fax*). A process that involves the transmission of an exact copy over communications lines; facsimile combines replication and distribution functions, since it duplicates exact copies of graphs, pictures, and other materials and transmits them to other locations.

Feasibility concepts. Aspects of the traditional office that must be examined by the feasibility study and what changes are likely to occur.

Fiber optics. The technique of converting communication signals to light pulses that are sent over strands of hair-thin glass fibers.

File. An organized, named collection of data records treated as a unit and stored on some external storage device.

File classification system. A logical and systematic arrangement of files into subject groups or categories based on some definite scheme of relationship using numbers or letters for identification.

File server. An extension of local disks in a personal computer environment that allows many workstations to share a common data library. A file server might be a large disk or disk pack to hold files accessible by all users with access to that library.

Filing. The activity and manner of keeping, organizing, and maintaining information in an orderly and retrievable form.

Financial lease. A lease arrangement whereby the lessor recovers the full cost of the equipment plus expenses and a profit. The lessee may receive title to the equipment at the end of the lease period.

First-line supervision. Management of ongoing operations at the department level.

Fixed information. Hard copy, microfilm, and other image storage that is unalterable in time and format.

Fixed-frame video. A video process in which a new picture is transmitted several times per minute; the monitor displays an image for a number of seconds, until the next frame is received.

Floppy disks.   A small flexible disk that has become the primary storage medium for personal computers.

Flowchart.   A diagram that uses symbols to illustrate the flow of work and paper through the office, from origin to completion.

Formatting.   The process of composing the basic form or style of text.

FORTRAN.   The first widely used procedure-oriented language (a way of expressing commands to a computer in a form somewhat similar to language) originating in the mid–1950s was labeled FORTRAN, an acronym from the words "formula translation."

Front-office processing.   Processing functions that are performed by end users who deal with the firm's clientele directly or with the firm's nontechnical personnel. Word processing, database management, and spreadsheet analysis are typical front-office activities.

Full duplex.   A communication attribute in which a given device can transmit and receive information simultaneously.

Full-motion video.   A closed-circuit television setup in which all activity is captured and transmitted to another location.

Gantt chart.   A graphic illustration (developed by Henry L. Gantt) of scheduled work on a vertical scale (function) and horizontal scale (estimated time).

Guideline method.   A technique for interpreting and reflecting the value of jobs in the marketplace.

Half-duplex.   A type of transmission in which signals travel in both directions, but only in one direction at a time. Half-duplex is satisfactory for most transmissions between computers and terminals.

Hard disks.   A disk resembling a phonograph record that is used to store large quantities of information that can be updated. Hard disks are used in personal microcomputers but are known primarily as the storage medium for minicomputers and larger mainframes.

Hard dollars.   Expenditures of money that can be measured and controlled (such as the salaries of employees or cost of equipment).

Hard-dollar savings.   Those salary and fringe benefit costs that can be saved through reduction of staff.

Hardware.   A basic piece of equipment.

Hierarchy of needs.   Abraham Maslow identified a hierarchy or ladder of needs and theorized that people can attempt to satisfy a higher-level need only after satisfying at least some of the lower-level needs.

Historical data approach.   An approach to studying an office that involves gathering information from past records about the time and amount of work associated with a certain job.

Horizontal software.   Generic software designed to perform a general application in any business.

Icon. A picture or symbol on a video display that depicts or symbolizes a computer function. When a user points to the icon with a "mouse" (a pointer displayed on the screen), the computer performs the function depicted.

Image copying. The process of replicating images through the use of OCR, laser copiers, or facsimile duplication.

Image network. See *electronic blackboard.*

Image printing. A printing process in which the entire image is produced in hard-copy form from a stored picture of that image in a cathode ray or an internal source.

Impact printer. An output unit that prints characters on paper by physical contact.

Inactive files. Files that must be retained only because of legal guidelines or that are awaiting destruction at a time specified by the company's retention schedule.

Inactive records. Records infrequently referred to. Inactive records often are transferred to a records center or other storage area.

Incident process. The presentation of an incident or a problem situation in only a few sentences, designed to force trainees to ask careful questions in order to obtain additional pertinent facts.

Incremental budget. A budget in which expenses for the coming year are based on the preceding year or on some average of preceding years.

Information management. Supervision and control over a system that creates, gathers, processes, replicates, distributes, stores, and destroys the information utilized by an organization.

Information processing. An integrated system created by the merger of data processing and word processing. In an information processing system, all forms of business information (data, text, image, and voice) are freely accessible to workers at all levels, within necessary security restrictions.

Informational-value records. Records that provide information that should be preserved for future generations.

Input. The entering of source data or text into a system for processing.

Instruction. A coded sequence of binary numbers that is interpreted by the processor and causes the computer to perform a primary function.

Integrated circuit. An electronic circuit made up of a large number of components, semiconductors, or transistors fabricated onto a computer chip. ICs are the building blocks of computer processors.

Integrated software. A type of software which is becoming increasingly dominant and which features programs that combine the functions of word processing, spreadsheets, graphics, communications, and sometimes accounting, often by using "windows" to promote ease of use and entry from one function to another.

Integrated systems. Systems that permit multiple functions to occur simultaneously and permit the user to combine text and data in a single application with little or no difficulty.

Intelligent copiers. Copiers that can electronically store materials such as often-used forms and thereby eliminate the need for hard-copy storage facilities.

Intelligent typewriter. An enhanced typewriter that has the ability to perform certain difficult typing tasks automatically, such as centering of characters and decimal alignment.

Interconnection. That part of the integrated electronic phase in which various electronic or technological components are tied together.

Interface. This term applies to an information exchange capability either between two machines, two people, or a machine and a person.

Internal information. Information generated within the organization (examples are production schedules, payrolls, policy manuals, and organizational directives).

Job classification. The analysis and rating of jobs according to predetermined classes (the same or similar task groupings).

Job description. A written, organized presentation of the duties involved in a specific job.

Job enrichment. The process of heightening both task efficiency and human satisfaction by providing greater scope for personal achievement and recognition in jobs, more challenging and responsible work, and more opportunity for individual advancement and growth.

Job evaluation. Any formal procedure for appraising, classifying, and weighing a set of functions.

Job redesign. The rethinking of a job and what it contains, with a view toward expanding the job by including in it more horizontal and vertical activities.

Job specifications. The minimum requirements of a job.

Keyboarding. The process of logging data into a system and assigning to the data an index designation for future distribution and retrieval.

Keystroke counters. Electronic counting devices that count the number of keystrokes produced on input devices.

Knowledge worker. Any management, professional, or clerical worker who processes information for use in decision-making.

LAN (local area network). A network that is designed for a particular installation to connect various elements of its office systems. A LAN could connect large computers, personal computers, remote terminals, or telephone lines.

LAN (local area network) duplex. An interlinked arrangement of computers (usually microprocessors) that permits a single computer in the network both to operate independently and to access directly other computers in a network over a limited area (1,500 feet to three miles).

Large-scale integration (LSI). A manufacturing technique in which large numbers of highly miniaturized electronic circuits are combined or integrated on a single chip of silicon or other semiconductor material. LSI has permitted very significant reductions in the cost of microprocessor and memory circuits.

Laser (light amplification by stimulated emission of radiation). A device that uses the natural oscillations of atoms to generate coherent, focused electromagnetic radiation. Lasers are used to cut optical disks and to read them.

Laser printing. A printing process similar to image printing, except that it operates by laser control rather than direct impact.

Lateral file. A drawer file turned sideways, with the side opening to the front.

Leader-member-relations task structure. The extent to which leaders and subordinates get along with each other.

Learning curve. A measure of the rate of learning in relation to the length of training.

Life cycle. A system that meets the objectives of the organization. When the office becomes too crowded, equipment is out of date, and procedures are no longer relevant, a new system cycle should be implemented.

Life span or cycle of a record. The successive stages undergone by a record (creation, processing, storage, retrieval, and retention or destruction).

Line counting. The electronic or manual process of counting typed lines.

Line graph. A chart that uses various types of lines to show fluctuations in a value or quantity over a period of time.

List management. In word processing systems, the ability to process a prerecorded list of names or other items, selecting only those that meet certain specified criteria.

Logging. The act of putting information onto a log sheet or into a system.

LSI (large-scale integration) circuits. The process of mass-producing electronic circuits by etching up to 10,000 transistors onto silicon chips.

Machine dictation. The act of speaking into a microphone and recording ideas on magnetic tape for later transcription onto paper by a secretary or word-processing operator.

Magnetic media. Any type of magnetically charged belt, card, disk, or tape used to store, make corrections, erase, or rewrite documents.

Mailgram. Correspondence sent via the E-COM system, an electronic mail facility.

Main memory. The storage capacity built into the computer itself.

Mainframe. The central processing unit (CPU) that houses the hardware, software, and operating controls of a computer.

Make-ready and put-away time. The time spent dealing with roughly drafted reports that can be eliminated through the use of proper equipment.

Management by objective (MBO). A management strategy that focuses on goals.

Managerial workstation. A work area designed for the professional knowledge worker. It usually contains a computer terminal with time management controls, text editing features, electronic mail capabilities, files processing capability, and other features.

Manipulation. The process of rearranging the format of text and data (for example, changing the order of the paragraphs) to come up with the most workable form in which to present the information.

Matrix management. An organizational setup that combines centralized and decentralized characteristics.

Memory. The capacity of a computer to store information electronically. Information in main memory may be accessed at any time to allow the computer processor to complete its functions.

Memory typewriter. An enhanced typewriter featuring the most basic text-editing capabilities and a nonremovable magnetic recording medium with capacity for 25 to 100 pages.

Menu. A list on a display screen that gives the extent of available choices in response to a prompt.

Message networks. See *electronic mail.*

Microcomputer. A small standalone computer that is operated from only one console and can perform only one task at a time. Personal computers are microcomputers.

Microfacsimile. The transmission and/or reception of microimages via facsimile communication.

Microforms. A variety of micrographic media that include microfiche and microfilm, containing highly reduced microimages for storage of records.

Micrographics. The process of recording and reducing paper documents or computer-generated information on film and providing a system to store and retrieve that information.

Microprocessor. A minuscule logic circuit on a microchip of silicon that can perform over 1 million calculations per second.

Minicomputer. A minicomputer comprises a central processor, a console, and also a number of peripheral devices such as disk drives and operating terminals. More than one user can perform tasks at the same time in either a real-time or time-sharing operating environment. The minicomputer is distinguished from larger mainframes by not being suitable for massive number-crunching tasks.

MIS. An acronym for management information systems.

Mobile storage system. A storage system in which files are put on tracks in order to eliminate the need for aisles for each set of files.

Modem. A device that converts analog signals to digital signals or vice versa for transmission over telephone lines or other communication facilities.

Mouse. The electronic pointer on a video display screen with which a user designates the function he or she wants the computer to perform.

MS-DOS. A microcomputer operating system developed by Microsoft for IBM and compatible microcomputers.

MTM (measure time and motion). The measurement of time by applying time measurement units (tmu) to each singular function or task to determine time and motion standards.

Multifunction terminals. Systems based on mainframe computers or minicomputers equipped with special software that provide specific services on computer terminals; such terminals generally are used for many functions.

Multi-tasking software. This software gives a computer the capacity to simultaneously perform two functions.

Needs assessment study. A study aimed at providing an overall perspective on an organization's needs as a basis for future planning.

Network. A system that interconnects a wide assortment of information processing devices through a communications line or data base.

Networking. The linking of various information processing devices, such as word processors and data entry units, storage devices, printers, processors, and other peripherals, to send, receive, exchange, store, or reproduce information.

Node. A terminus in any sort of network. In a computer it could be a terminal, a disk drive, or a communications interface. In a PBX it would be any telephone.

Nonaction information. Information on which no action is required.

Nondocumentary information. Information that is not recorded. Usually obtained through word of mouth or personal observation.

Nonimpact printers. A printing device in which the paper is not struck but imaged by other means such as ink jet, electrostatic, or laser.

Nonoriginal input. That information already existing in a system.

Nonrecord. A convenience copy that normally is discarded when no longer needed.

Nonrecurring information. Information that is reported and used once in its lifetime.

Objective data. Data that deal with things rather than with thoughts or feelings.

OCR (optical character reader). The overall concept of scanning a paper or microfilm document and converting the image to binary digital codes for storage, transmission, or some other use. Sometimes also used to denote optical character recognition.

OD (optical disk). The overall concept of storing and retrieving data on a plastic and metal composite circular medium by means of directed laser beams.

OEM. An acronym standing for original equipment manufacturers.

OCR (optical character recognition). The process by which a system scans typewritten pages and stores the scanned characters in digital form.

Off-the-shelf applications package. Software packages sold by computer vendors or by separate software outlets. Such packages provide freedom and flexibility to experiment, as they can be obtained and used or discarded quickly and easily.

Office automation (OA). The introduction to the office systems that offer word processing as part of a bundle of office functions that include electronic mail and message distribution, electronic filing, data access, data processing, and administrative functions such as calendaring, scheduling, and tickler systems.

Offset printing. A printing process in which copies are made from an original copy produced on either a paper or a metal plate.

Online. (1) Pertaining to equipment or devices under control of the central processing unit. (2) Pertaining to a user's ability to interact with a computer. (3) Pertaining to equipment or devices under control of a COM device.

Online data base.   An integrated accumulation of machine-readable data maintained on one or more direct-access storage devices.

Online terminal.   A device that permits the interactive transmission of data to, or the reception of data from, a computer or other information-processing device via electronic digital pulses transmitted over some medium.

Open-office planning.   Designing office space with minimal enclosed areas, using movable wall panels.

Operating lease.   A lease arrangement whereby equipment is leased for a fixed sum each month. The lessor does not normally recover the full cost of the equipment over the period of the lease.

Operating-systems software.   Sets of instructions used to tell the microprocessor how to act.

Optical character reader (OCR).   A device that scans hard copy printout, reads the characters, and writes them digitally onto a disk.

Optical disk.   A disk that uses laser technology to provide high-density storage of either data or image information.

Organization chart.   A graphic presentation of the organizational structure that points out responsibility relationships.

Organizational culture.   A company's values, attitudes, and degree of competitiveness and commitment, which reflect top management's approach to decision-making.

Organizational objectives.   Company goals.

Organizational structure.   The hierarchy of authority, span of control, and areas of responsibility within an organization.

Orientation or induction training.   Training that acquaints new employees with the company's history, philosophy, policy, practices, and procedures (such as office rules and regulations or employee benefits).

Original input.   Information put into a system for the first time.

Originators.   Individuals who create information or text.

Overhead transparency.   A clear plastic sheet that, when placed on a lighted glass surface, projects the image on the sheet in magnified form onto a screen.

Overlay.   A memory management process whereby certain segments of data share the same physical location in a computer's memory while being processed. When not being processed, the segments of data are stored on disk.

PBX (private branch exchange).   An electromechanical communications device—usually a staffed switchboard.

Peripheral device.   A device not central to the operation of a computer but which is connected to it and supports it functionally.

Personal computer.   A computer designed for use by managers and professionals rather than by computer specialists.

Phase-in process.   An area-by-area approach to office automation.

Phototypesetter.   A device that converts text in digital form to printed material.

Phototypesetting. A method by which information can be reproduced efficiently through a printing process that prints characters optically by taking pictures of them at high speeds.

Pie chart. A circular diagram divided into sections ("slices") that normally is used to present information in percentages.

Pilot. A prototype installation.

Pixels. In facsimile transmission, the individual picture elements of the subject copy which are analyzed successively for their light reflective values. An appropriate signal then is transmitted and directs the receiving device in the reconstruction of successive pixels.

Plotter. A computer-driven peripheral device designed to produce graphics output in paper form.

Point method. A method of evaluation in which a range of points is assigned to a set of common factors (for example, education or skill).

Presorted mail. Mail that is sorted according to zip codes, carrier routes, and so on before mailing.

Primary group. A close-knit group whose members know the norms that govern the conduct of each member.

Problem-oriented solution. The process of identifying and isolating a problem and providing a solution to that one problem.

Processing. The manipulation of information that has been input into a system for replication and for distribution in the form of communication.

Processor. The central device within a computer that executes the instructions provided by the user.

Productivity. Measurement of the ratio of work done to time spent doing it.

Productivity gains. Improvements in employee work output.

Programmed instruction. A self-instruction method in which information is systematically presented to the trainee.

Protocol. The language in which a message sent from one machine to another is packaged and handled.

Prototype. A test situation involving installations or equipment being considered for wider use in the company.

Qualitative data. Employee perceptions of how and why things are done within the system.

Quality circles (QC). A group or circle of employees that meets to discuss how to improve the quantity and quality of work.

Quality of work life (QWL). A factor of work life that can be enriched when employees are involved in decisions affecting their work environment.

Quantitative data. Measurable work being accomplished, the type of information required by management, and the time it takes to produce such information.

RAM (random access memory). A memory device from which information may be accessed by pointing directly to its location.

Random access.   A method of finding a piece of stored data by pointing to its location and picking it out.

Real labor costs.   All labor costs, including payroll costs.

Real-time processing.   A mode of computer processing in which information about a transaction or other event is processed at the time the event occurs, as opposed to batch processing in which there is an interval of time between the occurrence of an event and the processing of information about that event.

Record.   Official document that furnishes information that is stored for future reference.

Record series.   Documents that are related in their form or content and maintained under a single filing system or as a unit because (a) the same forms are used; (b) the information relates to the same subject; (c) the information results from the same activity; or (d) the physical characteristics of the records (maps, blueprints, for example) mandate that they be kept together for convenience.

Record center.   A low-cost centralized storage area maintained to store, process, serve, and protect inactive records.

Recording density.   A measure of how tightly data bits may be stored; a measure of the storage capacity of a medium for a given space occupied.

Records format.   Formats designed to meet requirements of paper systems, micrographics, and computerized systems.

Records inventory.   A detailed listing of the volume, scope, and complexity of an organization's records in order to evaluate, appraise, and organize the collection.

Records management.   The systematic handling of documents from creation to destruction, including filing and micrographics, archiving, and destruction.

Records retention schedule.   A timetable based on the administrative reference needs and fiscal, legal, and historical requirements for the location and handling of records. Retention schedules apply to records: when they are created, while they are in use, and when they are awaiting either destruction or storage as dictated by the retention schedule.

Records series.   Identical or related records that are normally used and filed as a unit and that can be evaluated as a unit for purposes of retention or destruction.

Recurring information.   Information that an organization regularly and frequently uses, such as sales, inventory, and production reports.

Reduction ratio.   The size ratio between a film image and the original document.

Reference documents.   Documents that contain or communicate information needed to carry on the business.

Reference rate.   The number of times within a given period that a records series is accessed for information.

Relative index.   A filing and finding aid for subject names which alphabetically lists each of the topics included in a subject outline and which usually includes many additional subjects under which a search for records might be carried out. Each entry shows the file designation for records on that subject.

Replication.   The duplication of information in another form.

Reprographics.   The various techniques of replicating information with the ultimate objective of distributing it in some form. Replication techniques include printing, phototypesetting, duplicating, and COM (computer output microfilm).

Resource sharing.   The facility that enables a number of users to operate the same piece of hardware or software.

Retention period.   The period of time during which records must be maintained before final disposition. The period is usually stated in terms of years, however, it can also be dependent on an event such as the completion of a contract or the retirement of an employee.

Results-centered leadership.   Leadership that is concerned with the "work itself" approach to motivation.

Retrieval.   The recalling of stored information for reuse.

RFP.   An acronym for a request for proposal—a document prepared by a potential user addressed to a vendor which delineates the user's needs and requirements.

Ring network.   A network in which individual devices are connected in a loop or ring via a string of signal repeaters. If one device in the ring breaks down or is added to, the entire network is put out of operation.

ROM (read-only memory).   (1) The overall concept of accessing information stored on a medium which has been loaded or programmed by a manufacturer or publisher. In such devices users cannot enter their own data or updates. This meaning is typically used to refer to a class of optical disk technology. (2) Semiconductor memory circuits that contain prewritten programs or data. The content of these ROM circuits is permanent, while the content of RAM circuits is volatile.

Run-length encoding.   In facsimile systems, a technique used to compress a digital signal to increase the speed of transmission and therefore reduce costs.

Satellite communications.   Electronic telecommunications via worldwide satellite transmission.

Self-paced instruction.   Instruction through individual learning packets that consists of a planned program through which an individual moves at his or her own pace.

Semiconductor.   A material that is neither a good conductor of electricity or a good insulator of the flow of electricity. It is used in transistors to permit the flow of electricity in one direction, but not in the other direction. Semiconductors allow the bifurcation of electrical current and are therefore essential to computer processors.

Sequential access.   See *serial access.*

Serial access.   A method of finding a piece of stored data by reading through the medium from the beginning until the desired piece is found.

Serial asynchronous transmission.   A method of transmission in which the individual bits which encode a given character are transmitted in sequence and framed (preceded and followed) by additional bits which separate successively transmitted characters from one another.

Shared-logic system.   A system in which multiple video display screens and output devices simultaneously use the memory and processing powers of one computer.

Shared resource system.   In word processing, a text-editing system that combines standalone input stations capable of local operation and text storage with other components, such as printers or large-capacity disk storage or CAR systems, which are shared by the various input stations. The purpose of shared resource systems is to maximize the use of infrequently used and expensive equipment components.

Small-office microfilm (SOM).   A term used to denote a group of micrographics products designed specifically for small organizations or decentralized microfilming operations within larger organizations. SOM equipment is typically low in cost and designed for simplified use by nontechnical personnel in an office.

Smart terminal.   A microprocessor-controlled terminal that offers display and printing features not found on conventional dumb terminals. Unlike intelligent terminals, however, smart terminals are not programmable and have no integral information-processing capabilities.

Short-range strategy.   A short-term plan for implementing office automation.

Silicon chip.   See *microprocessor*.

Single-element typewriter.   A typewriter that uses a typing ball containing characters (Selectric typewriters are one example).

SNA (Systems Network Architecture). A data network product offered by IBM that allows data transfer among different office machines.

Soft dollars.   Expenditures of money that can be estimated but not controlled (for example, improved productivity through conversion from longhand to machine dictation).

Soft-dollar savings.   Reductions in expenditures that come about when management delegates work and uses time-management techniques.

Software.   A program that instructs a computer to perform operations it ordinarily cannot perform.

Standalone display system.   A self-contained word processing unit that uses its own memory and processing powers for keyboarding, storage, text editing, and printing.

Star network.   A network in which all communications pass through some form of switcher at the hub of the configuration.

Statistical approach.   An approach to studying an office that uses one or all of the following methods: historical data, work sampling, and time studies.

Storage.   The systematic preservation of information within the system in some form.

Study team.   A group of people responsible for conducting a study. The team is usually made up of representatives from key office areas, such as data processing, records management, and reprographics.

Support-systems feasibility study. A study conducted to determine the volume and kind of work done in an office by both management and support employees.

Synchronous transmission. The mode of transmission between equipment with different protocols, in which each character must arrive at a predetermined time—which requires synchronization between sender and receiver.

System. A collection of office machines unified in their function and connected in some way to enable designated tasks to be accomplished and applications to be performed.

System software. Programs that enable a computer to function and control its own operation, as opposed to application programs which accomplish some user specified task. The most common example of system software is the computer's operating system.

Task-oriented responsibility. Responsibility without much opportunity for creativity or personal initiative.

Telecommunications. (1) The electronic transfer of data or information from one point in an information system to another through a unit that performs the necessary format conversion and controls the rate of transmissions, including transmission from one computer system or station to remotely located devices. (2) The ability to relay messages from one place to another without paper.

Telecommunications manager. A person who has total responsibility for the management of the personnel who plan, install, maintain, and create networks of communication and monitor the transmission lines for the communication functions of an organization.

Teleconferencing. Simultaneous processing of data messages and visual connections for the purpose of sending pictures and voices through telephone wires to screens and speakers in other locations.

Telex. A network of telegraph-grade lines and terminals designed for the interchange of domestic and international messages.

Text-editing systems. In word processing, systems designed to capture keystrokes on magnetic media for subsequent printing, correction, revision, or other manipulation.

Territoriality. The need for personal work space.

Text input. The keyboarding of text into an information system.

Theory X and theory Y. Two theories of management. Theory X assumes that successful management of people requires total control. Theory Y assumes that employee self-control and self-direction, with minimal managerial involvement, will result in successful management. A combination of both theories usually is required to perform daily supervisory functions.

Theory Z. William Ouchi's theory based on the belief that a management or company philosophy should be less rigidly structured than theories X or Y (for example, formal reporting relationships, job assignments, and divisions between departments are imprecise and unclear).

Third-party service. Service obtained from a company other than the equipment manufacturer.

Throughput. The volume of typing, including dictation, transcription, and revision.

Time ladder. A list of functions performed together with colored-in time periods indicating when employees performed each task.

Time sheet. A sheet that lists the functions performed each day and the length of time it took to perform them.

Time standards. The amount of work that should be done under specified conditions and methods.

Time studies approach. An approach to studying an office in which an individual job is analyzed or reduced to individual tasks, which are then timed to determine the average time per task.

Topology. The physical and logical configuration of networks; the way in which devices are connected to one another and to a traffic processing system.

Total support system. A planned structure for integrating all services formerly considered separate functions into a support staff under centralized supervision and control.

Total system solution. A comprehensive, integrated support system in which priority consideration is given to compatibility with a mainframe.

Transaction documents. Documents that record the individual day-to-day transactions of an organization.

Transaction processing. The processing of a specific business action such as a sale, a paycheck, or a change in inventory.

Transcribing. The keyboarding of information into a system for future access.

Transitional office. The conversion of a traditional office into an electronic office through a series of logical steps and strategic plans.

Turnkey. The total preparation of a facility by a contractor which includes the acquisition and setup of all necessary premises, equipment, supplies, software, and personnel so that a customer only needs to "turn the key" to begin full operation.

Typesetting. Methods of printing, such as handset, casting, typewriter composition, and photocomposition.

Typewriter-based text-editing system. A text-editing system that uses a modified typewriter as a combined input-output device.

Typing production. Typing volume measured in lines, pages, documents, or other criteria for a specific period of time.

Unbundled services. Services not included in the original purchase of equipment and provided by vendors for a separate charge.

Understaffing. The hiring of too few people to meet the demands of the work load.

Updatable microfiche system. A microfilm that permits the addition or deletion of images.

UNIX. An operating system for computers developed by Bell Laboratories.

Upgrades. Additions to or replacement of software or hardware that updates existing software or hardware.

User friendly. The attribute of a system that is easy to use.

User manual. A guidebook for principals describing the services that the support system provides.

Value added. Additional benefits that accrue to the user of a particular product or service that are not paid for directly.

VDT. An acronym for video display terminal.

Vendor. A company that sells technology, furniture, supplies, and services to meet the needs of the automated office.

Verbal input. The dictation of information into an electronic dictation system or the voice input of information into a voice recognition system.

Vertical files. Conventional file cabinets, whose drawers open at the front.

Vertical software. Software programs created for a specific industry or industry segment, and also those designed for a specific application, such as for attorneys, purchasing or sales agents, or research and development staffs.

Videoconferencing. The use of television monitors, cameras, and specially designed studios to conduct a conference among groups of persons in geographically separate locations.

Videodisk. A television recording on magnetic disk.

Videotape. A television recording on magnetic tape.

Videotex. Television-based information services that allow users to access publicly available data banks through modified television sets in the home or office.

Virtual memory. The storage capacity that the user of the computer can employ to accomplish a task. Virtual memory is larger than main memory when the architecture of the computer permits mapping onto storage media other than main memory.

Visual display. The process of displaying information on a cathode ray tube (CRT) or video display terminal (VDT).

Vital records. Information needed to establish or continue an organization in the event of a disaster.

VLSI (very-large-scale integration). Circuits that incorporate vast quantities of logic; the compression of more than 10,000 transistors on a single chip.

Voice activation. A feature on dictation equipment that activates the tape when a person speaks and deactivates it when there is a pause.

Voice mail. The storing of messages in digital form for transmission to a receiving point at a later time.

Voice recognition. The process by which systems "recognize" spoken words and convert them to digital signals sent to an attached system or display device.

Voice response.   The process by which systems "respond" to an inquiry by converting the answer stored digitally in computer memory.

Voice synthesis devices.   Machines that enable visually impaired workers to interact with computers or word processors.

Winchester-type disk.   In word processing and small computer systems, a hard surface disk often used as a high-capacity alternative to floppy disks.

Word processing.   The transcribing of an idea into a document by means of automatic equipment.

Work-count unit.   A standardized, predefined specific quantity, such as a character, a line, a page, or a document.

Work measurement.   A method for determining work load volumes and improvements in work or in work groups by comparing what has been accomplished against a standard.

Work sample.   A collection of sample materials for quantitative measurement by size, nature of the materials, and required format.

Work-sampling approach.   An approach to studying an office in which a manager observes work at random periods or gathers copies of work to determine the amount of work accomplished in sample periods.

Work standards.   Work measurement approaches—subjective, statistical, or engineering.

Workstation.   An office space equipped with automated technology that is designed either for a particular individual or a particular task. Typically, the central component is a personal computer.

WORM (write once read many).   The overall concept of information storage in which the user can store or encode data once on a medium and thereafter only access it. Additions are allowed if there is capacity, but no alterations or erasures can take place. Often used to refer to a class of optical disk technology.

Xerographic process.   The formation of a latent electrostatic image by action of light on a photoconducting insulating system. The latent image may be made visual by a number of methods, such as applying charged, pigmented powders or liquids that are attracted to the latent image. The particles, either directly or by transfer, may be applied and fixed to a suitable medium.

Index

About the Author

MILBURN D. SMITH III is a consultant with the Omni Group, Ltd.